Malawi and Scotland
Together in the Talking Place

Published by

Mzuni Press
P/Bag 201
Luwinga, Mzuzu 2
Malawi

ISBN 978-99960-27-07-9 (Mzuni Press)

Mzuni Press is represented outside Africa by:
African Books Collective Oxford (also for e-books)
(orders@africanbookscollective.com)

www.mzunipress.luviri.net
www.africanbookscollective.com

Cover: Shadreck Malekano
Printed in Malawi by Baptist Publications, P.O. Box 444, Lilongwe

Malawi and Scotland
Together in the Talking Place
since 1859

Kenneth R. Ross

Mzuni Books no. 8

2013

"This pioneering and fascinating book is the first to tell the story of the remarkably enduring bonds between Malawi and Scotland from the time of David Livingstone to the flourishing cultural, economic and religious relationships of the present day. Kenneth Ross is a Scot who has also worked for several years in Malawi. That experience and his own careful research has enabled him to produce a volume which manages to combine authority with readability. It will have very wide appeal in both countries."

Professor Tom Devine
Personal Senior Research Chair of History
University of Edinburgh

"I am absolutely convinced that this book demonstrates that the relationship between Scotland and Malawi is both very special and very important because of the deep and extensive shared history of 150 years. It should be required reading for all Malawians so that we know and understand our history and identity as a people, as well as appreciate the depth and extent of our connection with the history and identity of Scotland."

Prof Brighton Uledi-Kamanga
Professor of English, Chancellor College, University of Malawi

"Since the signing of the Co-operation Agreement between Scotland and Malawi in 2005, more and more Scots have discovered the remarkable history of the friendship between our two nations. Here, for the first time, Kenneth Ross tells that story - from the early encounters of David Livingstone to the partnership that exists today between our communities and the Warm Heart of Africa. This is a story of an enduring friendship established in the nineteenth century, developed through the ups and downs of the twentieth century, and now rekindled for the twenty-first.

Kenneth Ross is uniquely placed to write this history. His understanding of both Scotland and Malawi, and his commitment to our partnership, shines through the pages of this book. I hope it inspires even more of our people to share in the friendship, in the knowledge of all that has come before."

Rt Hon Lord McConnell of Glenscorrodale
First Minister of Scotland 2001-2007

"Enlightening and a BIG 'eye-opener' for everyone interested to understand the history and context behind the momentum generated by the special relationship between Scotland and Malawi. Particularly so for those of us involved on the Malawi side - this book helps in understanding what makes the relationship between Scotland and Malawi very different from any other conceivable relationship between any two nations."

Dr Matthews Mtumbuka
Chair, Malawi Scotland Partnership

"An excellent account of the development of the relationship between Scotland and Malawi from one of Scotland's leading advocates for Malawi. This book is essential reading for those who seek to understand the strengthening bond between our countries."

Fiona Hyslop, Cabinet Secretary
for Culture and External Affairs, Scottish Government

Acknowledgements

The knowledge on which this book is based has been formed primarily through conversations with friends over the many years since I first arrived in Malawi in 1988. First and foremost, I acknowledge my debt to my colleagues at the University of Malawi and in the Church of Central Africa Presbyterian who have immeasurably expanded my understanding by generously sharing their experiences and perspectives with me.

Likewise at the Scottish end I have been fortunate indeed to benefit from the knowledge and wisdom of many colleagues within the Scotland Malawi Partnership and the Church of Scotland. In particular, discerning readers of the following pages will not fail to notice the extent of my debt to three distinguished historians of Malawi: Andrew Ross, John McCracken and Jack Thompson. Not only their written works but also their willingness to converse at length about matters pertaining to Malawi and Scotland has exercised a strong formative influence on this book. Its deficiencies are, of course, entirely my own responsibility.

I am honoured to be able to include photographs taken from the private collection of Dr Jack Thompson and express my sincere gratitude to him for making these available for the purpose. I also acknowledge with sincere thanks the Scotland Malawi Partnership which provided me with the cover photograph and the two photographs which feature in Chapter 11.

Grateful acknowledgement is due to the Drummond Trust, 3 Pitt Terrace, Stirling, for a generous grant towards the cost of publishing this book in Malawi.

From beginning to end it has been a pleasure to work with Mzuni Press, not least because it provided the opportunity to work once again with Klaus Fiedler with whom I have been privileged to collaborate on many publishing projects over the past 20 years.

Kenneth R. Ross
Netherlorn, Argyll
November 2012

Table of Contents

1. Introduction: Two Nations in Conversation

Amidst the conflicts, wars, tensions and tumults of the early 21st century, one inter-national relationship which could easily be overlooked is the one between Malawi and Scotland. Why should there be any significant relationship between one small nation on Europe's north-western seaboard and another in the interior of Africa? How did it reach the stage where in 2012 Fiona Hyslop, Cabinet Secretary for Culture and External Affairs in the Scottish Government, could describe Malawi as Scotland's "sister nation"?[1] This book attempts an answer. It traces the way in which this relationship began and evolved across a century and a half. It recognises that the connections of the two nations have found a special place in the hearts of individuals and communities on both sides. It observes that today these underpin both an inter-Governmental Cooperation Agreement and a remarkable plethora of interaction at the level of civil society. It detects particular qualities which bring a distinctive character to the relationship and explains why these continue to have a compelling quality for the people of both nations today.

Its starting point is the very simple observation that Malawians and Scots have been in conversation since 1859. Apart from a short interlude at the beginning, the conversation has been continuous. From the time of the establishment of Scottish Missions in the mid-1870s it is safe to say that there has not been a single day when Malawians and Scots have not been talking to one another. Over the years they have found that they have much to discuss and this remains the case today. What have they been talking about all this time? This book will identify important episodes which have proved to be talking points but will also discern salient threads which run through the entirety of the conversation.

One Scot who had a particularly sympathetic understanding of Malawian community life was Thomas Cullen Young, a Livingstonia missionary during the first three decades of the 20th century. Young observed that at the heart of a Malawian village was found the "talking-

9

place" – a place where people would gather to discuss current affairs, settle disputes, arrange religious observance, air political issues and affirm community life and tradition. Many of the Scots who have shared his sympathy have had the privilege of being admitted, at least to some degree, to the "talking-place". This book aims to offer a brief summary of the talk which has taken place across more than one hundred and fifty years.

It makes no claim to be comprehensive. Inevitably, it is selective – edited highlights rather than the whole match. It is limited by the perspective of the author, a Scot closely involved with Malawi over the past twenty-five years, a mere one-sixth of the total. While this has been a wonderful vantage-point it is inevitably one from which some things are seen very clearly while others are hidden from view and others again are seen only in hazy outline. Therefore many of the by-ways – and some of the highways – of the Malawi-Scotland story have not been explored in this book. Future travellers across this terrain will find much ground that is still waiting to be explored.

Recognising these limitations, the book aims to be an introductory reader for anyone enquiring as to what the Malawi-Scotland relationship is all about. Its focus is on the major points at which the histories of Malawi and Scotland have intersected and exercised influence in both directions. If the relationship is to be regarded as a long conversation, this book identifies some of the main participants, some of the main topics, and some of the main conclusions which have emerged. It recognises disappointments and negative elements but its main focus is on the best moments from which lasting inspiration may be derived.

For a new generation of Malawians and Scots entering into this long-running relationship, as they are doing in large numbers today, this book aims to assemble the lore which gives particular content and meaning to the axis between the two nations. In doing so, it offers an example of what can be achieved through the determination of the people of two nations to listen, in depth, to each other's concerns over an extended period of time and in the context of profound mutual respect and affection. It is written out of the conviction that the contribution of such an engagement to peace, development and prosperity is not to be underestimated.

To avoid confusion in regard to nomenclature, it should be noted that prior to 1891 the area now known as Malawi had no defined borders and consequently no fixed name. From 1891 to 1907 it was known as British Central Africa. From 1907 to 1964 it was known as Nyasaland. Since independence in 1964 the nation has been called Malawi. The story told in this book spans all four periods so, for the sake of simplicity, the modern name "Malawi" will be used throughout.

---

[1]   Press Release, Scottish Government, 14 May 2012.

2. First Encounters: Livingstone and Friends in Malawi

A Momentous Arrival

The crowd at Kamuzu Stadium, Malawi's national football ground in Blantyre, on 11 April 2009 was bedecked in blue cloth bearing a portrait of David Livingstone and the words "gospel, peace, freedom and fair trade". Malawians had come in their thousands to mark the 150th anniversary of the arrival of David Livingstone in their country. They heard their State President, Ngwazi Dr Bingu wa Mutharika strongly stating his view that Livingstone is not to be confused with the colonialism which followed after his death. "Colonialism was far from his mind as he ministered the Word of God and fought to emancipate people from slavery." The President pointed out that the name of Malawi's largest commercial centre - the city of Blantyre (called after Livingstone's birthplace in Lanarkshire) - is living testimony to Malawians' appreciation of Livingstone's role in their country's history. "The people of Scotland have always stood behind the people of Malawi. The legacy of Dr Livingstone lives on in all of us."[1]

As a graduate himself of the Henry Henderson Institute in Blantyre, the President expressed appreciation both of the transformative power of the gospel of Jesus Christ and of the missionary approach which embraced the whole spectrum of human activity, including trade and industry. A procession of floats featured different aspects of Livingstone's contribution, the most striking being a dramatic representation of his liberation of a group of slaves. Choirs sang, preachers preached, poets recited and dancers danced until the day ended with football matches featuring Malawi's top two sides, Bata Bullets and MTL Wanderers. For an African nation to celebrate in this way the arrival of a European missionary in their country suggests that something unusual had occurred.

The event being remembered in the stadium was the first known encounter between Scots and Malawians. This occurred in 1859, a year after Livingstone, sponsored by the British Government, had embarked on his Zambesi Expedition – which aimed to introduce "commerce, civilization and Christianity" to the region. Frustrated by difficulties in navigating the Zambesi River, Livingstone recorded that: "Our attention was in the mean time turned to the exploration of the river Shire [pronounced Shee-ray], a northern tributary of the Zambesi, which joins it about a hundred miles from the sea. We could learn nothing satisfactory from the Portuguese regarding this affluent; no one, they said, had ever been up it, nor could they tell whence it came."[2] There was nothing Livingstone liked better than to lead his expedition into unknown territory. So it was that on 28 December 1858, the little ship *Ma-Robert* - bearing the name which the Tswana people had given to Livingstone's wife Mary ("the mother of Robert") – turned into the River Shire and began the journey which would bring, for the first time, a group of Scots to Malawi.

By late March 1859 they reached Malawi soil, arriving at Chibisa's village, named after its chief with whom Livingstone quickly formed a friendship. From there they left the village and struck out overland, climbing up from the river valley into the Shire Highlands. Livingstone was greatly struck by what he found: "We were all charmed with the splendid country, and looked with never-failing delight on its fertile plains, its numerous hills, and majestic mountains."[3] On 18 April 1859, they arrived at Lake Chilwa and Livingstone searched for words to describe the splendour of the scene "The country around is very beautiful, and clothed with rich vegetation; and the waves, at the time they were there, breaking and foaming over a rock on the south-eastern side, added to the beauty of the picture. Exceedingly lofty mountains, perhaps 8000 feet above the sea-level, stand near the eastern shore. When their lofty steep-sided summits appear, some above, some below the clouds, the scene is grand. This range is called Milanje; on the west stands Mount Zomba, 7000 feet in height, and some twenty miles long."[4]

Though delighted by the topography of the area around Lake Chilwa, Livingstone was intrigued by the accounts he heard from Malawians of a much larger lake to the north. He therefore returned to the area later in the year and recorded simply: "We discovered Lake Nyassa [now Lake Malawi] a little before noon of the 16th September, 1859."[5] Only his "discovery" of the Victoria Falls could rival this as the stand-out event in Livingstone's remarkable career as the premier explorer of inland southern Africa.

More importantly, Livingstone was deeply impressed by the people whom he met: "The Mang'anja are an industrious race; and in addition to working in iron, cotton, and basket-making, they cultivate the soil extensively. All the people of a village turn out to labour in the fields. It is no uncommon thing to see men, women and children hard at work, with the baby lying close by beneath a shady bush."[6] It was a populous area: "never before in Africa have we seen anything like the dense population on the shores of Lake Nyassa."[7] The fertile land and industrious people quickly led Livingstone to the conclusion that he may have found the area he had been seeking – a place where productive agriculture would create commercial possibilities which in due course would undermine the slave trade. His mind raced as he thought of the potential: "Water-carriage exists by the Shire and Zambesi all the way to England, with the single exception of a portage of about thirty-five miles past the Murchison Cataracts, along which a road of less than forty miles could be made at trifling expense; and it seems feasible that a legitimate and thriving trade might, in a short time, take the place of the present unlawful traffic."[8] Countering the slave trade was no theoretical matter. Its effects were all too evident as Livingstone travelled across the Shire Highlands and along the lakeshore. Malawi's Department of Antiquities preserves a tree at Mbame where Livingstone confronted a group of slavers as he reached the top of the Shire Valley escarpment and set free the slaves whom they were holding. As he remarked at the time: "Logic is out of place when the question with a true-hearted man is, whether his brother-man is to be saved or not."[9]

There is no escaping the fact that David Livingstone, more than any other single individual, is responsible for the special relationship which exists between Malawi and Scotland. Of course, no less responsible are the Malawians who received him and made friends with him and his little expeditionary group. At that time they were not able to put their impressions into print as Livingstone did. However, they did have a very strong oral tradition and this was used to convey within Malawian communities the sense that something extraordinary and decisive had occurred in 1859 as Scots and Malawians met one another under a shady tree or around the evening campfire. What was it in Livingstone that so quickly won the confidence of the African communities whom he encountered in the Shire Highlands? To answer this question we need to look into his background and identify the influences which made him the man he was.

By any reckoning David Livingstone was a colossal figure. Andrew Walls suggests that: "If any 'man in the street' – at least, in any British street – were asked at any time in the last century to name a Christian missionary, it is likely that he would name David Livingstone. This might indeed be the only missionary name he could think of. Somehow Livingstone has come to stand as the representative missionary, the missionary par excellence."[10] Of his stature there can be little doubt yet the question of what he actually stood for has proved to be a controversial one. In the years of the "scramble for Africa" which followed his death he was portrayed as the forerunner of British imperialism, an image which led to his statue beside the Victoria Falls being stoned by Zimbabwe's "war veterans" in the early 21st century. On the other hand, Zambia's first President Kenneth Kaunda famously described Livingstone as "Africa's first freedom fighter". Still capable of provoking such strong reactions, what was he really all about?

David Livingstone was a product of the Evangelical Revival which greatly influenced his native Scotland in the early 19th century and, in particular, of the great moral cause which Evangelicals like William

15

Wilberforce and Thomas Buxton took to heart: the need to defeat and eradicate the slave trade. As a young man Livingstone attended an Evangelical gathering in London and heard Fowell Buxton declare that: "… it was Christianity and commerce that would solve Africa's problems above all, these two together would eliminate the slave trade. Africans had a hunger now for European manufactured goods; and, in order to obtain these, chiefs sold other Africans as slaves. If legitimate European commerce could only penetrate Africa and promote the cultivation of products Europe wanted to buy, then these could be exchanged for European goods, uplifting African standards of living and ending the slave trade. At the same time, the work of Christian missions in preaching the Gospel and in developing schools would aid the process and in turn be aided by it."[11] This vision gripped the imagination of David Livingstone and never left him. As he marched on foot for mile upon mile through the African bush with ulcerated feet, constant anal bleeding, dysentery and gastrointestinal problems, it was this vision which drove him on. To heal the "open sore" of the slave trade it was necessary, in his view, to create the possibility of "honest" trade and extend the moral influence of the Christian faith.

Lithograph of David Livingstone from a photograph by Thomas Annan

To this cause he brought a formidable range of skills. A trained medical doctor who became expert in tropical medicine, he also developed the skills which made him one of the great geographers of his time. From boyhood an avid naturalist, he took European knowledge of Africa's flora and fauna to a new level. During his early years in Africa he learned the Sichuana language which honed his skills as a linguist and gave him a lasting appreciation of the richness, copiousness and subtlety of the Bantu languages. Famously, he was an explorer and did more than any other individual to expand understanding of the geography of central Africa. Though often criticised for having apparently abandoned his missionary vocation, in his own mind he was always a missionary, personally devout and ever ready to speak of his faith: "God had an only Son, and he was a missionary and a physician. A poor, poor imitation of Him I am. Or wish to be... In this service I hope to live; in it I wish to die."[12]

Above all, he had at heart the welfare of the African communities to which he had dedicated his life. No greater recognition of this commitment could have been given that the action of his African companions, Susi and Chuma, when he died in 1873. According to his wishes, they opened up his body and buried his heart and entrails at the spot in Ilala, Zambia, where he died. They then mummified his body in the sun and set off on the 8-month journey to carry it to the coast whence it could be taken by ship to Britain for interment in Westminster Abbey. There can be no question that Livingstone had qualities which earned him an extraordinary degree of loyalty and affection from the Africans among whom he lived and worked. It was these qualities which made his encounters with Malawians in the years from 1859 so portentous.

When he arrived in Malawi, David Livingstone was already a seasoned missionary with almost 20 years of African experience behind him. A Scot, of Highland stock, born and brought up in industrial Lanarkshire, he had enlisted as a young medical doctor with the London Missionary Society. During his early years in South Africa he imbibed the pro-African approach which had marked out the early involvement of the LMS. A particular influence was his fellow Scot and LMS colleague John Philip who stood so strongly for the rights of the African people that he became the target of the fury of European settlers who believed that the role of Africans was a subservient one.[13] Livingstone's lack of racism is indicated in his reflection on his own family history when he remarks that "the Highlanders ... were much like the Cape Caffres".[14] The fact that his great-grandfather had fought on the defeated Jacobite side at Culloden in 1745 gave Livingstone an instinctive sympathy with the African communities which engaged British forces in the so-called Kaffir Wars. As he commented: "No nation ever secured its liberty without fighting for it. And every nation on earth worthy of freedom is ready to shed its blood in its defence. In sympathising with the Caffres [sic] we side with the weak against the strong."[15] He insisted that the Xhosa had the right to fight for the freedom of their homeland and compared their cause with that of the widely admired Hungarian liberation struggle in 1848.

Livingstone's hostility to racism comes out in remarks which he made in the course of the Zambesi Expedition which took him to Malawi. He comments, for example: "Most writers believe the blacks to be savages, nearly all blacks believe the whites to be cannibals. The nursery hobgoblin of the one is black, of the other white. Without going further into these unwise comparisons, we must smile at the heaps of nonsense which have been written about the negro intellect."[16] This scornful attitude towards racism arose from the simple reality of having lived close to African communities, to the extent of becoming more comfortable among Africans than among Europeans. It is striking that Livingstone's relationships with fellow-Europeans were often stormy while his friendships with Africans were marked by a remarkable degree of affection and loyalty.

Both in the trans-African trek which took him and his Makololo companions to Luanda on the west coast and in his final journeys searching for the source of the Nile in Tanzania and Zambia, Livingstone spent many months entirely in African company. This gave him a closeness to African community life, and an appreciation of its qualities, which would become rarer in the later colonial era in Africa and reinforced the anti-racism which he had developed in his early days in South Africa.

During his time in the Shire Highlands he made a throwaway remark which reveals the way he thought on questions of race. Commenting on a Mang'anja village which had profited from participation in the slave trade, he said: "Nothing was more disheartening than this conduct of the Mang'anja, in profiting by the entire breaking up of their nation. It was nearly as bad as the behaviour of our own countrymen, who bought up muskets and sent them out to the Chinese engaged in war with our own soldiers; or those who, at the Cape, supplied ammunition to the Kaffirs, under similar circumstances..."[17] Moral failure was something which could be found equally in any race. Given the conflicts which would occur around questions of race during the next hundred years in central Africa, it is important to note the stance which Livingstone took. One of his many biographers, Andrew Ross, observes that, "his passionate belief in racial equality was ignored in the enormous body of literature about him that was produced shortly after his death."[18] It is therefore necessary to recall that Livingstone was able to say: "I have never met an African who did not know whose side I am on."

Livingstone's Vision for Africa

Livingstone related to Africans with a sympathy and fellow-feeling which were distinctive at the time and which have proved to be definitive for the relations of Scotland and Malawi in all the years which have followed. Above all, his approach was marked by confidence in the integrity and strength of African life and culture, not least when it came to the reception of the Christian faith which was close to his heart. His early missionary experience amongst the Tswana led him to the conviction that they were not bereft of a knowledge of God, a concept of the after life and a moral conscience. He also became deeply interested in traditional African methods of healing. "All of this already marked him out," comments Andrew Ross, "from most other missionaries in Africa at that time, who showed neither serious interest in nor any sympathetic understanding of African culture."[19]

Lamin Sanneh, in his re-assessment of the Western missionary movement, notes Livingstone's admiration for the richness and subtlety of the Bantu languages and his determination that the Christian faith should be expressed in the vernacular. This confidence in the inherent capabilities of the vernacular environment, Sanneh suggests, "brought Livingstone into radical tension with is own European cultural roots."[20] He sometimes suggested that, for the appropriation of Christianity, African culture might prove to be a better basis than European. Notwithstanding his commitment to the spread of British political influence, he held to the principle that the Christian faith in Africa must be built on indigenous foundations.

After his 750-mile trek into central Africa in 1841 Livingstone wrote many letters and, as Andrew Ross points out: "In all of them he was insistent that only what he called 'Native Agency' would bring about the conversion of Africa, that is only Africans would convert Africa."[21] This tension in Livingstone's thought – between the need for British influence and confidence in African agency - would only be resolved by subsequent history. As Sanneh writes: "an African Church, rooted in the vernacular, must inevitably come into conflict with a political system based on the superiority of foreign institutions."[22] The success of the translation enterprise initiated by Livingstone would ensure that a vernacular Christianity would remain and flourish long after the days of European colonial rule had come to an end.

However, what Livingstone had in mind was something very different from the white domination which would sweep southern Africa after his death. It is necessary to recognise that Livingstone's vision of a "colony" was of a settlement geared to trade and development which would interact on equal terms with the surrounding African communities. There was a period when he was in Britain in 1857 when he toyed with the idea of large-scale white immigration to central Africa and on this basis he has been portrayed as forerunner of the white settlers of the colonial era. Surveying his writing as a whole, however, Andrew Ross concludes that: "Whenever we find him writing about a definite plan, what he wanted was clearly not large-scale white migration. His colony was a missionary and commercial settlement, whose members would begin by spreading the gospel and also initiate the legitimate trade which would drive out slave raiding and trading."[23] At stake here are two very different ideas of a "colony".

Sanneh brings out the contrast when he compares Livingstone with his younger contemporary Cecil Rhodes: "Both dominated Central Africa: Rhodes left a legacy of white domination, Livingstone of rising African aspirations."[24] Whereas Rhodes was driven by the ambition to exploit Africa's abundant resources to the advantage of Britain, Livingstone worked to a different rhythm. He wanted to see African communities freed from the scourge of the slave trade and able to reach their full potential within the community of nations and the international trade system.

For our purposes, it is also important to note that David Livingstone was a Scot. Not only was he a Scot but he was very conscious of his Scottish identity. Notwithstanding the fact that he became, for a time, a prominent figure in the London establishment, was finally laid to rest in Westminster Abbey and became an icon of British imperialism, he never lost his sense of being Scottish – or "Scotch" to use the language of the time. In common with the usage of his day, Livingstone would often speak of "we English", meaning British. During his time in the Shire Highlands in 1859 he wrote that "there is room to spare for English emigrants to settle and work the virgin soil of the still untilled land of Ham." It is clear, however, that the settlers whom he particularly had in mind were Scots. Confiding in his fellow Scot Sir Roderick Murchison, the President of the Royal Geographical Society, he made it clear that he was thinking of "Scotch" settlers: "The interior of this country ought to be colonised by our own countrymen … I think twenty or thirty good Christian Scotch families with their ministers and elders would produce an impression in ten years that would rejoice the hearts of all lovers of our race."[25]

In the vision which Livingstone was forming for what was to become Malawi there was a special place for Scots to occupy. This is confirmed in a comment which Livingstone makes about the visit to the area made by James Stewart in 1862 when he was commissioned by the Free Church of Scotland to examine its possibilities. Stewart arrived just at the time when the effort by the (English) Universities Mission to Central Africa had proved a failure (see below). Livingstone remarked: "The time

… was inopportune; the disasters, which from inexperience had befallen the Mission of the Universities, had a depressing effect on the minds of many at home, and rendered new attempts inadvisable; though had the *Scotch perseverance and energy* been introduced it is highly probable that they would have reacted, most beneficially, on the zeal of our English brethren, and desertion would never have been heard of."[26]

Recent scholarship has underlined the importance of taking Livingstone's Scottish background into account in order to understand him properly. There is no question that his relationships, particularly with fellow-Europeans, could be stormy at times and there were many furious quarrels in the course of his various expeditions. Arthur Ransford suggested that these incidents might indicate a clinical case of manic-depressive personality.[27] Contesting this view, Andrew Ross has argued convincingly that: "Livingstone's readiness to take offence and to maintain a feud-like antagonism towards those who, in his eyes, had betrayed him can be explained by some consideration of the culture that helped shape him. The culture of the working class in the industrialised areas of the west of Scotland did not produce any understanding of shades of grey. Things were either black or white: he who is not with me is against me…. Ransford … clearly had never been in a pub in Coatbridge or Sauchiehall Street."[28] Given the significance of Livingstone's Scottish formation over the course of his life and career in Africa, this was clearly a factor in the encounters which took place in the Shire Highlands and along the lakeshore in 1859. His family background in the Highlands is also not to be underestimated in that it allowed him to draw on an experience of affinity between Scottish Highland life and culture and that which obtained in the African communities in which he now found himself.

This was the man who arrived, as the first known European to reach what is now Malawi, in 1859. The characteristics which mark him out would cast a long shadow over the century and a half to come, particularly in regard to the relations which would develop between Scotland and Malawi. He brought a deep sympathy with African life and culture, a steely determination to root out the slave trade, and a confidence that the combination of Christianity and successful commerce held the key to a prosperous future for the peoples of Africa. The thrill he experienced as he encountered Malawi for the first time was that it seemed to be the fulfilment of his vision: an area with a large African population, a healthy situation, good communications and beyond the baleful influence of the racist white domination prevailing further south.

Though Livingstone was a child of his time and not without an element of paternalism, it is remarkable to observe the degree to which Malawi's history has been a struggle to fulfil this vision. Long years were spent resisting the efforts of racist white regimes to extend their influence into Malawi. Today it is unjust trading rules which inhibit the full participation of Malawians in the global economy which is needed to free the country from the chains of poverty. At the Kamuzu Stadium celebration of the 150th anniversary of Livingstone's arrival, the loudest cheers from the crowd came at the point in a sermon when the preacher called for fair and just trade rules to be introduced. Malawi continues to be vexed by the need for effective transport links with the coast – the very concern which prompted Livingstone's arduous voyages on the great rivers of east-central Africa. In so many respects Livingstone brought new ways of thinking both to Malawi and to Scotland and these remain influential today.

Scots in Malawi: Livingstone and Friends

There is no escaping the fact that it was Livingstone who inspired and led the initial contact between Scotland and Malawi. He was not, however, alone. Though the Zambesi Expedition was a British initiative there was a high proportion of Scots on the team. The Expedition comprised a naval officer, a mining geologist, an economic botanist, an assistant and moral agent, an artist and store-keeper, and a ship's engineer. Livingstone sought out the best-qualified men regardless of their place of origin but it is significant that three Scots were among those appointed: Dr James Kirk as economic botanist and medical officer, George Rae as ship's engineer, and Livingstone's brother Charles as general assistant and moral agent. The Expedition was therefore significantly Scottish in complexion. Angus Calder comments: "It seems apt that four Scots – Livingstone, his brother Charles, John Kirk and George Rae – were the first white men known to have seen the glories of Lake Malawi…"[29]

While on leave in the UK in 1857 Livingstone had appealed for people to come forward to take up the work which he had begun in Africa. In the Senate House at the University of Cambridge he had created an electric effect when he ended his speech with words which became his epitaph: "I beg to direct your attention to Africa. I know in a few years I shall be cut off in that country which is now open. Do not let it be shut again. I go back to Africa to try to make an open path for commerce and Christianity. Do you carry out the work I have begun. I leave it with you!"[30] As a direct result of this appeal, the Universities Mission to Central Africa was founded. Encouraged by Livingstone's reports regarding the Shire Highlands, the UMCA decided to establish a first mission in the area.

To lead the mission they selected Charles Frederick Mackenzie, a Scot from Portmore in Perthshire who had been a distinguished mathematician at Cambridge University before ordination and service as Archdeacon of Natal. While in Natal he had been influenced by the deep identification with the Zulu people which marked the ministry of his bishop, John William Colenso. He therefore brought to his new assignment a commitment to identify with the people among whom he would work – to learn their language, to understand their culture, to share in their struggles. In January 1861 he was consecrated bishop "of the mission to the tribes dwelling in the neighbourhood of Lake Nyassa and the River Shire".

When Livingstone, Mackenzie and the mission party arrived in the Shire Highlands in July 1861, they encountered a very different situation from the one Livingstone had known two years earlier. Yao slave trading had greatly intensified, prompted in part by crop failures as a result of poor rains. On their way up from the Shire Valley the mission party encountered a group of slave traders who were taking their unfortunate captives, mainly women and children, to Tete. When the missionaries freed the slaves, the majority decided to remain with the bishop who "thus gained a ready-made constituency for his mission".[31] While this might have worked to Mackenzie's advantage, it introduced the problem that the mission was, from then on, identified with the Mang'anja in their conflict with the Yao.

Even before they had time to properly establish their mission station at the Magomero site which Livingstone had chosen, the missionaries and their Mang'anja followers encountered another group of apparently hostile Yao slavers. A fight took place in which the missionaries opened fire and killed six of the Yao. The result was that "... from then on the Mang'anja saw Mackenzie and his mission as an important military ally, and the Yao saw the mission as their enemy".[32] The mission never recovered from the disastrous effect of being drawn into inter-tribal conflicts.[33] Hopelessly vulnerable, the final blow to the mission came when Mackenzie died of malaria in January 1862. Soon afterwards the decision was taken to abandon the fledgling mission station at Magomero.

Certainly Mackenzie is vulnerable to criticism in regard to his tendency to be drawn into local conflicts and his willingness to use force. However, to put this in perspective, Jonathan Newell points out that missionaries over the years have often been evacuated from situations of unrest or threat. "Mackenzie never considered this option, but sought to live and work – and fight – in the most difficult of circumstances, in the hope that by doing so his example would win converts and the trust of the local people; an aspiration which does appear to a certain extent to have been fulfilled."[34] Although the mission which he led was both flawed and short-lived Mackenzie demonstrated the passion for justice and committed friendship which would unite the peoples of Scotland and Malawi in years to come. Though the UMCA mission at this point appeared to be a failure, it provided an opportunity for lessons to be learned when fresh attempts to establish mission stations were made by Scottish Presbyterians in the mid-1870s; and by the return of the UMCA in 1885.

Amidst the chaos and confusion of the social and political situation in 1861, a significant development was the decision of Livingstone's Makololo followers to settle permanently in the Shire Valley. Insisting for the rest of their lives that "they were still the men of Dotoro Livisto",[35] they took on a leadership role among the Mang'anja whose survival as a people has been attributed to the Makololo by a leading historian of the Mang'anja.[36] These were men who knew from long experience the justice, loyalty and friendship which Livingstone stood for in Africa. Later they would play an important part in resisting Portuguese influence and in sustaining the traditions which make Malawi what it is today. Alexander Hetherwick, who served at Blantyre from 1883 to 1928, knew the Makololo well and recalled that: "I heard from some of these men tales of their old leader, whom they always spoke of with intense veneration."[37]

He was vividly remembered also even by Malawians who had only a fleeting encounter with him, unsurprisingly given that he was invariably the first European they had met. When a new church was inaugurated at Kasonga in Mangochi in 1915 it was opened by Chief Kasonga who recalled his experience, as a young man, of speaking with Livingstone.[38] Though not a Christian himself, he was well disposed towards the church and the whole associated movement, at least in part, as a result of the favourable impression made by this early encounter. As Donald Fraser observed: "Wherever [Livingstone] went he spread and left behind him a gracious influence which made the path easy for any European who should follow."[39]

Above all, Livingstone brought a quality of friendship to the relations between Scotland and Malawi which has endured over generations and continues to inspire today. The nature of the discussion which took place as Livingstone used his knowledge of kindred languages to try to understand the Chinyanja in which he was addressed will never be known. It is clear, however, that a special chemistry developed between the people of the Shire Highlands and David Livingstone. As Patrick

26

Keatley has commented: "The best way to make contact today with David Livingstone is simply to talk to Africans. You could do this anywhere but perhaps best in Nyasaland (Malawi), his beloved land by the lake, where his influence remains most profound.... He gave himself no airs, was never pompous, and never underrated the ability of his African students to make excellent missionaries themselves. 'I have no hesitation in saying one or two pious native agents are equal if not superior to Europeans.'"[40]

Yuraya Chatonda Chirwa was someone who became such an agent and who was able to recall Livingstone's arrival in his home district of Bandawe in 1859. Among several amazing actions Livingstone had gone down to the lakeshore in the evening and had rubbed his head in such a way that "his brains oozed out".[41] This was the first sighting of the use of soap to occur in Bandawe. Such memories remained vivid and, along with them, lay a deeper consciousness of the values for which Livingstone stood, particularly as the outright opponent of the slave trade.

His confidence in Malawians seems to have engendered a mutual confidence which is unusual in the relations between Europeans and Africans. It brought to Malawi a sense that in the threatening new world which was breaking in upon Africa there was a nation in Europe to which it would be particularly and beneficially related. It brought to Scotland a sense of there being a part of Africa to which it had a special relationship and for which it had special responsibilities in the imperial age which was to follow. Amidst the turbulence of Livingstone's time in what is now Malawi, a relationship was formed which would shape the history of both Scotland and Malawi in lasting ways.

So far as Scotland is concerned, controversy has continually raged as to how Livingstone should be remembered. Not in doubt is his status as one of the iconic figures in Scottish national identity. His activity in Africa had a reflexive effect on Scotland's self-understanding. As Tom Devine observes:

> Much was made of Livingstone's joint Highland and Lowland ancestry. His great-grandfather was a Gael who was said to have

fought at Culloden. On his mother's side, however, he was descended from Lowland Covenanters. It was common to explain his sympathy for the African people by recourse to his Highland heritage as the Scottish clan system was portrayed as similar to the tribal structures of Africa. Thus, so it was said, Livingstone the Scot would understand African society in a way that no Englishman could.[42]

Whether such perceptions were a matter of myth or reality, or a blend of the two, Scotland's connection with Malawi, which owes its origins to Livingstone, would bring its influence to bear not only on events in Malawi but also on developments in Scotland.

Late in 2009 a letter arrived by surface mail at the Church of Scotland headquarters in Edinburgh. It was from Stafford K. Soko, a Malawian who was trying to establish contact with a Scot whom he had known in Malawi fifty years earlier. It concluded: "Greetings to all Scottish people, they are very kind. They gave us Dr Livingstone who opened the whole Central Africa."[43] The memory has not faded with the passing of the years. The verdict passed by Donald Fraser has stood the test of time:

> What then was the secret of Livingstone's wonderful achievement? He set out ... alone, unsupported by wealth or worldly influence, with no experience to guide him, and yet in the space of a fleeting generation set forces working whose power and limits no sage observer would dare to estimate, whose effects are for all time. Amongst the various conclusions that may be drawn one is unquestionable. Livingstone's attitude towards Africa breathed a wider and higher spirit than any of his predecessors had reached. He came to give, not to get, and the measureless bounty of his spirit left inexhaustible treasures behind.[44]

---

[1] Personal observation.

[2] David and Charles Livingstone, *Narrative of an Expedition to the Zambesi and its Tributaries; and of the Discovery of the Lakes Shirwa and Nyassa*, London: John Murray, 1865, pp. 74-75.

[3] *Ibid.*, p. 107.

[4] *Ibid.*, p. 82.

[5]   *Ibid.*, p. 123.

[6]   *Ibid.*, p. 110.

[7]   *Ibid.*, p. 372.

[8]   *Ibid.*, p. 129.

[9]   *Ibid.*, p. 357.

[10]   Andrew F. Walls, "David Livingstone 1813-1873: Awakening the Western World to Africa", in Gerald H. Anderson et al. ed., *Mission Legacies: Biographical Studies of Leaders of the Modern Missionary Movement*, Maryknoll NY: Orbis Books, 1994, pp. 140-47, at p. 140.

[11]   Cit. Andrew C. Ross, *David Livingstone: Mission and Empire*, London & New York: Hambledon & London, 2002, p. 25.

[12]   Cit. Dana L. Robert, *Christian Mission: How Christianity Became a World Religion*, Oxford: Wiley-Blackwell, 2009, p. 84.

[13]   See Andrew C. Ross, *John Philip: Missions, Race, and Politics in South Africa*, Aberdeen: Aberdeen University Press, 1986.

[14]   David Livingstone, *Missionary Travels and Researches in South Africa*, New York: Harper & Bros., 1858, p. 2.

[15]   National Archives of Zimbabwe, L 1/1/1; cit. Ross, *David Livingstone*, p. 75.

[16]   Livingstone, *Expedition to the Zambesi*, p. 67.

[17]   *Ibid.*, p. 398

[18]   Andrew C. Ross, "Livingstone, David", in Daniel Patte ed., *The Cambridge Dictionary of Christianity*, Cambridge: Cambridge University Press, 2010, p. 736.

[19]   Ross, *David Livingstone*, p. 44.

[20]   Lamin Sanneh, *Translating the Message: the Missionary Impact on Culture*, Maryknoll NY: Orbis, 1989, p. 109.

[21]   Ross, *David Livingstone*, p. 43.

[22]   Lamin Sanneh, *Translating the Message*, p. 106.

[23]   Ross, *David Livingstone*, p. 167.

[24]   Sanneh, *Translating the Message*, p. 113.

[25]   Cit. Angus Calder, *Scotlands of the Mind*, Edinburgh: Luath Press, 2002, p. 118.

[26] Livingstone, *Expedition to the Zambesi*, p. 414, my italics.

[27] Arthur Ransford, *David Livingstone: The Dark Interior*, London: John Murray, 1978, pp. 1-5.

[28] Ross, *David Livingstone*, p. 52.

[29] Calder, *Scotlands of the Mind*, p. 119.

[30] G.H. Wilson, *The History of the Universities Mission to Central Africa*, London: UMCA, 1936, p. 4.

[31] Ross, *David Livingstone*, p. 172.

[32] *Ibid.*, p. 173.

[33] See Owen Chadwick, *Mackenzie's Grave*, London: Hodder & Stoughton, 1959.

[34] Jonathan Newell, "'Not War but Defence of the Oppressed'? Bishop Mackenzie's Skirmishes with the Yao in 1861", in Kenneth R. Ross ed., *Faith at the Frontiers of Knowledge*, Blantyre: CLAIM, 1998, pp. 129-43, at pp. 142-43.

[35] Ross, *David Livingstone*, p. 175.

[36] J.M. Schoffeleers, "Livingstone and the Mang'anja Chiefs", in Bridglal Pachai, *Livingstone: Man of Africa*, London: Longman, 1973.

[37] A. Hetherwick, "Livingstone's Makololo: Pioneers of Empire before Cecil Rhodes", *Other Lands*, April 1935, pp. 115-16.

[38] *Life and Work in British Central Africa*, January-March 1915.

[39] Donald Fraser, *The Future of Africa*, Edinburgh: The Foreign Mission Committee of the Church of Scotland and the Mission Study Council of the United Free Church of Scotland, 1911, p. 57.

[40] Patrick Keatley, *The Politics of Partnership*, Harmondsworth: Penguin, 1963, pp. 124-25.

[41] T. Cullen Young, "End of an Era at Livingstonia: Death of Two Men Who Remembered Livingstone", *Other Lands*, July 1951, pp. 83-84, at p. 83.

[42] T.M. Devine, *To the Ends of the Earth: Scotland's Global Diaspora*, London: Allen Lane, 2011, p. 204.

[43] Stafford K. Soko to The Moderator, Free Church of Scotland, 19 May 2009.

[44] Fraser, *The Future of Africa*, pp. 57-58.

3. Scots in Malawi: the Early Days

Launch of the Livingstonia Mission

The idea of a Scottish mission to Malawi had been canvassed during Livingstone's lifetime by James Stewart who had accompanied the celebrated explorer on some of his Central African journeys and who was inspired to champion the idea of establishing an industrial mission there. His initial approach to his own church, the Free Church of Scotland, did not bring much encouragement so he began seeking financial support from businessmen, academics and local politicians. He formed an eighteen-strong committee, chaired by the Lord Provost of Edinburgh, to drive forward the initiative to launch the mission.[1] Though its efforts did not bear fruit at that time, a seed had been planted. Meanwhile, throughout the 1860s, the Free Church continued to actively consider the possibility of beginning mission work in eastern Africa. Livingstone's death in 1873 provided fresh impetus and Stewart found that the moment of opportunity had now arrived. Financial backing was offered mainly by Glasgow-based industrialists and businessmen who provided a committed support base for Livingstonia during its early decades, to the extent that they formed the effective governing body, with the Free Church Foreign Mission Committee invariably ratifying their decisions.[2]

Livingstonia's expeditionary party was led by E.D. Young, a warrant officer in the Royal Navy with experience of travelling with Livingstone. Amongst his team was a young man who had recently qualified both as a minister and medical doctor. Robert Laws was to spend the next fifty-two years in Malawi, his name becoming synonymous with that of Livingstonia. "Always austere, sometimes obstinate," wrote John McCracken, "he possessed an appetite for work that was almost unbelievable."[3] The first base established by the Mission was at Cape Maclear, near the southern end of Lake Malawi. "Livingstonia is begun," wrote Laws, "though at present a piece of canvas stretched between two trees is all that stands for the future city of that name."[4]

The small party of Scots faced many challenges as they adapted themselves to the African environment but steadily they began to enjoy the sustained daily contact through which relationships were formed and lasting mutual influence exercised. Africans from a variety of backgrounds were drawn to the fledgling Mission. Lorenzo Johnston, Thomas Bokwito, Samuel Sambani and Frederick Zarakuti were former slaves who had been freed by David Livingstone and Bishop Mackenzie in 1861. Others had been recruited by the Mission to assist with its initial journey from the coast. Others again were recruited from coastal communities on later expeditions, such as Joseph Bismarck, the son of an African planter from Quelimane who would go on to become an influential farmer and church leader in the Blantyre area. The significant role played by the Africans drawn to Livingstonia during its earliest years has been highlighted by John McCracken:

> Unjustly ignored in official histories of the mission, the contribution made by members of this group in the pioneer years was undoubtedly of considerable importance. At a time when the Scots were isolated from their neighbours by the barriers of language and custom, it was Boquito, Sambani, Bismarck and the others who supervised work gangs at the station, kept open communication with the coast, interpreted for missionaries on their travels and explained to potentates like [local chief] Mponda the purpose of the mission and the reasons for its presence.[5]

Besides being a magnet for immigrants, the Livingstonia Mission also began to make its first tentative contacts with the Yao, Mang'anja, Ngoni and Chewa people who were living in fairly close proximity to Cape Maclear. The presence of the Scots at Cape Maclear from 1875 to 1881 marked the beginning of relationships which would prove influential. Nonetheless, poor health and political difficulties convinced Laws that a better base might be found further north and in 1880 the Mission transferred its headquarters to Bandawe, a lakeshore centre near Nkhata Bay.

In this he was influenced by James Stevenson, one of Livingstonia's most committed financial backers, who suggested establishing a station towards the north of the lake as he contemplated the potential for a northward trade route. In 1878 small posts had been established at Bandawe on the lakeshore and at Kaning'ina in the foothills inland (close to the modern city of Mzuzu). This brought the Mission into contact with the Tonga people and opened the chapter which led to Livingstonia concentrating its efforts on northern Malawi. Early discussion often revolved around the resolution of disputes with the Mission being called upon to act as arbiter. Only gradually did its leaders become aware that they were thus being drawn into the exercise of civil powers to the extent that their missionary purpose might be compromised. Nonetheless, their early embroilment in disputes and conflicts was an education in the social, cultural and political dynamics which shaped the African communities with which they were now engaged.

Beginnings of the Blantyre Mission

Running in parallel to the Free Church Livingstonia Mission was a missionary initiative of the established Church of Scotland which was similarly inspired by Livingstone's death. Despite their ecclesiastical differences, there was talk of the two churches jointly mounting a central African mission. Though this did not happen it was agreed that the two would cooperate closely and offer each other all possible assistance. Henry Henderson of the Church of Scotland accompanied the initial Free Church expedition led by E.D. Young and shared with them in the arduous journey from the coast to Lake Malawi. From there he set off, accompanied by Tom Bokwito as his interpreter, to find a suitable site for the establishment of the Church of Scotland mission.

Bokwito was familiar with the Shire Highlands, having been there previously with Livingstone and Mackenzie, so was able to introduce Henderson to significant chiefs. After spending some time with Malemia and Kalimbuka in the Zomba area, they proceeded towards Blantyre. Near Nguludi Hill a little boy named Kambwiri saw Henderson and heard the name of Jesus for the first time.[6] Little did he know that some thirty-five years later, as Rev Harry Kambwiri Matecheta, he would become the first Presbyterian minister to be ordained in Malawi and the pioneer of Blantyre Mission's work among the southern Ngoni. Something was stirring as Scots and Malawians encountered one another in these early days. Henderson and Bokwito arrived finally at the village of Chief Kapeni, an area which Livingstone had recommended as a favourable spot for a mission. By now the initial staff of the Mission had arrived at the coast where Henderson met them and led them to their chosen site on Nyambadwe Hill. They arrived on 23 October 1876 and named the place Blantyre.

The Church of Scotland had struggled to find recruits for their central African venture and the initial party were a mixed bag. On the assessment of Andrew Ross: "They ranged from Dr [Thornton] Macklin and John Buchanan, dedicated Christian men with a passionate zeal to end the slave trade ... to George Fenwick, an adventurer who would not have been out of place among the mercenaries from Scotland who played such a role in the Swedish and German armies in the 17th century." [7] The Mission at first lacked a minister to provide leadership and little tangible progress had been made by the time Rev Duff Macdonald arrived in 1878. He, however, quickly began to form friendships with local people and to develop the school which had been begun by William Koyi, the Xhosa evangelist on loan from the Livingstonia Mission. Meanwhile Chief Malemia gave the Mission some land in Zomba where John Buchanan pioneered the growing of coffee as a cash crop and gathered a regular congregation to whom he preached in Yao.

Macdonald and Buchanan were able to take up where Livingstone had left off in terms of relationships with local Africans, particularly the Makololo who had accompanied the latter on his expeditions. Duff Macdonald recalled the visit of Maseo, one of the Makololo chiefs, when a magic lantern show included a slide of David Livingstone and "the chief recognised Dr Livingstone, and stood up before the screen to have a good view."[8] Macdonald lost no time in establishing strong relationships with nearby chiefs, learning the Yao language, and developing the impressive understanding of local life and culture which is evident in his two-volume *Africana*. All the indications are that he would have met with success as a missionary were it not for the invidious position in which he was placed by the expectation that the Mission would exercise civil jurisdiction.

In the unsettled conditions created by the slave trade, numerous freed slaves and other refugees gravitated to the Blantyre Mission which quickly became a community several hundred strong. Whether they liked it or not, the missionaries found that they were expected to settle disputes and, in effect, provide government for their small settlement. Under pressure of this expectation they set up a rudimentary judicial system which could try cases and administer punishments, including flogging and imprisonment. At this early stage the function of the Mission as a civil colony seemed to its Scottish promoters to be inherent in its role in countering the slave trade. It was only when excessive and sometimes unjust punishments attracted hostile publicity in Scotland that the Church's Foreign Mission Committee turned away from any attempt to exercise civil jurisdiction.[9]

Ironically, it was Duff Macdonald, who had been the first to express misgivings about the civil authority being wielded by the Mission, who was made the scapegoat for the scandal and required to resign his position.[10] The other members of the original staff were either dismissed or left the service of the Mission so that by 1880 its future was very much in question. Where Macdonald left foundations on which others would build was in the relationships which he had formed during his brief tenure in Blantyre. As Andrew Ross has stated: "He left to his successors very good notes on the Yao language, as well as some good translations, good relations with many people, Mpama, Malemia, Kalimbuka and Kapeni, to name a few. He also left a flourishing school and a group of African men, Bismarck, Kagaso Rondau, Nacho and others who, like the children of the school, had a great affection for him..."[11]

The African Lakes Company

The Glasgow industrialists who funded the Livingstonia Mission were very much aware that Livingstone's vision for the development of central

Africa involved not only Christianity but also commerce. They therefore founded a commercial company which aimed to operate in close association with the Livingstonia Mission. At its foundation in 1878 it took the name Livingstonia Central Africa Company, changing in 1883 to the African Lakes Company. By this time it was known in Malawi as "Mandala", the nickname given to John Moir who, together with his brother Fred, was the Company's first manager. John was nicknamed "Mandala" on account of the way the sun reflected from his spectacles while Fred was nicknamed "Chindevu" on account of his long, bushy beard. For many Malawians, the Moirs were the first Europeans they had ever met and the pair became legendary figures. Their influence extended from developing a modern transport system for Malawi to introducing Virginia tobacco to fighting a war against "Arab" slavers to importing the first bicycle into Malawi. They established their headquarters at Blantyre where in 1881 they completed the construction of Mudi House, Malawi's oldest building.[12]

The African Lakes Company was a Scottish-based Company with a Scottish Board of Directors. John and Fred Moir were the sons of a prominent Edinburgh physician, John Moir, who was a member of the Free Church Foreign Mission Committee.[13] Of the fifty-two staff recruited by the Company between 1878 and 1887, all but eight from Scotland.[14] These business-oriented Scots recruited a large Malawian workforce to develop the infrastructure needed by the Company for its operations. This created an environment in which not only a working relationship but deep friendship could develop between Malawians and Scots. When Frederick and John died within six months of each other in 1939-40, Hastings K. Banda, future President of Malawi, lamented the loss in these terms: "In the death of these two brothers Nyasaland has lost her elder architects; the Africans of Nyasaland, the pioneer champions of their cause."[15] Banda commented particularly on the quality of their relationships in the Malawi context: "By tact and diplomacy John and Frederick converted the bitter enmity of many chiefs into firm and lasting friendship. Many Chewa and Nyanja chiefs, who had originally opposed them, became the close personal friends of the brothers.... The love which

36

the brothers had for Africans found equal reciprocity in the hearts of the people of Nyasaland."[16]

Staff of Blantyre Mission and the African Lakes Company at Blantyre c1886

In terms of commercial success, it cannot be claimed that the ALC fulfilled the high hopes which Livingstone had inspired. In its early years, ivory trading was the only truly profitable part of the business. Otherwise its operations had meagre results in terms of income for producers or dividends for shareholders. This does not necessarily indicate any lack of enterprise or ability on the part of the Company since the challenges with which it was struggling have proved to be perennial. As Hugh Macmillan remarks: "The central problem which the Company faced, of how to reduce the cost of transport to the level where people throughout the area could profitably sell their produce to the outside world, and pay for what they imported from it without leaving their homes, remains to be solved."[17]

Where the ALC did make an unmistakable impact on Malawian history was in the "war" which they fought against the "Arabs" at Karonga from 1887 to 1889. Always described by contemporaries as the "Arabs" these were in fact Swahili-speaking Africans with trading connections to the Arab world. They had arrived at the north end of Lake Malawi at roughly the same time as the Company, attracted by possibilities of ivory trading and slave trading. They built stockaded villages in the Karonga area, striking fear into the hearts of the indigenous Ngonde people. Large numbers of the Ngonde took refuge with the ALC whose local agent Monteith Fotheringham hastily constructed a fort for their protection. Since the creation of the Company had been inspired by Livingstone's vision of the eradication of the slave trade, it felt it had no option but to protect people who were in imminent danger of being captured by slavers. The result was more than two years of intermittent fighting in which there were many fatalities and both John and Fred Moir were seriously wounded. The outcome of this conflict hung in the balance until the strengthening forces of the ALC persuaded Mlozi, the Arab leader, to sign a peace agreement in 1889.

It was, in the words of Fred Moir: "a small but historic fight for freedom, conducted largely by the volunteer staff of the African Lakes Company, and almost entirely at that Company's expense."[18] This "North End War" did much to arouse support for Malawi in the UK and helped to move public opinion towards favouring a British Protectorate. It also had a great impact on Malawian public opinion as Fred Moir discovered when he returned to Malawi, after a thirty-year absence, in 1921, and was addressed in these terms: "The people of this country look upon you as their saviour who liberated them from the Arabs.... We are glad that we are free now and the country is free from the slave trade, these are due to your efforts and sufferings..."[19] In subsequent years the ALC "gradually became just another transport and trading company"[20] but its role in the "North End War", together with its major contribution to the early development of basic infrastructure, secured it a unique place in Malawi's history.

The Stevenson Road

Among those who responded to Livingstone's vision of opening up the interior of Africa to legitimate trade, none was more committed than the Glasgow industrialist James Stevenson. The strategic move which he sought to make was to link the lakes and rivers of eastern Africa in such a way as to enable commercial interaction over a very extensive area. He saw the potential to create a great "water route" linking the lakes to the Zambezi river and the Indian ocean, covering a distance of almost 1,500 miles with only 275 miles of overland transport.[21] He therefore promoted the idea of building a road to connect the northern end of Lake Malawi with Lake Tanganyika. When his attempts to convince the Livingstonia Mission and London Missionary Society to take responsibility for construction of the road were unsuccessful, he offered to put up £4,000 of his own money for the project, on condition that the two Missions would each establish a mission station at either end of the road. Livingstonia accepted the proposal and made plans to establish a base at Chirenje, near Mweniwamba's village, some fifty miles inland from the lake.

Stevenson recruited James Stewart, civil engineer, to lead the construction project. Stewart was the cousin of his namesake James Stewart of Lovedale who had played a prominent role in the launch of the Livingstonia Mission. It was at the latter's instigation that the young civil engineer had first come from India to join the fledgling Scottish missionary project in Malawi. Both Livingstonia and Blantyre had benefitted from his engineering skills. While at Blantyre he not only laid out the central square of the Mission but designed Malawi's first road from Chikwawa to Matope, connecting Blantyre with the lower Shire.[22] Now he took up the further challenge of the road to Lake Tanganyika. Starting in 1881 he worked for some two years on the project, surveying and supervising the construction of some seventy miles of the road, with the help of his assistant Donald Munro. He was still working on its construction when he died of fever in August 1883. The following April his successor William McEwan arrived and continued the work but, after little more than a year, he too died, at the early age of 22.

Construction of the road was, of course, entirely dependent on the recruitment of local labour and on effective interaction between the Scottish engineers and the Malawian workers. A flavour of the discussions that transpired is found in a diary entry of William McEwan: "McE and Munro had a long meeting with the men – arguments about how much payment in cloth to chief and men in advance – how long the men were to remain at the end of the day and getting back to their gardens – worried about going via Angoni land..."[23]

In terms of relationships it was, of course, a matter of managers and workers. Nonetheless bonds were established at the human level, poignantly illustrated by a description Donald Munro gives of the reaction of Patris, personal servant of James Stewart CE, on the latter's death: "I showed them the body covered in the tent. Poor Patris burst out crying like a child, he is the first black fellow I ever saw shedding a tear through grief."[24] On a lighter note, William McEwan was prone to making comparisons between the land forms of Scotland and Malawi, something to which innumerable Scots and Malawians have succumbed over the years. Of the road construction near Karamba's village he remarks: "It reminded me very much of the cuttings along Loch Awe on the C & O [Callender and Oban] Railway and the formation of the ground that had to be faced is very similar."[25] So Scots and Malawians began to share their experience at a variety of levels.

The road was never completed in the form which Stevenson and Stewart had envisaged. Even at its best it was what Jack Thompson describes as "essentially a dirt track, suitable for ox-carts or porters."[26] Nonetheless it was significant in a number of ways. It helped to move the centre of gravity of Livingstonia Mission to the northern part of Malawi, with far-reaching consequences. This in turn proved to have a political importance which has been highlighted by Thompson: "When, in 1889, Britain and Germany began negotiating a treaty to define their respective spheres of influence in Central Africa, the original draft would have given most of what is now the Northern region of Malawi to the Germans. It was the Scottish missionary presence in the north, and, to some extent, the myth of the Stevenson Road, which enabled their supporters in Britain to pressurize the British government to negotiate changes to the proposed treaty.... Thus, at least indirectly, the work of James Stewart in the north of the country might be said to have helped to bring about the present boundaries of Malawi."[27] Finally, it may be noted that recent analysis of the factors which cause countries to be caught in the poverty trap has highlighted the importance of trade links. Paul Collier identifies being landlocked as one of four key factors which prevent a country from achieving development.[28] Stevenson's agenda therefore remains important for Malawi even in the very different world of today.

Livingstonia: Forging Friendship with Tonga and Ngoni

During its early years, the Livingstonia Mission was vexed by the same problem of civil power as proved to be such a stumbling block at Blantyre. Early encounters with the Tonga people around Bandawe frequently revolved around appeals to the Mission to arbitrate in local disputes. It took the clear vision and firm leadership of Robert Laws to see that: "The exercise of Magisterial Functions by the head of the Mission I think rather hinders than furthers his work as a minister of the Gospel. In the eyes of the natives he is apt to be looked upon more in the character of a chief than as a teacher and friend to whom they can come for instruction and guidance."[29] Having learnt this lesson from experience Laws was able to apply it to the activity of the Mission as it established itself in northern Malawi during the 1880s.

Another important step for the Mission was the development of contacts with the Ngoni people in the district now known as Mzimba. Key to this was William Koyi, one of four Xhosa "evangelists" recruited for service with Livingstonia Mission by James Stewart at Lovedale. The Ngoni, who had only recently arrived in Malawi, came originally from South Africa and had travelled northwards as a result of the

41

fragmentation of the Zulu people which occurred in the mid-19th century. Koyi was familiar with their language and culture and soon earned the nickname of "Mtusane" – the "bridge-builder" or "go-between". As Jack Thompson has stated, he was "a man who could co-exist in two very different worlds and represent one to the other. In the extremely delicate and sometimes dangerous conditions of uNgoni in the 1880s such a quality was vitally important."[30] By winning the confidence of M'mbelwa, the paramount chief, and other significant leaders Koyi enabled Laws to establish the cordial relations which led to the establishment of a mission station at Njuyu, near Hoho village, in 1882. Thus began an engagement between the Ngoni people and the Livingstonia Mission which would have profound effects on both.

Prior to the arrival of the Livingstonia Mission relations between the Tonga and Ngoni were marked by suspicion and tension, leading to frequent outbreaks of violence. By attempting to establish friendship with both communities Livingstonia pursued a high-risk strategy. If it succeeded, the Mission could be a force for reconciliation in northern Malawi. If it failed, hostilities could deepen and the Mission could be caught in the cross-fire. Not without many an anxious moment, the Mission did prove to be a force for peace and reconciliation. Key to this was the quality of personal relationships which were established at leadership level. Angus Elmslie, who lived and worked as a medical missionary in uNgoni from 1885 recalled his eventful early days: "Living, as I did, with Mombera [M'mbelwa] for six years before he died, I never knew of his having stopped a single war party from attacking the helpless Tonga around Dr Laws' station at Bandawe because of his belief in God; but over and over again because of his attachment to Dr Laws he refused to sanction war."[31] As a "third side" the Mission proved to be an agent of change in Tonga-Ngoni relations. As relationships deepened, Livingstonia not only enabled the Tonga and Ngoni to come to terms with each other but also prepared them to engage with the wider world, something which both communities would do with conspicuous success during the 20th century.

The missionary appointed to take forward the work of Blantyre Mission, after its near-collapse in 1880, was David Clement Scott, a man of strong personality and formidable intellect. From his arrival in 1881 Scott worked closely with the small group of Africans who had been attracted to the Blantyre Mission during its troubled early period in the late 1870s. Men like Joseph Bismarck, Rondau Kaferanjila and Donald Malota proved to be able leaders and took prominent roles in starting the Mission's work in other parts of the Shire Highlands, such as Domasi and Chiradzulu. Particularly through the school, Scott was also able to capitalize on friendships and contacts which had been developed over the twenty years since Livingstone and his party had first entered the Malawi area. Scott's close colleague and eventual successor, Alexander Hetherwick, recalled his first day in Blantyre in 1883: "The day closed with a visit to the Dormitories and a chat with the boys sitting round their fire; most of them were Makololo lads from the River, sons of Livingstone's Makololo..."[32] It was through such chats that the distinctive ethos of Blantyre Mission was developed.

From his conversations with Rev Harry Matecheta and Mr Lewis Bandawe many years afterwards, Andrew Ross learned that: "Every Saturday afternoon ... senior boys or girls were invited to the Manse for tea. These were meant to be relaxed friendly occasions which Scott hoped to use in a twofold way. First he taught the young folk how to behave easily in European company, secondly, he got a chance to have them talk and learn from them not only customs and traditions of African life, but also their ideas and feelings about what was going on around them."[33] Another unusual feature of Blantyre Mission was the practice of everyone gathering outdoors on cloudless moonlit nights to dance, play games and sing. Such gatherings were commonplace in African villages but almost unheard of in the context of a mission station. Underpinning them in the mind of David Clement Scott was the philosophy of anti-racism and confidence in the African vernacular world which he had imbibed from David Livingstone.

Scott's confidence in the African vernacular world can be seen in relation to language. The extent of his success in learning the local language of the Blantyre area is evident in his *Cyclopaedic Dictionary of the Mang'anja Language*, published in 1892.[34] This was a magisterial work demonstrating not only great philological skill but profound understanding of Mang'anja culture and idiom. Scott's vision for the emerging church was that its life and worship would be conducted in the Mang'anja language which Europeans in the country would be expected to learn. This early encounter of Scots and Malawians was marked by a sense of confidence in the contribution which would be made by Malawian life and culture.

The appreciation of local language and culture found expression in a philosophy of mission which was wary of alien imposition and confident about the potential of the local vernacular world to provide the soil in which a truly African church could grow and develop. This confidence was forged through extensive involvement in *mlandu* – dispute resolution – to which Scott devoted much time without falling into the trap of attempting to exercise civil jurisdiction. Through this experience he came to recognise the strength of the society in which he was working and which he believed offered a sound basis for further development.

At a time when racist ideology and settler economics prescribed menial roles for Africans, Scott set out in an entirely different direction:

> People will not believe how much an African is capable of until they have tried. Our aim is always to teach how to bear responsibility, and, at the proper time to lay it upon those who are able to bear it. In many ways that time has come now. It is a fatal mistake to keep the African in leading strings. We cannot too soon teach him to realise that he has a part to play in the education and life of Christ's Church and kingdom.[35]

Scott sought to put these principles into effect in the everyday life of the Blantyre Mission. Convention at the time generally required that Africans remove their hats in the presence of Europeans, as a mark of respect. On one occasion Scott encountered Joseph Bismarck standing with his hat in hand as he waited to speak with John McIlwain, the head of carpentry. In a remark which revealed both his paternalism and his anti-racism, Scott said: "No, no Bismarck, when McIlwain comes up you simply raise your hat, that's all, you and he are brothers. You both keep your hats off while speaking to me because I am your Father, but you two, no, you are brothers."[36] Such symbolic gestures were potent in a social context where relations between the races would become a defining issue.

Given the number of Scots and Malawians by now encountering one another, it would be surprising if there were never any moments of friction. The low point came in February 1884 with an altercation between Chipatula, one of the Makololo chiefs, and George Fenwick, one of the original staff of the Blantyre Mission who was by now an independent trader. The two had long been drinking companions and Fenwick had become well-known for his bad temper and violence. An argument about the price paid for a consignment of ivory got out of hand and Fenwick killed Chipatula. Retribution for the murder was swift as people of Chipatula's village caught and killed Fenwick, mounting his head on a stake.[37] Understandably this issue shook the sense of confidence which had been growing between Scots and local African communities. However, the movement associated with the Mission was now strong enough to surmount such a crisis.

Besides the rapid development of Blantyre Mission as a headquarters, the 1880s also witnessed the beginnings of contacts and connections throughout southern Malawi from which the work of the Mission would grow in future years. Stations were begun at Domasi and Chiradzulu, extending the Mission's influence among the Yao and Mang'anja people of the Shire Highlands. Contact was also established with the southern or "Maseko" Ngoni of Ntcheu district. Chikuse Kaphatikiza, the paramount chief, and Clement Scott developed a personal friendship which was analogous to that between M'mbelwa and Robert Laws in the north. In a context where Ngoni raids were still feared by the Yao and Mang'anja, such a friendship carried strategic significance. Another important step was the beginning of Mulanje Mission, on the lower slopes of the Mulanje Massif, in 1890.

Meanwhile at Blantyre itself construction was advancing on the central church which would become known in later years as St Michael and All Angels. The extraordinarily ambitious architect of this remarkable structure – the first permanent church building between the Limpopo and the Nile – was David Clement Scott. As Andrew Ross explains: "Its catholic cruciform shape surmounted by Byzantine towers, were meant by Scott to symbolise his hopes for an African Christianity free from the petty quarrels of Europe."[38] For the design to be given effect required a very close understanding between Scott and the Malawian workforce. A key figure in the enterprise was the carpenter John McIlwain of whom his colleague William Affleck Scott remarked:

St Michael and All Angels Church in Blantyre

"He has all the charge of the workmen, and the brickmaking, and the carpentry in the place, and so he is '*weel kent*'."[39] Together they succeeded, by 1891, in building the beautiful church which continues to attract admiration from both locals and visitors in Blantyre today.

Nkhoma: Scottish Roots and Chewa Connections

When the history of Malawi's influential Presbyterian Church (CCAP) is told, it is often explained that the Livingstonia Synod in the north and the Blantyre Synod in the south have Scottish origins while the Nkhoma Synod in the Central Region originates with the Cape Synod of the Dutch Reformed Church in South Africa. This is quite true but it can easily obscure the fact that the South African roots of the Nkhoma Synod in turn drew their roots from Scotland. In 1821 a young Scottish minister

46

named Andrew Charles Murray responded to an appeal by the British Governor of the Cape Colony, Charles Somerset, for ministers and teachers to promote English amongst the Dutch-dominated community in South Africa.[40] It was a move which was to have far-reaching effects both on South Africa and Malawi. Murray married Maria Susanna Stegman, an Afrikaner woman, and together they created a deeply religious home into which their sixteen children were born.

Amongst them were John Murray who founded the Dutch Reformed seminary at Stellenbosch and Andrew Murray who became one of the most influential devotional writers of his generation. Amongst the next generation was Andrew Charles Murray's grandson and namesake who pioneered the establishment of what became the Nkhoma Synod of the CCAP. The family had retained its Scottish connections and A.C. Murray had undertaken his theological training in Scotland. It was therefore entirely natural for him to spend time with Laws and Elmslie in the north of Malawi before beginning his own missionary work in the central region. Here they quickly formed the connections with the Chewa people of central Malawi which would lead in subsequent years to a fast-growing church movement as well as major educational and medical institutions.

As the work became established, no less than five of Murray's siblings joined him. As Janet Parsons remarks: "Mission work for the Dutch Reformed, to a far greater extent than the Scots at Blantyre and Livingstonia, was becoming a family affair."[41] Moreover, it was a family with a distinctive Scots-Afrikaner pedigree, adding a new dimension to the Scotland-Malawi connection. They continued to cherish their Scottish connection. When William Hoppe Murray, a cousin of A.C. Murray, completed the translation of the New Testament into Chinyanja (a task on which he collaborated with Blantyre missionaries Alexander Hetherwick and Robert Napier), he took his manuscript to Scotland where he arranged with the National Bible Society for its publication. While their South African experience tended to give the Dutch Reformed missionaries views on race, education and agriculture which differed from those of the Blantyre and Livingstonia missionaries, the Scottish heritage which united the three missions, and which still today provides an important strand in the unity of the CCAP, is not to be underestimated.

Conclusion

It is beyond question that the establishment of the Livingstonia, Blantyre and Nkhoma Missions heralded a new era for the people who would come to form the nation of Malawi. What has less often been recognised is that it was a profoundly significant development for the people of Scotland as well. As Alexander Duff's biographer remarks: "In 1874 Dr Duff and James Stevenson ... launched the Livingstonia Mission, the greatest national enterprise, it has been truly said, since Scotland sent forth the very different Darien expedition."[42] This comparison looked back to the closing years of the 17th century when a huge national effort by Scotland was put into the establishment of a colony in Panama. As much as half the national wealth was invested in the initiative but it proved to be a complete failure resulting in economic catastrophe and leading to the union with England in 1707. Almost two hundred years later, according to Robert Laws' biographer, "the bitter ignominy and shame of its failure still haunted the national memory."[43] The Livingstonia Mission was set in this context – as a national effort which might redeem the failure of the Darien scheme. It was seen as having the moral power to do this. Whereas the Darien scheme had aimed simply for commercial returns, Livingstonia aimed to open up Africa and free its people from the curse of the slave trade.

This high purpose was understood to be uniting the nation once again in seeking to establish a centre of influence far from home, but this time on an altruistic basis. In this way developments in Malawi were shaping Scottish identity and destiny in important ways. This is evident from the extensive coverage which the Livingstonia expedition received in the national press, with a plethora of reports and letters appearing in all the major Scottish papers.[44] When James Jack wrote the history of the first twenty-five years of the Livingstonia Mission, he set it in this framework: "Many countries were moved by this wave of missionary enthusiasm

48

produced by Livingstone's labours; but Scotland in particular felt the power of it. Livingstone was a son of Scotland, born and bred amid her rugged scenes, and she felt more profoundly impressed by his labours than any other civilised country. She awoke to a new missionary life. She became specifically interested in Africa, and manifested a profound desire for the highest welfare of the African people."[45] Involvement in Malawi was bringing renewal to Scotland's identity and purpose at an important time in her history.

---

[1]   John McCracken, *Politics and Christianity in Malawi 1875-1940: The Impact of the Livingstonia Mission in the Northern Province*, 2nd ed., Blantyre: CLAIM, 2000, p. 52.

[2]   *Ibid*, pp. 62-63.

[3]   John McCracken, "Livingstone and the Aftermath: the Origins and Development of Livingstonia Mission", in Pachai., *Livingstone: Man of Africa*, pp. 218-34 at p. 225.

[4]   Robert Laws to "a friend at home", 19 October 1875; cit McCracken, *Politics and Christianity*, p. 66.

[5]   McCracken, *Politics and Christianity*, p. 80.

[6]   H.K. Matecheta, *Blantyre Mission: Nkani ya Ciyambi Cace*, Blantyre: Hetherwick Press, 1951, p. 1; cit. Andrew C. Ross, *Blantyre Mission and the Making of Modern Malawi*, Blantyre: CLAIM, 1996, p. 42

[7]   Ross, *Blantyre Mission*, pp. 19-20.

[8]   Duff Macdonald, *Africana*, Vol. II, London: Simpkin Marshall & Co, 1882; repr. New York: Negro Universities Press, 1969, p. 99.

[9]   See A. Chirnside, *The Blantyre Missionaries: Discreditable Disclosures*, London: Ridgeway, 1880.

[10] See Ross, *Blantyre Mission*, pp. 52-57.

[11] Ross, *Blantyre Mission*, p. 60.

[12] H.W. Macmillan, "The Origins and Development of the African Lakes Company 1878-1908", PhD, University of Edinburgh, 1970, p. 116.

[13] *Ibid.*, p. 95

[14] *Ibid.*, p. 129.

[15] Hastings K. Banda, "The Moirs of Nyasaland: An African's Tribute", *Other Lands*, July 1940, pp. 144-45.

[16] *Ibid.*, p. 144.

[17] Macmillan, "Origins and Development", p. 438.

[18] Fred L.M. Moir, *After Livingstone: An African Trade Romance*, London: Hodder & Stoughton, n.d., p. 150.

[19] *Ibid.*, p. 195.

[20] Macmillan, "Origins and Development", p. 342.

[21] James McCarthy ed., *The Road to Tanganyika: The Diaries of Donald Munro and William McEwan*, Zomba: Kachere, 2006, p. 16.

[22] P.A. Cole-King, "Transport and Communications in Malawi", University of Malawi, Conference on the Early History of Malawi, 20-24 July 1970, pp. 9-10.

[23] McCarthy, *The Road to Tanganyika*, p. 124.

[24] *Ibid.*, p. 53.

[25] *Ibid.*, p. 97.

[26] T. Jack Thompson ed., *From Nyassa to Tanganyika: The Journal of James Stewart CE in Central Africa 1876-1879*, Blantyre: Central Africana, 1989, p. 3.

[27] *Ibid.*, pp. 15-16.

[28] Paul Collier, *The Bottom Billion: Why the Poorest Countries Are Failing and What Can Be Done About It*, Oxford: Oxford University Press, 2007, pp. 53-63.

[29] Robert Laws to George Smith, 3 February 1880, quoted in Livingstonia Sub-committee minutes, entry for 2 June 1880, NLS 7912, cit., McCracken, *Politics and Christianity*, p. 97.

[30] T. Jack Thompson, *Touching the Heart: Xhosa Missionaries to Malawi, 1876-1888*, Pretoria: University of South Africa, 2000, p. 133.

[31] W.A. Elmslie, *Among the Wild Ngoni*, Edinburgh: Oliphant, Anderson & Ferrier, 1899, p. 94, cit. McCracken, *Politics and Christianity*, pp. 129-30.

[32] Alexander Hetherwick, "My First Day in Blantyre", *Central Africa News and Views*, Vol. 2 No. 1 (July 1936), p. 5.

[33] Ross, *Blantyre Mission*, p. 75.

[34] D.C. Scott, *A Cyclopaedic Dictionary of the Mang'anja Language*, Edinburgh: Foreign Missions Committee of the Church of Scotland, 1892.

[35] *Life and Work in British Central Africa*, June 1895.

[36] Ross, *Blantyre Mission*, p. 66.

[37] *Ibid.*, pp.77-78.

[38] Andrew C. Ross, "Livingstone and the Aftermath: The Origins and Development of the Blantyre Mission", in Pachai, *Livingstone: Man of Africa*, pp. 191-217 at 214.

[39] Stephen Green, "Blantyre Mission", *The Nyasaland Journal*, Vol. X No. 2 (July 1957), pp. 6-17 at p. 11.

[40] See Janet Wagner Parsons, "Scots and Afrikaners in Central Africa: Andrew Charles Murray and the Dutch Reformed Church Mission in Malawi", *The Society of Malawi Journal*, Vol. 51 No. 1 (1998), pp. 21-40, at p. 22.

[41] *Ibid.*, p. 26

[42] George Smith, *Life of Alexander Duff*, London: Hodder & Stoughton, 1899, p. 337; cit. Esther Breitenbach, *Empire and Scottish Society: The Impact of Foreign Missions at Home c. 1790 to c. 1914*, Edinburgh: Edinburgh University Press, 2009, p. 138.

[43] W.P. Livingstone, *Laws of Livingstonia: A Narrative of Missionary Adventure and Achievement*, London: Hodder & Stoughton, 1921, p. 9.

[44] Esther Breitenbach lists *The Scotsman, Dundee Courier, Glasgow Herald, Daily Review, Edinburgh Courant, Aberdeen Weekly Herald and Free Press* and *Wick Gazette*. Breitenbach, *Empire and Scottish Society*, p. 156.

[45] James W. Jack, *Daybreak in Livingstonia: The Story of the Livingstonia Mission, British Central Africa*, Edinburgh & London: Oliphant, Anderson & Ferrier, 1900, pp. 18-19.

4. Encounter and Transformation

By the time the British Protectorate was established in 1891, it was clear that the initial contact made by Livingstone and his friends thirty years earlier had been consolidated. Even by the 1880s it was clear, as James McCarthy remarks, that "there never was a region of Africa more replete with Scots whether missionaries, administrators, traders, or engineers, most if not all answering Livingstone's call."[1] When a German traveller, Tom von Prince, visited Blantyre in the early 1890s, he noted the cold and un-African fog and described the place as "African Scotland". He went on to observe that; "all around was the unmistakable accent of that kind of Englishmen. What is more, Livingston, who discovered that area, was a Scotsman. Almost all the inhabitants there seem to be Scottish, a breed of men which is very clever in monetary affairs. They combine the pleasant with the useful, are the best soldiers of England, and are very precise as businessmen."[2] Attention is naturally often focussed on the Blantyre and Livingstonia Missions which provided the outstanding institutional expression of Scottish influence but Scots made their mark in other spheres also, such as "Pitgaveny" the military officer who often led the forces of the British administration, invariably scorning the standard uniform and charging into battle in his Cameron Highlanders kilt;[3] or John Buchanan and his brothers who were pioneers of estate agriculture well before the British Protectorate was established.[4] Scots formed a clear majority of the 57 Europeans resident in Malawi in 1891.[5]

Scotland and the British Protectorate

During the 1870s and 1880s the Livingstonia Mission, Blantyre Mission and African Lakes Company established Scottish influence in Malawi in a context where there was no overarching civil authority. As has been seen, this was not without its problems, particularly in the early days of the Missions when they succumbed to pressures to exercise civil authority themselves. They learned from their mistakes, however, and gradually developed their diplomatic skills in forming good working relationships with the chiefs of the surrounding communities. In fact, they gained understanding of the structure of African societies and respect for chiefs who exercised their authority effectively. In turn, men such as Robert Laws and David Clement Scott won the respect and affection of chiefs with whom they were in contact. It is important to recognise that these early interactions took place in a pre-colonial political context. Malawians and Scots had already established relationships of mutual respect prior to the advent of British colonial rule.

Had there been no external pressures to consider, it is possible that the Scottish Missions would have been quite happy to continue operating as they did in the 1880s. Towards the end of that decade, however, they became gravely concerned about the territorial ambitions of the Arabs and the Portuguese. An increase in Swahili-inspired slave-raiding led to the slaver Mlozi attempting to set up a new Swahili-controlled state at Karonga at the north end of the Lake. Meanwhile, the Portuguese claimed as their territory a large part of what is now southern Malawi, including the Shire Highlands, where Blantyre Mission was based. By 1889 David Clement Scott was ringing alarm bells: "Rumours from home speak of a division of territory between Portugal and Britain in which the Shire is the dividing line. This is disastrous if it is true: it is indeed 'keeping the shell and giving Portugal the kernel'. We must hold fast to this stronghold and gateway of African civilization whatever comes..."[6] The two threats were inter-linked in that it appeared as though it would be very difficult to confront the claims of Mlozi if the Portuguese were able to cut off the Scottish presence in Malawi from the outside world. It was only in January 1889 that D.J. Rankin discovered the Chinde mouth of the Zambesi which allowed the Zambesi-Shire route to be recognised as an international waterway.

Meanwhile from 1886 Mlozi was seeking to impose his authority over the Ngonde people around Karonga, with increasing violence. A number of Ngonde took refuge at the Karonga station of the African Lakes Company, appealing to the Scots as their friends to come to their aid. The outcome, as described by Andrew Ross, was that:

The Livingstonia Mission, backed up the African Lakes Company in siding with the Ngonde people, and its supporters in Scotland through the press and pulpit told Scotland that this war was one in which Scots were standing shoulder to shoulder with the African people against an attack by Arab slavers.... From 1887 to 1889 there was desultory fighting at Karonga. The Ngonde and Scots could not take the stockaded strongholds of Mlozi, while he in turn failed to subdue the Ngonde or drive off their Scottish allies.[7]

Meanwhile the Portuguese stepped up their insistence that only Portuguese traffic could be allowed on the Zambesi and Shire; and reiterated their claim to sovereignty over all the territory between the Zambesi and the southern end of Lake Malawi. As Ross concludes: "The African Lakes Company, the Scottish missions and their African allies and friends appeared to be helpless between the jaws of the Swahili-Portuguese nutcracker."[8]

The Scottish missionaries believed that Portuguese annexation would be injurious both to their own work and to the Malawian people with whom they were by now very familiar. A British Protectorate seemed the only viable alternative. They therefore launched a vigorous and finally successful campaign to persuade the British Government to withdraw from its initial willingness to cede the area to Portugal, and to establish a formal British Protectorate. This included a series of public meetings in Aberdeen, Glasgow, Edinburgh and Dundee and culminated in "a monster petition" signed by over 11,000 ministers and elders of the Scottish churches who demanded British intervention in the Lake Malawi area."[9] The campaign even involved collaboration between members of the Free and Established Churches in a way which was unprecedented since the "Disruption" which had divided the two churches in 1843. The Convention of Royal Burghs and several Chambers of Commerce lent their support.[10] When Archibald Scott, Convener of the Church of Scotland Foreign Mission Committee, presented the petition to the Prime Minister, Lord Salisbury, he was able to say: "My Lord, this is the voice of Scotland".[11]

To this extent, Scots played a significant role in the advent of colonial rule in Malawi. It should be noted, however, that it was not British rule which was sought by the missionaries but rather an intervention from Britain to ensure that neither the Portuguese nor the Swahili were allowed to take over the area. "It was not to make a state that Sir Harry Johnston was sent out," wrote Clement Scott, "but to deliver from Portuguese occupation a state already made."[12] The conditions under which British protection was offered were, in fact, a matter of much concern to the Scottish missionaries. In their view what was required was protection from outside interference but the minimum of disruption to the internal affairs of the people of the territory. It seems clear that it was the intense pressure from Scotland which convinced Salisbury that he would have to review his initial inclination to allow Portugal to gain control of southern Malawi. "In all of this long period of campaigning," comments Andrew Ross, "the Scottish lobbyists adopted a consistent line in their approaches to the government in London.... The future of the land and people of the Lake Malawi area was a Scottish issue, united Scots of different Churches and of different political persuasions."[13] As Richard Finlay concludes, "... it was probably the only time that Scottish public opinion changed British foreign policy in the nineteenth century."[14]

Once Salisbury's mind was made up, events moved swiftly. Harry Johnston was appointed Consul and ordered to proceed to Blantyre via the Chinde mouth of the Zambesi, thus establishing the Zambesi-Shire route as an international waterway. Johnston then travelled north to make treaties of friendship with various chiefs, including Mlozi. Meanwhile, his Vice Consul John Buchanan, who had been one of the first staff of the Blantyre Mission at its inception, was faced by an advance of Portuguese troops up the Shire valley. He responded by raising the Union Jack at Blantyre and declaring both the Shire Valley and the Shire Highlands to be under British Protection. An ultimatum from Salisbury to the Portuguese Government in February 1890 forced the withdrawal of the Portuguese troops. Finally, in May 1891 came the formal declaration of the British Central African Protectorate, with Harry Johnston named as the first Commissioner.

The Scottish missionaries were relieved that the serious threats posed by the Arabs and Portuguese had been successfully addressed but they were immediately anxious about new threats entailed in the Protectorate status now enjoyed by Malawi. In particular, they were dismayed by the prospect of Cecil Rhodes' British South Africa Company being given the responsibility of ruling the country. Rhodes had provided a subvention to meet the costs of the administration of the new Protectorate for its first three years. It was believed that this might pave the way for the Protectorate to be ruled by the Company. Clement Scott at Blantyre was trenchant in his response to this prospect: "A Chartered Company is not a government and never can be. To be ruled by such is to be ruled for commercial ends by absentee directors and shareholders whose real interests are only served by tangible dividends."[15]

For years Rhodes manoeuvred to establish his influence in Nyasaland but at every turn he was met by the inflexible opposition of Clement Scott and his colleagues. In 1894, when Rhodes made a gift of £17,000 to the government of the Protectorate, the comment in the Blantyre Mission newspaper was as follows: "The government by £17,000 of alien money must be exercised to that amount in the interests of that alien influence, and that alien influence lacks the essential elements, the dignity, the impartiality, the esprit de coeur of a British government. The effects *cannot be good*."[16] In the judgement of Sir Harry Johnston, the pioneering British Consul and an associate of Rhodes, it was the Blantyre missionaries who were mainly responsible for the failure of Rhodes' efforts to embrace Nyasaland within his empire. In 1893 Johnston wrote to Rhodes as follows:

> I don't think you have ever realised the bitter hatred borne you by these Scotch missionaries of Blantyre. They hate you because you are an Englishman because you threaten to overshadow their own petty meddling and muddling with grander schemes that will outshine mission work in popular favour. Remember it was mainly Scott and Hetherwick who baulked the scheme in 1890 of all BCA coming

under the Company's Charter. They are now up and at it again and the most serious enemies you possess.[17]

The commitment of the Blantyre missionaries to the interests of the Malawian population made them always suspicious of the commercial ambitions of Cecil Rhodes. As Roland Oliver summarises: "Nyasaland (later Malawi) was a shaving from the north-eastern corner of Rhodes' empire, which Lord Salisbury took under direct imperial control, because British missionaries were already established there … who have made plain their antipathy to Chartered Company rule."[18]

In 1900 when the possibility of Chartered Company rule was again being canvassed the Scottish Missions were no less implacable in their opposition. In a context where it was often argued that transfer of power to a chartered company would be economically beneficial, Blantyre Mission stated its position unequivocally: "The principle involved here is radically wrong. The prosperity of any country should always be in the possession of its inhabitants."[19] Underlying this robust approach was an awareness that South Africa, already emerging as the dominant power of the southern African region, was taking a very different approach to its "natives". Again, the position of Blantyre Mission was very clear: "No worse fate could befall the native than to be thrown aside as a useless factor in the development of the country. Central Africa [Nyasaland] would then become another South Africa. A worse doom could not befall either the Protectorate or its inhabitants."[20] So far as Blantyre Mission was concerned the South African approach represented "a system of ideas on things African and native that are entirely foreign to the original foundations of our community."[21]

Strong awareness of these "original foundations" also disposed the Scottish missionaries to be critical towards the first British administration on certain points. While they had supported the establishment of the Protectorate they were by no means complacent as to the policy on which it would run. Land, labour and taxation were the crucial issues faced by the African community during the early years of British rule and on each of these the Scottish Missions took a very different view to that adopted by the Government. On the question of land, for example, in a context

57

where European planters were establishing estates on more and more of the best land, Blantyre Mission made its position clear as early as 1892:

> We have always held that land belongs to the people, and have ever questioned the legal and moral right of the chief to sell any part of his territory over the heads of those dwelling on it without safe-guarding to them the right to have room to plant and build. A very large part of the Shire Highlands is claimed by European purchasers.... Where is the native community soon to find room to hoe and plant its food crop?[22]

It also offered a robust response to the planters and traders within the Protectorate who were complaining about the difficulty of securing sufficient labour and blaming the supposed laziness of the "natives": "Does a 'European colonist' imagine that the native is unwilling to work and that he can be made to do so by presents and threats? Let him go and see the plantations of Buchanan Brothers at Michiru, Lunza, Chiradzulu and Zomba. These are the products of free labour. The African can work without compulsion of any kind."[23]

So persistent were the Blantyre missionaries in questioning the policies of the British Administration on such matters as land, labour and taxation that in 1894 Acting Commissioner Alfred Sharpe reported that:

> Mr Commissioner Johnston in his despatches advised that there would be no permanent and satisfactory state of things with regard to this Mission until two missionaries, The Rev D.C. Scott and the Rev Alexander Hetherwick, were removed from the country.... The missionaries are taking a course that makes them appear in the eyes of the natives of this Protectorate as an Opposition Party to H.M. Administration.[24]

Sharpe had detected the awareness of Malawians that the Scottish missionaries had a very different approach from the British Administration on a number of matters which gave them cause for concern.

It was an approach which they were to consistently maintain across the years. When a Legislative Council was established in 1908, Alexander Hetherwick was appointed to sit on it as representative for missionary and native interests. He used his position to champion the concern for justice in relation to land distribution which the Mission had been expressing since the establishment of the Protectorate. In 1910, for example, he told the Legislative Council that if Africans were to be induced to remain on the soil, they should be given security and an adequate amount of land. Although government allowed free use of Crown land and excluded African villages and plantations from alienation, yet Africans did not feel assured. Hetherwick mentioned instances of Africans being moved from one place to another to make room for Europeans.[25]

Nor was it only a matter of particular issues. At a time when British military force was being widely used to impose the authority of the new Administration, the Blantyre missionaries championed an alternative approach. They had confidence in the culture and institutions through which African communities operated and believed that it was through these long-established channels that the Administration would work most effectively:

> We ask too for a constitutional mode of dealing with the native life about us. We ask that the authority and influence of the native chiefs in the country be recognised and their counsel sought in dealing with the people. The African if he is anything is constitutional – no change or step of any importance is taken without first open *mlandu* in which the opinion of all is fully sought and expressed. We hope to see the same constitutional methods continued in all future changes. The native recognises them and obeys them, and when similar modes are followed he will obey the new power as readily as the old. The native and native life must be developed and not crushed.[26]

Andrew Ross grasped the nub of the issue when he stated: "... the critical position of the mission in regard to the Administration was based on fundamental differences over principle. The issue of principle was twofold: first was the African of the day capable of becoming a responsible and civilised individual, and secondly, was African culture capable of becoming the foundation of modern development."[27]

59

At Livingstonia, Scottish missionaries also took the view that British rule was the least bad option available to the communities among which they were working. The annexation of Ngoniland in 1904 was cautiously welcomed by the Livingstonia missionaries who made it clear at the same time that they did not want their own work to be identified with British rule. This is well illustrated in a letter which Angus Elmslie wrote to Robert Laws in 1895:

> As for Ngoniland and the Government I believe it would be for the good of the people and good for us in view of changes inevitably coming if the country were under the Government rather than under the B.S.A. Co. [British South Africa Company] As to helping the Government further than neutrality, that may or may not be wise for us. There are dangers in taking part, even by countenancing arrangements, and there might be worse dangers in holding aloof. I should like to see the treaty before committing myself, and I should also want to know how far, if assistance were given, our opinion would rule the *modus operandi*.... But I do not like the idea of being mixed up with Government business.[28]

While the Mission kept its distance from the colonial regime, its work among the Ngoni over the preceding twenty-five years was an essential precursor to the peaceful and mutually satisfactory negotiations which led to agreement between the Ngoni chiefs and the British administration. The confidence between Scottish missionaries and African communities, grounded in deep personal relationships, was a vital resource for the latter as they navigated changing times. As Andrew Ross reflects on the situation around Blantyre: "The coming of the Boma and the increase in the number of European planters meant that the old world was being shaken for a large number of people. Perhaps Scott and his people could provide a help in dealing with this new world of the Boma with its demand for taxes and of the planters with their demands for work at the most inconvenient times of the year. He was the one representative of this new world that they knew and could approach."[29] Personal confidence, built up through meeting crises together, was a key characteristic of the relationships developed between Malawians and Scots during this period.

While the political ramifications of the Scottish presence in Malawi unfolded, on a day-to-day basis encounter took place on the intersection between the rapidly developing institutions of the Missions and the African community life within which they were set. The late 19th and early 20th century proved to be a period of rapid growth particularly in regard to mission schools. Among the Tonga, for example, the number of Livingstonia Mission schools increased from 18 in early 1895 to 53 in 1898, with average attendance rising from 1,600 to around 5,000. Likewise among the Ngoni, in 1893 there were ten schools with a total enrolment of 630. By 1904 Loudon Mission alone maintained 134 schools in the Embangweni area, with up to 9,000 pupils. By 1909 it had opened a further 150 out-schools with a total of some 12,000 pupils. Donald Fraser, the missionary in charge, could ask, "whether there is another mission in the world with so great school systems attached to one station as you will find in the Livingstonia Mission?"[30] The training of teachers to staff this extensive school network and the running of its administration involved extensive contact and collaboration of Scots and Malawians as they worked together on this rapid expansion. A parallel development was well underway at Blantyre Mission.

The increased provision of educational opportunity was not only a matter of quantity but also of quality. As the colonial administration and modern economy created demand for skilled labour it was noted that: "posts of middle-grade administrative responsibility fell open to Africans in Malawi earlier and in greater numbers than anywhere else in Central Africa."[31] As early as 1897 Robert Laws observed that: "from many quarters, comes the demand for natives who can be put in positions of trust and responsibility of a subordinate nature."[32]

A hugely significant step taken by the Livingstonia Mission was the establishment of the Overtoun Institution on a site on the Khondowe plateau which took the name "Livingstonia". The brainchild of Robert Laws, the aim of the Institution was to offer post-primary education in a variety of fields, training leaders for church and society. The range of the curriculum, the discipline with which it was pursued and the high level which it sought to reach meant that the Institution brought something quite new to Malawi and its influence would be felt for a century and more. By 1921 the trade unionist Clements Kadalie, himself a product of the Overtoun Institution, could write that, "The work of both the Nyasaland and Northern Rhodesian Governments is largely being done by those black men trained at a college established by Dr and Mrs Laws."[33] Besides the quality of the education it offered, the Institution also played a distinctive role by bringing together the most able Malawians from different districts and ethnicities. To a considerable extent, Livingstonia proved to be the melting pot within which Malawian national unity was forged. Its influence is further evident in the fact that the descendents of its first graduates have continued to take leading roles in national life right down to the present day.

Scottish missionaries, of course, had the primary purpose of introducing Christianity to Malawi. This meant that there was a spiritual dimension to the expanding engagement between the Missions and the African communities within their sphere of influence. In the early years Africans who embraced the Christian faith were few and far between but it was clear by the mid-1890s that a popular movement was underway. Congregations of more than 1,000 became common at church services at Bandawe, with many eager to be baptised and become church members.[34] At Ekwendeni in May 1898 a five day "communion season" was held which saw congregations of between three and four thousand responding with intense emotion to the Christian message.[35] Blantyre too saw remarkable church growth during this period. A church membership of 30 in 1891 had increased to 6,500 by 1914.[36] The movement was underway which would lead to a majority of Malawians professing to be Christians. Many different influences contributed to this outcome but the role of the Scottish Missions, especially in the early years of Malawian Christianity, is not to be underestimated. The spread of the faith was largely undertaken by Malawians but its original inspiration arose from their encounter with the Scots and the new ideas which they brought to Malawi.

As Malawians embraced Christianity the question arose as to how far they would be expected to adopt a prescribed form of religion and how far they would be free to work out on their own terms how it might best be expressed in their context. At a time when most European missions in Africa were preoccupied with replicating the church life of their home constituency, Clement Scott took quite a different approach: "Our purpose we lay down as the foundation of all our work that we are building the African Church – not Scotch or English – but African.... The African has a part to play in the Church of Christ universal. His character and influence have still to be reckoned with."[37]

A similar approach was adopted by Donald Fraser who lived and worked among the Ngoni of Mzimba from 1896 to 1925. On the basis of extensive study of Fraser and the Ngoni, Jack Thompson has concluded that: "... the genuinely African church which was created in Mzimba district in the first twenty-five years of the twentieth century, was made possible precisely because Fraser was willing to listen to his Ngoni colleagues, and to encourage at least some aspects of African culture, rather than imposing an entirely European form of Christianity on them."[38] In thinking through the forms of expression which would be appropriate for the Christian church among the Ngoni, Fraser became convinced that a more "emotional" form of worship would be required. Framing what this would mean in relation to the Scots, Fraser suggested that: "It is not the 'canny Scot' but the fervid Celt who is most closely allied to the African."[39]

Consideration of the voluminous writings of Fraser reveals that, overall, his attitude to the Ngoni was one of respect and admiration. In an age when it was normal for Europeans to denigrate African life and culture, Fraser struck an entirely different note: "Our Ngoni came to Nyasaland as a moral blessing. The aristocratic Ngoni is a gentleman through and through. His word is absolute. When he gives a promise you may fearlessly rely upon it. He does not steal, nor does he intrude on your privacy."[40] Such warmth of admiration led quite naturally to empathy and affection. This deep personal sympathy created an environment in which it was natural to encourage Ngoni Christians to express their faith in ways which would carry resonance within their own culture. Perhaps even more strikingly, it also found expression in relation to the Ngoni who declined to take part in the new Christian movement. In 1908 two outstanding Ngoni leaders, Ng'onomo Makamu and *Nkosi* Mabulabo, died. Fraser took the trouble to write an article entitled "The Passing of Two Great Angoni Chiefs",

Emily Nhlane and Mary Chipeta – elders (balalakazi) in the first generation Ngoni church, around 1900

which he published in the *United Free Church Missionary Record*. He observed that: "to the end they lived and died polygamists, drunkards, heathen, yet brave and honourable gentlemen."[41] Here was the emergence of mutual respect, friendship and solidarity between Scots and Malawians which could transcend even differences in matters of faith.

One area where Malawians and Scots worked creatively on African interpretation of the Christian faith was in the composition and adaptation of hymns for use in worship. Donald Fraser's sympathetic attitude to Ngoni culture was important in this regard. As Jack Thompson remarks: "Fraser ... found an already thriving tradition of Ngoni Christian music by the time he arrived in uNgoni in 1897.... Soon after his return in 1901 he was already organising musical competitions between the different schools. At Hora in 1901 about two dozen new hymns were heard; the following year fifty new compositions were submitted, and Fraser commented: 'Some pieces were particularly beautiful, and it was felt that a valuable contribution had been made to the hymnology of the Central African Church.'"[42] Research conducted by Andrew Ross in the Blantyre area reveals that there too hymn-singing was an influential medium in communicating the Christian message and attracting people to the church.[43]

Both Missions actively promoted African leadership. At Blantyre in 1893 Clement Scott announced: "a deacons' class of seven but representative of many more, who will in like manner devote themselves to service..."[44] The class was composed of John Macrae Chipuliko, Mungo Murray Chisuse, Thomas Mpeni, James Gray Kamlinje, James Auldearn Mwembe, John Gray Kufa and Harry Kambwiri Matecheta. All seven successfully completed their course and were ordained as deacons on 4th November 1894. The office of deacon is not a familiar one in the Presbyterian churches and it seems that Scott deliberately sought to create a new office: "there is no office at home exactly like it: it is distinctly African".[45] Though they operated in a subordinate capacity, the deacons were entrusted by Scott with considerable responsibility. When a mission station was opened in Angoniland (Ntcheu) in 1893 it was Harry Kambwiri Matecheta who was chosen to lead the work. Though the structures of missionary control would be asserted in subsequent years, the confidence which Scott invested in local African leadership had already begun a movement at village level which would continue to advance with its own momentum, regardless of trends at HQ.

Two Revealing Episodes

Two dramatic episodes serve to reveal the distinctive attitudes which leading Scots brought to the early years of British administration. In January 1899 a European trader named William Robert Ziehl entered Ngoni territory in the north of Malawi, with a group of African employees, in order to buy cattle. When he departed a few weeks later there was uproar among the Ngoni who accused him and his followers of murder, rape, theft and various other offences. Ziehl's account of events indicated that he was on good terms with the Ngoni and was trading successfully until he was subject to an unprovoked attack by Daniel

Nhlane, a teacher employed by Livingstonia Mission. The Ngoni account was very different. As Jack Thompson summarises, they, "accused Ziehl and his followers of forcing the sale of cattle against the will of their owners, seizing cattle without payment, whipping villagers with a *chikoti* [whip], and raping several women."[46] According to the Ngoni it was Ziehl who had lost his temper and struck Daniel Nhlane with his whip. In response, Nhlane and others had beaten him up. He had drawn a revolver and opened fire, slightly wounding two of the Ngoni. On their way out of the area, Ziehl's men had shot and killed two men and wounded an elderly woman.

Nhlane was responsible to the young Scottish missionary Donald Fraser who was based at Ekwendeni at this time. When Fraser got word of the altercation between Nhlane and Ziehl he sent a message to C.A. Cardew, the British administration Collector who was based on the lakeshore asking him to arrest the white man. Meanwhile feeling was running high among the Ngoni who urged Fraser to make the twenty mile journey to Engalaweni where the incident had occurred. On arrival he quickly concluded that the Ngoni could not be restrained from pursuing Ziehl and suggested that he himself would accompany a specially chosen *impi*. As final preparations were made for the pursuit, Cardew and his police arrived and thus, according to Thompson, "averted by a few hours what would have been the unprecedented sight of a Scottish missionary leading out an Ngoni army."[47]

Ziehl was eventually tried by the British Administration and, while the judgement recognised that he had been subject to a degree of provocation, he was found guilty on eight of nine charges and sentenced to six months imprisonment or a £50 fine. He was also required to pay compensation to those he had wronged. Thousands of Ngoni gathered at Ekwendeni to witness the trial. They were deeply impressed that Ziehl was brought to trial at all and, even more so, that he was convicted of his offences by a European court. It has been cited as one of the reasons that the Ngoni were willing to accede to British rule a few years later. It also highlighted the particular relationship which had been formed between the Ngoni and the Livingstonia Mission as they navigated changing times. Donald Fraser's unequivocal identification with the Ngoni side in the dispute presaged an affinity between Scots and Malawians which found expression in resisting together hostile actions by other Europeans during the colonial era.

The distinctive position of the Scottish missionaries in relation to the African community was also demonstrated by disturbances which took place in the Blantyre area in October 1902. The British administration was recruiting troops to join units of the Kings African Rifles which were on their way to Somaliland where they would be involved in attempts to quell the revolt of Muhammad Abdullah Hassan, known to the British as the "Mad Mullah". Villagers were press-ganged, causing many to flee their homes and take refuge either at the Blantyre Mission or in the bush. Women were assaulted and raped. Some were abducted by troops and police. It was described by the Central African Times as a "Reign of Terror under the British Government".[48]

It was Alexander Hetherwick who called for a special meeting of the Committee of the Chamber of Agriculture and Commerce, the organ of the planting community, to be held to consider these events. At the meeting Hetherwick successfully proposed a motion protesting against the actions of Government forces, urging an immediate official enquiry, and demanding compensation for those who suffered damages. A court of enquiry was duly established by the Administration with Judge Joseph John Nunan presiding over its seven days of meeting from 5 November 1902. In his judgement Nunan "largely cleared the army of blame but upheld many charges against the Blantyre police while playing down their significance."[49]

The debate in the Enquiry reached its height when Hetherwick and Nunan clashed on the nature of sexual morality in the African community. In his evidence, Hetherwick "gave it as his deliberate opinion after 19 years experience in the country... that [women] ... were faithful to their husbands." He claimed never to have seen or heard immodest acts or words in that time and he commented on the ferocity of traditional African punishments for adultery.[50] Nunan by contrast believed that sexual morality was low among African women: he was "well aware of the worth of the virginity of the native women in this country" and suggested that indiscriminate sexual intercourse before marriage was commonly practised.[51] As Sean Morrow summarises: "Hetherwick posited an extraordinarily sexually continent female African population – needing to be kept in line however by allegedly draconian punishment. This tradition should, he felt, be used and reinforced by Christian missionaries. Nunan posited so promiscuous and unfettered an African female sexuality that even 'rape' lost its meaning in relation to it."[52]

What stood out was Hetherwick's deep respect for the moral standards of the African community, in contrast to the contempt in which they were held by Judge Nunan. The former's passion for justice was expressed soon afterwards in an article in the Blantyre Mission newspaper: "If the arm of British law and justice is to be felt anywhere it must be in the protection of the native woman. Under the old regime ... the mutual rights of husband and wife are stringently guarded by an unwritten code that exceeds in severity even our own.... Here if anywhere the law must step in to strengthen the foundations of native morality already laid deep in the life of the people."[53] Clearly, for Hetherwick, the new order should be a matter of building on the strengths of the old and working on a basis of admiration for the moral standards of the African community. This demonstrated the strength of the relationship which had been formed between Scots and Africans in the early days of the Blantyre Mission.

Mutually Shaping Identity

It was not only Malawi's identity and destiny, however, which were shaped by the shared experience of Malawians and Scots. George Shepperson observed that "... the Scots' pioneering of British Central Africa and their spirited opposition to the possibility of its passing to Portugal in the late 1880's may be envisaged, from one angle, as the attempt by a group of peoples who had all the aspirations of a nation but little of the structure and substance of one to make a final fling at nationhood by acquiring at last the Caledonian colony which had been denied them since the failure of the seventeenth century Darien venture."[54] If so, the extent of their success may be gauged from Lord Lugard's remark that, "Scotsmen have made Nyasaland".[55]

While the Scottish missionaries welcomed the advent of the British administration in Malawi, they were clear that their own involvement rested on an entirely different basis and were not at all afraid to voice trenchant criticisms of the Government when occasion required. The fact that "Scotland" was playing a distinctive role in Malawi served to sharpen its sense of its own identity at this time. At the Union with England in 1707, civil society in Scotland carried forward a distinct Scottish national identity, particularly through the church, education and law. Scotland's Presbyterian church life was secured under the terms of the Union and now this distinctiveness was bolstered as Presbyterianism took root in Malawi. The Presbyterian democratic ethos underpinned the egalitarian and anti-privilege orientation of the Scottish educational system and, again, this distinctive character was highlighted through the development of a Scottish-inspired educational system in the new context of Malawi.[56] At a time when there were pressures for Scotland to dissolve its distinct national identity and become "North Britain", the development of institutions with a distinctly Scottish character in the new context of Malawi was one initiative which fostered a strong sense of national identity.

---

[1] McCarthy, *The Road to Tanganyika*, p. 28.

[2] Tom von Prince, *Gegen Araber und Wahehe: Erinnerungen aus meiner ostafrikanischen Leutnantszeit 1890-1895*, Berlin, 1914, p. 238; cit. John M. Mackenzie with Nigel R. Dalziel, *The Scots in South Africa: Ethnicity, Identity, Gender and Race, 1772-1914*, Manchester and New York: Manchester University Press, 2007, p. 5.

[3] M.E. Leslie, "Pitgaveny, 1899-1905", *The Nyasaland Journal*, Vol. 4 No. 1 (January 1951), pp. 40-53.

[4] John Buchanan, *The Shire Highlands (East Central Africa) as Colony and Mission*, Edinburgh & London: William Blackwood, 1885; repr. Blantyre: Blantyre Printing and Publishing, 1982.

[5] Bridglal Pachai, *Malawi: The History of the Nation*, London: Longman, 1973, p. 83.

[6] *LWBCA*, June 1889.

[7] Andrew C. Ross, "Scotland and Malawi 1859-1964", in Stewart J. Brown & George Newlands ed., *Scottish Christianity in the Modern World*, Edinburgh: T. & T. Clark, 2000, pp. 283-309, at 288-89

[8] *Ibid.*, p. 289.

[9] Breitenbach, *Empire and Scottish Society*, p. 158.

[10] John D. Hargreaves, *Aberdeenshire to Africa: Northeast Scots and British Overseas Expansion*, Aberdeen: Aberdeen University Press, 1981, p. 36.

[11] W.P. Livingstone, *A Prince of Missionaries: Alexander Hetherwick*, London: James Clarke, n.d., p. 52.

[12] *LWBCA*, August-December 1897; cit. Ross, *Blantyre Mission*, p. 124.

[13] Ross, "Scotland and Malawi", p. 292.

[14] Richard J. Finlay, "National Identity, Union and Empire, c.1850 – c.1970", in John M. Mackenzie and T.M. Devine ed., *Scotland and the British Empire*, Oxford: Oxford University Press, 2011, p. 298.

[15] *LWBCA*, October 1890.

[16] *LWBCA*, July 1894.

[17] Johnston to Rhodes 7 June 1893, Salisbury Rhodesia Archives LT/1/16/4/1; cit. Ross, *Blantyre Mission*, pp. 115-16.

[18] Roland Oliver, *The African Experience*, London: Weidenfeld and Nicolson, 1991, p. 181.

[19] *LWBCA*, April 1900, pp. 6-7; cit Mufuka, *Missions and Politics*, p. 148.

[20] *Ibid.*

[21] *LWBCA*, March 1900, p.7; cit Mufuka, *Missions and Politics*, p. 149

[22] *LWBCA*, February 1892.

[23] *LWBCA*, March 1892.

[24] Alfred Sharpe (to Kimberley, 31 October 1894, F.O. 2/67); cit. Ross, *Blantyre Mission*, pp. 114-15.

[25] Proceedings, Nyasaland Legislative Council, January 1910, cit. B.S. Krishnamurthy, "Aspects of Land and Labour Policies in Malawi 1890-1914", University of Malawi, Conference on the Early History of Malawi, 20-24 July 1970, p. 6.

[26] *LWBCA*, November 1891.

[27] Andrew C. Ross, "The African – 'A Child or a Man'; - the quarrel between the Blantyre Mission of the Church of Scotland and the British Central Africa Administration, 1890-1905", in Eric Stokes and Richard Brown ed., *The Zambesian Past: Studies in Central African History*, Manchester: Manchester University Press, 1966, pp. 332-51, at p. 351.

[28] W.A. Elmslie to Robert Laws, 13 August 1895; cit. Jack Thompson, *Ngoni, Xhosa and Scot: Religious and Cultural Interaction in Malawi*, Zomba: Kachere, 2007, p. 127.

[29] Ross, *Blantyre Mission*, p. 149.

[30] Livingstonia Mission Report, 1909, p. 23, cit. McCracken, *Christianity and Politics*, p. 156.

[31] McCracken, *Christianity and Politics*, p. 155.

[32] *Aurora*, August 1897, p. 25, cit. McCracken, *Christianity and Politics*, p. 155.

[33] Newspaper cutting from Cape Times, 1921, cit. McCracken, *Christianity and Politics*, p. 180.

[34] McCracken, *A History of Malawi*, p. 104.

[35] See McCracken, *Christianity and Politics*, p. 160.

[36] Ross, *Blantyre Mission*, pp.173-74.

[37] *LWBCA*, April 1895.

[38] Thompson, *Ngoni, Xhosa and Scot*, p. 75.

[39] Donald Fraser, "Heathenism", in Proceedings of the Third Federation of Missions Conference, Blantyre, 1910; cit. Thompson, *Ngoni, Xhosa and Scot*, p. 151.

[40] Donald Fraser, "The Zulu of Nyasaland: their Manners and Customs", in Proceedings of the Philosophical Society of Glasgow, Vol. XXXII (1900-01), p. 71; cit. Thompson, *Ngoni, Xhosa and Scot*, p. 141.

[41] Donald Fraser, "The Passing of two Great Angoni Chiefs", *United Free Church of Scotland Monthly Record*, February 1908, p. 64; cit. Thompson, *Ngoni, Xhosa and Scot*, pp. 152-53.

[42] Thompson, *Christianity in Northern Malawi*, p. 149.

[43] Ross, *Blantyre Mission*, p. 148.

[44] *LWBCA*, May 1893.

[45] *Life and Work in British Central Africa*, November 1894.

[46] Thompson, *Ngoni, Xhosa and Scot*, p. 114.

[47] *Ibid.*, p. 116.

[48] *Central African Times*, Vol. VI, 5 (1 November 1902); cit. Sean Morrow, "'War Came from the Boma' Military and Police Disturbances in Blantyre, 1902", *The Society of Malawi Journal*, Vol. 41 No. 2 (1988), pp. 16-29, at p. 17.

[49] Morrow, "War Came from the Boma", p. 17.

[50] *Ibid.*, pp. 25-26.

[51] *Ibid.*, p. 26.

[52] *Ibid.*

[53] *LWBCA*, Vol. December 1902.

[54] George A. Shepperson, "External Factors in the Development of African Nationalism, with Particular Reference to British Central Africa", *Phylon: The Atlanta University Review of Race and Culture*, Vol. XXII/3 (1961), pp. 207-28, at 212.

[55] Frederick Lugard, Lecture to the Royal Scottish Geographical Society, 15 November 1892; cit. Hargreaves, *Aberdeenshire to Africa*, p. 36.

[56] See Graham Walker, "Empire, Religion and Nationality in Scotland and Ulster before the First World War", in Ian S. Wood ed., *Scotland and Ulster*, Edinburgh: Mercat Press, 1994, pp. 97-115.

5. War and Peace

The period which stretched from the establishment of the British Protectorate in 1891 to the outbreak of the First World War in 1914 saw increasing opportunity for Malawians and Scots to encounter one another, albeit within the constraints of a colonial age. Both the Livingstonia and Blantyre Missions grew exponentially during these years, with Scottish-Malawian interaction being at the core of their work. At Livingstonia between 1891 and 1914, the number of Scottish missionaries increased from 13 to 48, the number of Malawian teachers from 52 to 1,674 and the number of baptised Christians from 106 to 9,513.[1] The schools which were just getting started in 1891 had expanded to a network of 907 schools with an enrolment of 58,656 students.[2] During the same period at Blantyre, the number of Scottish missionaries had increased from 13 to 25, the number of Malawian teachers from 46 to 447, and the number of baptised Christians from 1,132 to 11,630.[3] The network of schools had increased from 7 to 220, with student enrolment rising from 971 to 11,630.[4] Through church life and educational institutions large numbers of Malawians were encountering Scots and many cordial relationships were formed.

The growth of the Scottish Missions took place in a context where the total European presence was relatively small. John McCracken calculates that: "On the eve of the First World War, missionaries in Nyasaland numbered around 200, compared with only 107 planters and 100 government officials. The Scots Presbyterians, with their substantial congregations and impressively constructed stations, remained the dominant group."[5] The Missions remained a primary point of engagement for Scots and Malawians but they were no longer the only one. Scots were also prominent in the development of estate agriculture, with results which, as we shall see, led to sharp differences between settlers and missionaries. Meanwhile the military sector was another where Malawians and Scots found themselves working closely together.

On the establishment of the British Protectorate, one of the first actions of the Administration was to recruit Malawians to serve as soldiers in its service. These troops played an indispensable role in establishing the authority of the British Administration and subduing any chiefs who resisted it. From this time onwards the military provided a context in which Europeans and Africans worked closely together, usually with the former as officers and the latter as "men". The experience of being together under a common discipline and sharing together in meeting the rigours of combat created an environment in which mutual respect and friendship could develop. Malawi's first modern army, the Central African Rifles, was founded in Zomba in 1895. They became the King's African Rifles in 1902 when they were incorporated as a regional force. Their first exposure to international warfare came when the First World War broke out in 1914.

One of the earliest actions fought anywhere in Africa in the Great War was the Battle of Karonga which took place in September 1914 after German forces crossed the Songwe River on Malawi's northern border and commenced an invasion. Cullen Young recalls the force which was mustered to resist the incoming German troops:

> In Karonga, Captain Barton, commanding the little defence force, had as the bulk of his strength the available companies of his own battalion, the 1st King's African Rifles, a force well seasoned to African warfare and commanded by Imperial officers. In addition he had a small body, roughly one fifth of his total, drawn from the white community. In this body were a number of men whose acquaintance with the country and with Africans qualified them to render the most effective assistance. Several of these, working with local Africans formed the Intelligence branch and the remainder were either attached to the askari companies or were detailed to the machine and light field gun sections or to transport.[6]

Young goes on to recount how this Nyasaland force succeeded in routing the German troops, driving them back across the Songwe River and securing Malawi's territory for Britain for the duration of the war. His high opinion of the African soldiers of the KAR remained with him and a new level of solidarity was introduced by the experience of having stood together in the heat of battle. He was particularly aware of the vital role which had been played by the *tenga-tenga* – the thousands of porters who had supported the troops: "without exaggeration, they carried us to victory on their backs".[7]

It is estimated that almost 200,000 porters were recruited in Malawi to support the British military effort as well as up to 19,000 Malawian soldiers. These men suffered greatly in course of the four-year conflict and proved their worth in the campaigns fought in Tanganyika and Mozambique in the latter stages of the war. Malawian troops built up a "commanding reputation throughout Africa".[8] Despite their strength as a fighting force the memories of Malawians who participated were dominated by the extent of their suffering: poor rations often leaving them hungry, lack of equipment, especially lack of boots on their frequent long marches, often leaving them vulnerable, and the many deaths leaving them traumatised and terrorised. Those who survived the war had not reached the end of their sufferings: "Even with an end to the fighting, there were sorrows, as men crippled in mind and body struggled home, and a new devastation, influenza, swept the land."[9]

Many Malawians were embittered by their experiences. As Melvin Page observed: "They had gone to war with at least passing, and perhaps self-serving, assurances from their European rulers of the necessity to defend the country. In the process, though, many had died, on the battlefields, along the lines of communications, as well as in Nyasaland. Afterwards the sacrifices seemed to bring few rewards, and some expressed in song their deep-seated frustrations: At Karonga / People perished there / Why did they perish? At Karonga / Many young men died there / Why did many die?"[10] This question, posed in song, proved to be a powerful force in subsequent Malawian history. It resulted in a new view of Europeans, whose folly and vulnerability had been exposed by the war. It resulted in a new sense of common cause among Malawians who now had a shared experience of suffering which transcended ethnic identity. It resulted in a new sense of entitlement on the part of Malawians, as expressed for example by G.M. Kayima Wavyenji in a submission to the Mzimba district commissioner during the 1930s:

> We have died for you, but you have no gratitude, you are only grateful to strangers. Alas but all have died for nothing. We have died in the war and there have been strangers who have not died like ourselves.... Now at the end of your wars our children have been finished. Can't you give us something, say honour?[11]

This sense of entitlement would make its mark on subsequent Malawian history and Scots, among others, would have to recognise that the First World War was a watershed event for Malawi.

There were times during the war when Malawians and Scots stood together and suffered together. A notable case was the patrol commanded by Robert Hellier Napier, a Blantyre missionary who followed in the tradition of David Clement Scott and had a genius for friendship which enabled him to form relationships of mutual confidence, not least with the Nyasaland soldiers in his patrol. Tragically, on 12 February 1918 Napier and his entire patrol were shot and killed by German adversaries as they carried out their duties in Portuguese East Africa.

Prior to his premature death Napier had written a poem entitled "Nyasaland Volunteer Reserve" which reveals something of the spirit of comradeship which he enjoyed across the racial divide that was so prominent at that time.[12]

Forth, side by side with K.A.R.
Africa's sons and you,
Rankers approved in affrays afar,
Officers brave and true!
As one against the bold invader,
One beneath the standard dear,
Britain and Black, met the attack
Till they swept the Border clear.

Napier's surviving colleague Alexander Hetherwick witnessed around Blantyre the return of many of the porters who had provided essential logistical support to the King's African Rifles and hailed: "... the native carriers, the *tenga-tenga*, as they are called in the native tongue, the men who, in their tens and tens of thousands fell on the line of communications, stricken by hardship and disease – the men of whom General Northey said, 'the *tenga-tenga* won the war' – those of them who survived, battered, broken and maimed for life many of them, crept home to their villages, unpensioned, unmedalled, undecorated, uncheered, the heroes of the war, the saviours of the Empire in Africa."[13] While Hetherwick could recognise their sacrifice and courage, it is readily understandable why the *tenga-tenga* themselves questioned why they were suffering so gravely by taking part in a war which was not of their own making and from which they could expect to derive little, if any, benefit. Their sense of grievance would influence events in Malawi itself during the war years and beyond.

The Chilembwe Rising

The sharp differences which emerged between the Scottish missionaries and the British Administration during the early years of the Protectorate in the 1890s revolved, to a large degree, around the inter-linked issues of land, labour and taxation. Europeans, many of them Scots, were arriving in Malawi in rapidly growing numbers and many of them were acquiring land to develop plantation agriculture. This was particularly apparent in the Shire Highlands, the area where the Blantyre Mission had been working over the previous twenty years and where its leaders were well-connected to local Malawian communities. This meant that they were sensitive to Malawians' experience of these new developments and willing to advocate their interests, notably through the columns of *Life and Work in British Central Africa*, at that time the only newspaper being published in Malawi. Essentially, Malawian communities were being squeezed by the alienation of their land and the imposition of taxes which left them no alternative to working for low wages on European-owned estates at the expense of their own agricultural productivity.

The combination of British rule with settler plantations very quickly created a very different political and economic environment from that which had prevailed in the 1870s and 1880s when Scots had first arrived in Malawi with the Livingstonia and Blantyre Missions and the African Lakes Company. As Hugh Macmillan explains:

> Military occupation had replaced commercial contact at a critical moment. The development of peasant-produced commodities had been delayed by the early difficulties of transport, and a plantation system had grown up in the Shire Highlands. While this was beneficial in that it provided opportunities for employment, it was based on the payment of very low wages, and was not the development which had been intended. The alienation of very large tracts of land, and inadequate provision for the residents on it, had sown the seeds of discontent which were soon to erupt in John Chilembwe's Rising of 1915.[14]

Malawi was no different in this respect from many other African and Asian countries which were subject to colonial rule at this time. Being reduced to the status of serfs in their own ancestral homeland quite naturally gave rise to an acute sense of grievance.

Scottish involvement in Malawi was decidedly ambivalent during these years of rapid change. While the Blantyre Mission was conspicuous for its vigour in advocating the interests of Malawian communities, there were also a significant number of Scots among the European planters whose arrival had created the difficulties now being experienced. Indeed, the pioneer of estate agriculture was none other than the ex-missionary John Buchanan, a member of the original staff of the Blantyre Mission, who had gone on to acquire land in Zomba on which he developed Malawi's first commercial plantation, growing coffee, tobacco and sugar. Through his years with the Mission Buchanan had built up good relationships with chiefs and people in the surrounding area. This was not always the case with Europeans arriving to establish estates from the late 1880s who often came into conflict with local communities. By 1900, John McCracken observes, there were, "some 100 European planters, all but twelve of them British, most of these Scots, were said to be working on estates in the Shire Highlands".[15] Amongst them was R.S. Hynde, the most vigorous advocate of settler interests, described by McCracken as: "a pugnacious Scot".[16]

On the establishment of the British Protectorate Sir Harry Johnston sought to regulate land ownership with due regard to the land rights of existing Malawian communities. Much of the best land, however, ended up either in the ownership of European planters or of "the Crown". The outcome for Malawian residents of the Shire Highlands was miserable. As one settler admitted to Alfred Sharpe, the Commissioner, "I venture to say that our domestic animals receive more attention and better treatment than our human beasts of burden, and when working in our plantations their existence is almost as bad as it can be."[17] Ironically the British involvement, which had originally been inspired by opposition to the slave trade, had resulted in a situation where many Malawians were reduced to conditions of near-slavery in their own country.

Prominent among the estate-owners subjecting Malawians to such conditions was Alexander Livingstone Bruce, grandson of David Livingstone, whose father Alexander Low Bruce had established a large plantation in the Magomero area where Livingstone and Mackenzie had earlier established Malawi's first Christian mission station. Bruce was one of the most outspoken settlers on the issue of the importance of the estate sector having sufficient provision of labour. As Bridglal Pachai observes: "A.L. Bruce and the other estate owners were emphatic about the labour requirements. Their tenants were there to provide for labour alone."[18] Even the Government Commission of Inquiry into the Rising, which had no sympathy whatsoever for its protagonists, acknowledged that, "the treatment of labour and the system of tenancy on the Bruce Estates ... were in several respects illegal and oppressive."[19]

It happened that close to the Bruce estates was the Providence Industrial Mission, supported and inspired by the black community in the USA and led by the Revd John Chilembwe who had developed ideas about the dignity and rights of Africans which could hardly have been more different to those espoused by Bruce. It is likely that as a child Chilembwe had been exposed to the work of the Blantyre Mission in his

79

home area of Chiradzulu but the outstanding influence on his life was Joseph Booth, an independent English missionary who had settled in the Blantyre area in the early 1890s and had taken a radical line in championing the rights of the indigenous Malawian population. Booth was Chilembwe's mentor and had sponsored his education in the USA.

The labour force on the Bruce estates were dissatisfied with their conditions and found in the Providence Industrial Mission a champion of their cause. Their discontent came to be focussed particularly on the Scottish manager of the estates, William Jervis Livingstone. As Shepperson and Price point out, in their magisterial account of the Chilembwe Rising, "... he was the most tangible representative of the administration of what the rebels conceived the most typical and threatening of the new European units which had come to challenge their traditional way of life on one hand, and their hopes of surmounting this by emulation of the Europeans themselves on the other.... Thus not only his own often domineering attitude towards his employees and local Africans, but actual economic forces within the Protectorate and on the Estates themselves were making it more likely that if a rising was decided on, the blow would, in all probability, fall first of all on him."[20] Bennett Ntambo, who was Chilembwe's house servant, has recalled that Livingstone, upon meeting well-dressed Malawians, was accustomed to ask them, "*Kapolo wandani?*" ("Whose slave are you?")[21] He had also ordered the destruction of three Providence Industrial Mission churches in 1912-13. When the dissatisfaction of the Malawian community with conditions on the estates was compounded by the sufferings endured by the troops and *tenga-tenga* following the outbreak of war, and when peaceful forms of protest had proved ineffectual, Chilembwe and his followers determined to resort to force.

W.J. Livingstone was indeed the initial target. On the evening of 23 January 1915 armed men broke into his bedroom and, after a fierce fight, he was killed and beheaded in front of his distraught wife Kitty and two small children. In a coordinated operation, two other Scottish staff of the Bruce estate, Duncan MacCormick and Robert Ferguson, were speared to death. On Chilembwe's strict instructions, the women and children of their households were unharmed but did have the terrifying experience of being captured and taken on a night march through the bush while traumatised by the sudden and violent deaths of their menfolk. A simultaneous attack on the Mandala headquarters of the African Lakes Corporation in Blantyre was repulsed. Thereafter the tide turned quickly against the "rebels" with troops and volunteers loyal to the British Administration gaining the upper hand. Within a week many of Chilembwe's men had been captured, tried and either executed or imprisoned. A few days later Chilembwe himself was shot and killed. The Rising proved to be short-lived and ineffectual. Nonetheless it gave a message which would long carry resonance in Malawi. In due course Chilembwe would take his place in history as the forerunner and pioneer of the nationalist struggle.

Chilembwe's associations with the Scots in Malawi were somewhat tenuous. The main influences on his thinking were his mentor Joseph Booth and the black community in the USA. Many of his followers, however, were products of the Scottish Missions, a point which was not lost on the Administration and settlers when they sought to analyze the underlying causes of the episode. Shepperson and Price point out that, "... almost all of the ringleaders in the Rising had begun their early education in the Scottish missions, although later they may have deserted to one of the more sectarian bodies. And that John Gray Kufa had been until the very last a trusted elder in the Blantyre Church was for many of the critics of the missions something of a trump card."[22] Kufa, in fact, had been one of the first converts to be baptised at Blantyre Mission and had gone on to become one of the "deacons" to be trained and ordained by David Clement Scott. He later worked in the dispensary at Blantyre Mission where he was one of the first Malawians to become skilled in Western medicine. He was condemned to death and executed for his part in the Rising. From death row he wrote to his cousin Johnstone Sazuze: "Here are my children. I leave them with you and Dr Hetherwick."[23] The fact that he was one of eighty-four "rebels" who were found to be baptised members of the Church of Scotland Blantyre Mission put the

Scottish Missions very much on the defensive in the aftermath of the Rising.

The reaction of the Government and the settlers focussed on the fact that it was educated "natives" who had led the Rising. Their education, of course, had been provided by the missions, with the Blantyre and Livingstonia Missions in a league of their own for both quantity and quality of education being offered. When the Government established a Commission of Inquiry its terms of reference included the question of "the effects of mission teaching ... on the native mind and character."[24] When the issue came to be debated in the Legislative Council, the two main protagonists were both Scots: Alexander Livingstone Bruce and Robert Laws. Bruce moved, "That pending the finding of the Commission ... all schools in charge of native teachers in the Protectorate be closed at once."[25] This was a direct attack on mission education and Robert Laws, as representative of missionary interests on the Council, offered a robust defence of the value of the education offered by the missions for Malawi's advancement. Though Bruce ultimately withdrew his motion, it had demonstrated the extent of the suspicion and distrust of the missions which was felt in the settler community in the aftermath of the Rising.

When the Commission of Inquiry convened in May 1915, it was clear that it was the Scottish Missions which were particularly under suspicion. Alexander Hetherwick was questioned for four and a half hours. To put his evidence in context, Nyamayaro Mufuka first provides extracts from other missionaries who appeared. J.J. Ferreira of the Dutch Reformed Church of South Africa was questioned on "native abilities":

Q: What is the object of ordaining a native minister, is it not to make them quite independent?

A: Oh no, it is only to get assistance, that is all. To tell you the honest truth, it is very doubtful we will ordain a native here. We are South Africans and we are dead against natives.

Roman Catholic missionaries were questioned on a similar point:

Q: In teaching natives, do you teach them that they are on the same equality as Europeans?

A: No, we teach them that they must submit to the Europeans who are very much wiser than they, and they must obey them as they are placed over them.

Q: Is there any social equality?

A: None whatever.

Q: Have they never raised this point?

A: No they never ask on this point.

The questioning of Alexander Hetherwick was as follows:

Q: Do you think the native, educated or otherwise, is capable of understanding the Holy Scriptures?

A: Yes, as capable as any ordinary Christian.

Q: If a teacher selects an isolated portion or a verse, may he misapply it?

A: Yes, as a European might.

Q: [Do] ... native teachers ... sometimes discuss among themselves texts of the Bible?

A: And why not?

Q: Can the native interpret it correctly to others?

A: The native is as able to interpret the Bible as you are.

Q: You do not expect the place of the European to be fully supplied?

A: Not meanwhile, but I have no objection to it.

Q: In the governing body has the native an equal vote?

A: Yes.

Q: Are you prepared for the Church of Scotland to be governed by a native majority?

A: It may be.

Q: Is there not a danger in giving the native so soon such powers?

A: We have seen nothing of danger as yet and I fear none.[26]

When Hetherwick was challenged by one of the Commission members who rehearsed the familiar European complaint that Africans were no longer showing due respect to Europeans by raising their hats when they passed, he replied "in high dudgeon" that it was the Europeans who were to blame: "I have seen many Europeans absolutely ignore a boy's salutation. The smallest drummer boy in the British army if he salutes Lord Kitchener receives a salute in return. There will be no difficulty if the European makes acknowledgement: it indicates that two gentlemen have met and not only one."[27]

Besides robustly defending themselves through every available means in Malawi, the Scottish Missions also called on their home constituency to rally to their support. They sought to apply political pressure on the Colonial Office of the British Government to ensure that the hostility and suspicion of the settler community in Malawi did not result in punitive or restrictive measures being taken against the Scottish missions. A key figure in this regard was Arthur Steel-Maitland, Under-Secretary of State for the Colonies, who was also a prominent elder of the Church of Scotland. He was finally able to give the assurance that the Governor of Nyasaland's dispatches on the Report of Inquiry into the Rising had been read, and that they showed that he was "absolutely satisfied with the work and teaching of the Scottish missions."[28] This gave the missionaries at Blantyre and Livingstonia the confidence that they would be unimpeded in their work.

The Rising was a major event, on any reckoning, in Malawian history. Indeed, it has been described by a leading historian as the only significant rebellion in the whole of Africa to be inspired by Christianity prior to the First World War.[29] One thing which it demonstrated was the extent to which Scottish involvement in Malawi had become ambivalent to the point of contradiction. So far as attitudes to Malawian development are concerned, it would be hard to find two environments more contrasting than the estates of Alexander Livingstone Bruce and the schools of the Scottish Missions. Both were strongly Scottish in character and drew their inspiration from David Livingstone's travels in the Shire Highlands. But they represented quite opposite visions of the role and destiny of the Malawian community which would be resolved only through the further passage of history. Meanwhile the occurrence of the Chilembwe Rising cannot be accounted for without some appreciation that, as Shepperson and Price observe: "It was Nyasaland's privilege and its perplexity that its taste for education had been formed by men from a country which had pioneered the spread of common schools: Scotland."[30] It also provides abundant evidence to support Nyamayaro Mufuka's conclusion that: "... on the whole Scottish missionaries behaved differently from other missionaries with respect to questions that had a bearing on the political aspirations of the African people of the Protectorate."[31]

The events of 23 January 1915 were not forgotten, either in Malawi or in Scotland. In 2004, Deirdre Hornyold-Strickland, grand-daughter of William Jervis Livingstone, was surprised and delighted to receive an invitation from Risen Lord Ministries to travel to Malawi to participate in a special ceremony of reconciliation and healing which aimed to minister to those whose parents or grandparents had been caught up in the violence of that fateful night. Deirdre's 90-year old father Alastair, who as a baby of just four months had been abducted (with his mother Kitty Livingstone) and carried through the bush following the assassination of his father, was not able to travel to Malawi but recorded a video message for the occasion. Ten members of the family of Duncan MacCormick who, like the Livingstones, came from the Hebridean island of Lismore off the west coast of Scotland, agreed to join Deirdre in travelling to the ceremony.

When the Scottish contingent arrived at the house where the Livingstone family had lived in Magomero, they met with members of the families of John Chilembwe and John Gray Kufa and joined in worship with a large Malawian congregation. Malawian clergy offered prayers and readings in Chichewa while Rev Moira MacCormick led prayers in Gaelic, the native language of the people of Lismore. When Deirdre's chosen hymn "How Great Thou Art" was sung, she recalls that "the Malawian singing was simply divine and very moving." The congregation then proceeded to the nearby graves of William Jervis Livingstone and Duncan MacCormick where more prayers were offered, interspersed with songs from groups of Malawian women gathered around the graves. When the MacCormick family offered their own sung worship, with an *a cappella* rendition of the 23rd Psalm in Gaelic, it was said that "each and every one who was present could feel the healing taking place." It is hoped that an appropriate centenary ceremony in 2015 will further heal the wounds of the past and make even greater moves towards reconciliation.[32] In this way Malawians and Scots have been able to come together in order to come to terms with one of the darkest moments in their shared history, to affirm their friendship and to look to the future in unity and with confidence.

Together in the Talking-Place

Besides the tumultuous events which unfolded during the First World War, the early decades of the 20th century included also less eventful times when Scots and Malawians encountered one another. Few were able to articulate their experience as well as Thomas Cullen Young who served with the Livingstonia Mission from 1902 to 1931, and who would later make a distinguished contribution as an anthropologist. His enquiring mind led him to raise significant questions:

What is central to the pattern of life within the living community? Is it not the "talking place of the village"? Is it not the primitive "moot" or "house of representatives," where every communal matter is discussed; the place where the "elders" sit around the "ruling elder," who is yet not "ruler" apart from the united wisdom of the group as a whole? Is it not the place of graded status in eldership, to the outer circle of which come the younger members as, one by one, they achieve adulthood with marriage, to serve apprenticeship in statecraft?[33]

Young knew the value of the "talking-place" out of personal experience – he had so often been there himself. So much was he at home in local community life that when he was given responsibilities which tied him to the Overtoun Institution at Livingstonia, he requested that he should be given duties in the villages.[34]

He came to have a well-defined philosophy of African village life and was able to recall the day when this had first begun to form in his mind:

The occasion of enlightenment which I most clearly remember in my own experience was a day when there was desultory conversation at the men's "talking-place" of a village in Northern Nyasaland. It was a village far from any beaten track and rarely visited by any European.... Talk had been of this and that, but had swung round – as it often does in Africa – to regrets and complaints about the European and his ways. The oldest of the men, an almost toothless mumbler, was talking, and I had nearly fallen asleep into a doze in my chair. But I became conscious of a phrase repeated and repeated, *muzi uweme*, "a good village".[35]

Struck by the phrase Young asked the old man what it meant. He offers a literal translation of the reply to his question:

A good village is where the head-man and the elders are respected by all; and where they have regard for all, even for the children. It is a good village where the young respect parents and where no one tries to harm another. If there is even one person who belittles another person or works harm, then the village is spoiled.[36]

It was a defining moment for Young: "To 'build a village,' I discovered, is a key-phrase in the language, and the words 'one who will build a village,' describes the character of an ideal male. Proverbially in Northern Nyasaland the village is built and maintained by 'the open hand'.... The fact is accepted that the open-handed and open-hearted build a village, the selfish never."[37] Such remarks exposed Young to criticisms that he was taking an excessively rosy view of African community life.[38] He, however, remained convinced of the integrity of African life and of the value of the contribution which it offered.[39]

Of the many conversations Young enjoyed during his visits to Malawian villages, one from the 1920s can be taken as an example:

"We have heard," said one of the local inhabitants, "that black men are allowed to have a union so that they can speak to the whites as one clan speaks to another – through the leaders." "Yes," broke in a small boy, of about 13 or 14. "Kerementi, you know." For a moment I was beaten. Who or what was Kerementi? Then it came to me; this insignificant goatherd was referring to Clements Kadalie [the Tonga immigrant from Malawi who founded and brought to its peak of power the first important South African Native trade union, the Industrial and Commercial Workers union]. He did not even belong to the same tribe or territory as Kadalie, yet this boy knew about the labour leader who had gone out from Nyasaland.[40]

Kadalie had been a student at Livingstonia and attributed his core values to the teaching of "good missionaries". It appears that Young fell into this category since it was he who escorted the great trade unionist on a sightseeing tour of Edinburgh when he paid a visit to Scotland in 1927.[41]

Young's friendships with such brilliant Malawians as Saulos Nyirenda, Andrew Nkhonjera and Levi Mumba formed the basis on which he built the knowledge of the history and culture of the people of northern Malawi which found expression in such pioneering works as *Notes on the History of the Tumbuka-Kamanga Peoples in the Northern Province of Nyasaland* which he published in 1932.[42] They also taught him a lesson often overlooked in the history books: "The cry in Africa ... is for the feel of human relationships and comradely activities at all costs, even if great schemes for political or educational or economic amelioration seem to be pushed into an inferior place."[43] The extent to which Scots have been able to respond to this cry is perhaps what has given Malawi-Scotland relations a distinctive character.

Sport was another area of interaction between Scots and Malawians during these years. As Hokkanen and Mangan have commented: "Although the games ethic was not dominant in the Scottish educational institutions at Blantyre and Livingstonia, both of which laid more stress on industrial training and manual work in their pedagogical programmes, the Scottish missionaries were disseminators of modern sport in the region, introducing cricket, rugby (without much success) and association football (with much greater success).[44] In fact, the first description of modern sport in Malawi is found in Duff Macdonald's account of his time in Blantyre from 1878 to 1881: "Each Friday afternoon we had races and gave small prizes. After a time they began to enjoy swings and football, but the favourite game was cricket."[45] During the 1880s and 1890s this early initiative was further developed by David Clement Scott who was a keen sportsman and had excelled at running while a student at

Edinburgh University. He was keen to promote cricket but it was his brother Willie's passion for football which was to have the greater lasting influence. By 1898 the Blantyre Mission had a "well-trampled football field" with daily games.[46]

Modern games came later to Livingstonia than to Blantyre. In its early days the Overtoun Institution had an intensely academic programme with no provision for sport or recreation. Gradually its leadership came to see the need for a more balanced curriculum. The appointment of Peter Kirkwood, a passionate sportsman, to the teaching staff in 1906 brought a new emphasis, especially on cricket. His report for 1907 included the comment that: "The cricket during the year was a success indeed. The boys took to it enthusiastically, and many of them developed into good all-round players."[47] By 1908 he had successfully introduced football. A pattern was established where cricket was played in the dry season and football in the wet season. Sport thus became another dimension of life where there was a significant sharing of experience between Scots and Malawians.

Unresolved Ambivalence

Prior to the First World War it was a proud boast of many Nyasaland settlers that their relations with the "natives" were better than anywhere else in Africa. This was the legacy, at least to some extent, of the relationships developed by the Scottish Missions in the pre-colonial period. This confidence was shaken by the experience of the Great War and, in particular, by the Rising led by John Chilembwe. The fact that a Scottish-owned estate, the property of none other than David Livingstone's grandson, became the primary focus of African discontent, demanded pause for thought on the part of those who assumed that Scots were playing an entirely beneficent role in Malawi at this time. Even more pointedly, the chosen symbolic target of the Rising was a well-established Scottish plantation manager, William Jervis Livingstone, not a blood relative of the great explorer but from a similar Hebridean background as David Livingstone's father.

The assassination of W.J. Livingstone and his colleagues, and the harsh reprisals against Chilembwe's followers which it provoked, marks the low point in Malawian-Scottish relations. George Fenwick had met a similar fate after his murder of Chipatula a generation earlier but he could be disowned as a rogue adventurer. W.J. Livingstone was a leading figure in the new economic order being established in Malawi and his death demonstrated the acute sense of injustice experienced by many Malawians as they came to terms with the implications of this new order. Scottish involvement in Malawi by now had a decidedly ambivalent character. Alexander Hetherwick at Blantyre Mission was the strongest voice advocating the interests of Malawian communities in regard to the crucial interlinked issues of land, labour and taxation. W.J. Livingstone stood for a settler-dominated economy which provoked deep resentment among thoughtful Malawians, notably those who were themselves best placed to participate in the new order now emerging. Another half-century would be needed for this ambivalence to be resolved.

---

[1] *Proceedings and Debates of the General Assembly of the Free Church of Scotland 1892*, Edinburgh: Ballantyne, Hanson & Co, 1892, pp.81-84; *Reports to the General Assembly of the United Free Church of Scotland 1915*, Edinburgh: Constable, 1915, p. 106.

[2] *Ibid.*

[3] *Reports of the Schemes of the Church of Scotland 1892*, Edinburgh: William Blackwood, 1892, pp. 163-64: *Reports of the Schemes of the Church of Scotland 1915*, Edinburgh: William Blackwood, 1915, pp. 297-98.

[4] *Ibid.*

[5] John McCracken, *A History of Malawi 1859-1966*, Rochester NY: James Currey, 2012, p. 108.

[6] T. Cullen Young, "The Battle of Karonga", *The Nyasaland Journal*, Vol. VIII No. 2 (July 1955), pp. 27-30, at p. 28.

[7] Cit. Peter G. Forster, *T. Cullen Young: Missionary and Anthropologist*, Hull: Hull University Press, 1989, p. 20.

[8]   L.S. Norman, *Nyasaland without Prejudice*, London: East Africa, 1934, p. 134, cit. Melvin Eugene Page, "Malawians in the Great War and After, 1914-1925", Ph.D., Michigan State University, 1977, p. 115.

[9]   Page, "Malawians in the Great War", p. 203.

[10] *Ibid.*, p. 234.

[11] Undated, untitled ms by G.M. Kayima Wavyenji, with English translation, MNA, NMM1/14/6, cit. Page, "Malawians in the Great War", p. 259.

[12] Robert Hellier Napier, "Nyasaland Native Reserve", cit. George Shepperson, "Malawi and the Poetry of Two World Wars", *The Society of Malawi Journal*, Vol. 53 No. 1 (2000), pp.144-55, at p. 150.

[13] Alexander Hetherwick, *The Romance of Blantyre: How Livingstone's Dream Came True*, London: James Clarke, n.d.

[14] Macmillan, "Origins and Development", p. 438.

[15] See McCracken, *History of Malawi*, pp. 78-79.

[16] *Ibid.*, p. 92.

[17] Teixeira de Maltos to Alfred Sharpe, 2 May 1903, cit. Harvey J. Sindima, *The Legacy of Scottish Missionaries in Malawi*, Lewiston/Lampeter/Queenston: Edwin Mellen Press, 1992, pp. 117-18.

[18] Bridglal Pachai, *Land and Politics in Malawi 1875-1975*, Kingston, Ontario: The Limestone Press, 1978, p. 98.

[19] *Report of the Commission appointed ... to inquire into various matters and questions concerned with the Native Rising within the Nyasaland Protectorate*, Zomba: 1916; cit. McCracken, *History of Malawi*, p. 145.

[20] George Shepperson and Thomas Price, *Independent African: John Chilembwe and the Origins, Setting and Significance of the Nyasaland Native Rising of 1915*, Edinburgh: Edinburgh University Press, 1958; repr. Blantyre: CLAIM, 2000, p. 225.

[21] Cit. Joey Power, *Political Culture and Nationalism in Malawi: Building Kwacha*, New York: University of Rochester Press, 2010, p. 17.

[22] Shepperson and Price, *Independent African*, p. 364.

[23] Cit. Pachai, *Malawi: The History of the Nation*, p. 253.

[24] Cit. *ibid.*, p. 368.

[25]   Cit. *ibid.*, p. 365.

[26]   *Evidence before the Commission of Enquiry into the Native Uprising of 1915;* cit. Mufuka, *Missions and Politics*, p. 200.

[27]   Cit., Shepperson and Price, *Independent African*, p. 369.

[28]   Cit. *ibid.*, p. 375.

[29]   John Iliffe, *Africans: the History of a Continent*, Cambridge: Cambridge University Press, 1995, p. 196; cit McCracken, *History of Malawi*, p. 127.

[30]   Shepperson and Price, *Independent African*, p. 242.

[31]   K. Nyamayaro Mufuka, *Missions and Politics in Malawi*, Kingston, Ontario: The Limestone Press, 1977, p. 4.

[32]   Email from Deirdre Hornyold-Strickland, 17 June 2012.

[33]   Cullen Young, *Contemporary Ancestors*, London: Lutterworth Press, n.d., pp. 155-56.

[34]   Forster, *T. Cullen Young*, p. 22.

[35]   T. Cullen Young, *African Ways and Wisdom: A Contribution Towards Understanding*, London: United Society for Christian Literature, 1937, pp. 11-12.

[36]   *Ibid.*, p. 12.

[37]   *Ibid.*, pp. 12-13.

[38]   See Forster, *T. Cullen Young*, pp. 63-64.

[39]   See e.g. T. Cullen Young, "The New African", *Other Lands*, Vol. 7 (1927), pp. 27-30.

[40]   T. Cullen Young, "The 'Native' Newspaper", *Africa*, Vol. XI (1938), pp. 63-72 at p. 60; cit. George Shepperson, *Myth and Reality in Malawi*, Evanston: Northwestern University Press, 1966, p. 5.

[41]   Clements Kadalie, *My Life with the ICU*, London, 1970, pp. 116-17; cit Forster, *T. Cullen Young*, p. 148.

[42]   T. Cullen Young, *Notes on the History of the Tumbuka-Kamanga Peoples in the Northern Province of Nyasaland*, London: Religious Tract Society, 1932; 2nd. ed., London: Frank Cass, 1970.

[43]   Young, *African Ways and Wisdom*, p. 40.

[44] Markku Hokkanen and J.A. Mangan, "Further Variations on a Theme: The Games Ethic Further Adapted – Scottish Moral Missionaries and Muscular Christians in Malawi" in *The International Journal of the History of Sport*, Vol. 23 No. 8 (December 2006), pp. 1257-74 at p. 1259.

[45] Macdonald, *Africana*, p. 224; cit. Hokkanen and Mangan, "Further Variations", p. 1266.

[46] See *LWBCA*, February 1898.

[47] Annual Report of the Livingstonia Mission of the Free Church of Scotland 1907, pp. 10-12, cit. Hokkanen and Mangan, "Further Variations", p. 1268.

6. Colonialism and Resistance

The Chilembwe Rising exposed a deep ambivalence in the Scottish involvement in Malawi, personified by Alexander Livingstone Bruce on the one hand and Alexander Hetherwick on the other. There can be no doubt that, of the two, Hetherwick was much closer to upholding the understanding of African dignity and destiny which David Livingstone had championed and which had originally inspired the Scottish involvement. However, even those who took Hetherwick's side in the crisis which followed the Rising, were themselves becoming more and more at home with the prevailing ethos and attitudes of the European community in a colonial age.

Ironically, this had been evident at Blantyre's celebration of the centenary of the birth of David Livingstone in 1913. Without betraying the slightest sense of irony, Hetherwick offered the following account of the arrangements:

> A joint committee of the various public bodies met in the Queen Victoria Memorial Hall and resolved that the European celebration should take the form of a service in the Blantyre Church to which the general public should be invited. The heads of the various business firms intimated the closing of their places of business so as to enable the members of their staffs to be present. The Government also was asked to close the Government offices at the hour of the Memorial Service, that the Government officials might be free to attend. Arrangements for a native celebration were left to the mission to make.[1]

That Hetherwick should be so complacent about the Blantyre celebration of Livingstone's birth being a segregated affair indicates how far he had come since the days when he and Scott had insisted that worship in the Blantyre Church would be an occasion when Africans and Europeans participated together. The intervening years had seen the establishment of a European community which was increasingly reluctant to mix socially with Malawians and even Blantyre Mission was accommodating itself to

94

the new order. Possibly the crowning irony was that the high point of the European celebration was the presentation by Alexander Livingstone Bruce of a memorial tablet which had been subscribed by Livingstone's grandchildren, himself included. Only two years later, Bruce's Magomero Estate would be the focal point of the "Native Rising" which would show how far was the plantation economy now developing in the Shire Highlands from the vision which David Livingstone had formed for the people of this area.

We have seen that, when that crisis broke, the Scottish Missions did stand up for their founding vision in face of settler hostility. Nonetheless, they themselves were far from impervious to the assumptions and prejudices which entrenched themselves in the minds of Europeans as colonial rule became the established order. In fact, they accommodated themselves to the new situation all too successfully. As John McCracken observes: "Adrian Hastings' description of missionary societies between the wars as 'rather too obviously the contented house cats of the colonial system' applies less well to the Scottish missions than to a number of other societies. Nevertheless, by the 1930s it was only on such relatively insignificant issues as what language was to be used in schools that there was any major disagreement between the churches and the government."[2]

Facing the Colour Bar

The fact that attitudes were changing was not lost on the Malawians who were most closely related to the Scots and other Europeans. Among them was Lewis Mataka Bandawe, a leading figure in the Blantyre Mission from the 1920s until the 1960s. He recalled the kind of relationships which had prevailed in the early days of the Mission:

> The very first missionaries, especially D.C. Scott and his brother really did get on with the people – they slept on *mphasa* [reed mats used as beds] in the houses and ate what the people gave them. My father-in-law, Mr Joseph Bismarck had many stories about this ... Napier was the missionary whom I saw and knew who was like that. He above the others really loved and was one with the people. Wherever he went he simply slept where space was offered and ate

whatever was going, like the first ones. Whenever there was any
tension or difficulty with teachers or other staff it was he who resolved
it.[3]

Implicit in such recollection is the recognition that by the inter-war years,
when Bandawe was active in leadership, the Scottish missionaries were
no longer close to the people in this way. Though inter-racial relations
were generally gentler than was the case in South Africa and Rhodesia,
nonetheless the "colour bar" was increasingly a reality. Not even the
Scottish Missions were exempt.

The extent of the racism which was allowed to develop within the
Livingstonia Mission is exposed in the autobiography of Paul Bwembya
Mushindo who worked for many years as an evangelist and minister in
the Livingstonia sphere in eastern Zambia.[4] Among the prevailing
customs to which he draws attention are the requirement for Africans
approaching a European house to stand some way off and wait until
called, the refusal of some missionaries to eat with Africans, the fact that
in Lubwa church separate seats were reserved for Europeans, and that
they drank from the communion cup before it was passed to the African
congregation. Mushindo was particularly critical of R.D. McMinn with
whom he had worked for many years at Lubwa, pointing out that
McMinn had forced him to travel in the back of their lorry even when
there was space in the cab, and that McMinn had ordered him not to wear
shoes and to remain barefoot.[5]

Vera Chirwa belonged to a family which included leading figures
within the Livingstonia Mission. She was therefore well-placed, as a
child growing up in the context of 1930s mission stations, to observe
prevailing attitudes. She recalls: "When I was a child, we did not know
what the inside of a European house looked like. The Europeans were
like gods to us. If you went to see relatives, who were working for them,
you could hardly enter the kitchen. But my mother, Elizabeth Chibambo,
stood up against all that. In the church at Ekwendeni Mission there were
separate doors and benches for the African and the Europeans. There
were only a few whites, among whom were Mr and Mrs Larkin, but they
nevertheless had their own door. My mother was exceptionally well

dressed for an African woman and carried herself in a European way, with hat, stockings and high heels. One day Mr Larkin summoned her after church. She could not enter his house and he confronted her on the veranda:

> 'Do you want to be like European women? I see you are dressing up in church and doing your hair like a European. What are you up to?'
>
> 'What is your problem,' my mother asked, 'This is my body and I do my hair as I please. My husband buys me dresses and I can dress as I want.'
>
> 'Oh, you are being very rude, Elizabeth!' Mr Larkin said.
>
> 'No, you are being rude, questioning me like that!' my mother snapped back, and the missionaries soon marked her out as a troublemaker who would 'spoil' other African women."[6]

Many such anecdotes can be recounted, showing that racist attitudes became quite mainstream in the Scottish missions, to the chagrin of spirited Malawians like Elizabeth Chibambo.

As an idealistic young Scottish missionary arriving in Malawi in 1950, Anne Hepburn did not fail to notice how the pervasive racism and colonialism of the day conditioned even the life of the mission stations. She recalls that: "In 1950 Nyasaland had Protectorate status under the Foreign and Commonwealth Office in London and the paternalistic colonial attitude of the Government was mirrored among the Scottish missionaries. On each of the three stations, Blantyre, Zomba and Mulanje, missionaries were in charge as Head of Station. There was very little social mixing with African colleagues."[7]

Paternalism and Racism

While it is possible to detect a deepening complicity with colonialism in the attitudes of Scots in Malawi in the inter-war years, it is also necessary to recognise that, somewhat in tension with their higher ideals, elements of paternalism and racism were built into the Scottish involvement from the very beginning. In several of his books Jack Thompson has drawn attention to the significance of the Xhosa evangelists who played a prominent role in the early years of the Livingstonia Mission.[8] The missionary encounter was not simply a matter of European expatriates on the one hand and indigenous Africans on the other. There was a third dimension represented by the five Xhosa who travelled from the Eastern Cape in South Africa to join the Livingstonia Mission. They were Africans who could readily understand the language and culture of the communities they now encountered in Malawi while, at the same time, their high-level education at the Lovedale Institution had introduced them to European ways. How were they regarded by their Scottish fellow-missionaries?

Xhosa missionaries to Malawi: (front) William Koyi and Isaac Williams Wauchope; (back) Mapassa Ntintili and Shadrach Mngunana

It is clear that they occupied an ambiguous position, in some respects treated as colleagues while in other respects regarded as inferior, in accordance with the prevailing racial attitudes of the time. With a telling analogy Thompson concludes that: "In general ... the Xhosa evangelists were treated with something like the same distance that a teacher might adopt towards a prefect in a Victorian school."[9] The importance of this for our purposes is that the relations between the Scottish missionaries and the Xhosa evangelists within the Livingstonia Mission would be paradigmatic for the way in which Scots and

Malawians would interact in the decades to come. On the one hand, the "teacher-prefect" relationship represents a degree of mutual confidence and collaboration which, at that time, would have been unthinkable in the political or commercial sphere. On the other hand, it carried a sense of paternalism which, however benevolent, would rankle with the able and assertive Malawian leaders who would emerge within the Livingstonia Mission during the early years of the 20th century.

Only with the advent of new attitudes, in the years after the Second World War, would friendship on a genuinely equal basis become possible. Nonetheless, even in the early years of missionary engagement in northern Malawi, on occasion deep friendships could be formed across the racial barrier. This is well illustrated by the case of William Koyi, the most influential of the Xhosa evangelists to whose work the beginnings of Christianity among the Ngoni owed much. When Koyi died in 1886 James Stewart, his Principal at Lovedale, wrote of him as: "a personal friend whom I greatly esteemed and loved."[10] In a curious phrase which perhaps reveals both the extent to which he was captive to the racism of the time and the extent to which he could transcend it, Angus Elmslie, whose own relations with Koyi had not always been easy, stated that: "no white man would have degraded himself if he had taken off his hat to him."[11] This inherently self-contradictory attitude would characterise the relationships of Scots and Malawians throughout much of the colonial period.

Malawian Voices of Protest

It meant that, inevitably, Malawian attitudes to Scots were double-edged. Admiration and respect were mixed with outrage and resentment. Among the first Africans to raise a voice of protest about racist attitudes among Scottish missionaries was Charles Domingo. Brought to Malawi by William Koyi in 1881, he was associated for many years with Livingstonia Mission. He studied at Lovedale for two years in the early 1890s and was a member of the party which established the new Livingstonia headquarters at Khondowe in 1894. He was one of the first two theological students to be enrolled at the Overtoun Institution in

April 1899, the other being Yakobe Msusa Muwamba. Domingo graduated in 1900 and spent the next six years as a teacher at the Institution where he became a highly respected figure. In May 1903 he was licensed to preach and in 1907 was transferred to Loudon to prepare for ordination to the ministry under the guidance of Donald Fraser. By this time Domingo was becoming exasperated by the length of time it was taking for him to achieve his goal of ordination. The last straw came when he was publicly reprimanded by Fraser for a speech he made which met with the latter's disapproval. As Harvey Sindima comments: "Domingo could no longer take paternalistic missionary attitudes and public humiliation towards Africans."[12]

Domingo was not alone in experiencing this kind of frustration. The high level of education offered by Livingstonia Mission created aspirations among Malawian students which it proved unable to fulfil. A running sore was the reluctance of the Scottish missionaries to ordain those who had trained for ministry, an action which would make them, ecclesiastically, fully equal to their European counterparts. As Daniel Nhlane exclaimed in 1915, after many years of ministerial training: "let us be ordained before we die!"[13] After making his break with the Livingstonia Mission, Domingo was forthright in his criticism, pointing out that the missionaries had no respect for an African "White fellows have been here for nearly 36 years, and not one of them sees a native as his Brother, but as his boy, tho' a native is somehow wiser than he in managing God's work".[14] This sense of injustice and grievance prompted Domingo to advance a sharp critique of the colonial system and to highlight the degree to which missionaries colluded with it:

> There is too much failure among all Europeans in Nyasaland. The Three Combined Bodies: - Missionaries – Government – and Companies or Gainers of Money do form the same rule to look on a Native with mockery eyes.... The life of the Three Combined Bodies is altogether too cheaty, too thefty, too mockery. Instead of "Give" they say "Take away from".[15]

These words, extracted from a letter written by Domingo to Joseph Booth in 1911, are among the first to articulate in English the acute sense of injustice which Africans would experience during the years of colonial rule. Without the education offered by the Livingstonia Mission, it is unlikely that Domingo would have had the critical acumen and linguistic fluency to prepare such an indictment of the colonial system. To that extent, Scottish influence contributed to resistance to colonialism. Yet, ironically, the critical faculties nurtured at the Overtoun Institution were employed to expose how far Livingstonia itself was an agent of colonialism. The attitudes of Scots, even those most deeply committed to Malawi and its people, were tainted by racism, paternalism and colonialism. Domingo would not be the last to raise a voice of protest.

Both of Vera Chirwa's grandfathers, Jonathan Chirwa and Yesaya Chibambo, were among the first African ministers in the Livingstonia Mission. She recalls that: "Even my grandparents, who were sincere Christians, would integrate criticism of the inequalities we were experiencing in their prayers and sermons."[16] Chibambo was an outstanding student at the Overtoun Institution and in 1920 was the first recipient of the Honours Diploma for Schoolmasters. He went on to complete a distinguished career as an ordained minister, Ngoni historian and advisor to the Ngoni paramount chief. In 1921 he wrote a letter to the Livingstonia Mission Council in order to register dissatisfaction with the conditions of service applied to African employees of the Mission. While much of the letter was concerned with such matters as contracts of employment, expenses, equipment and pensions, running through the letter is the conviction that the underlying reason for the lack of adequate conditions of service was a lack of respect for the African staff of the Mission. Among the points which he raised were:

The native is not regarded as a co-worker with the missionary.

The native worker is commonly called "boy" by his missionary without any distinction.

The native does not see the way to believe that the work on which he is placed is his, and that with his aid, he will enable his missionary and master, to bring up indigenously the growth of his native country, to an intellectual and spiritual ability, for serving God and man; but by threats he works with fear.

One sees that he is slightly esteemed, so is his work.

No native is allowed to report about his own work. There are some offices and departments which originally were held by European staff only, but which are now entrusted to natives. The report which comes to the Mission Council from a native is only taken through a missionary; and sometimes the missionary who writes the same report perhaps does not understand really about the work done by the native. This is especially the case where a missionary holds a temporary place.

Lastly the native is not encouraged to attend Mission Council. The missionary is in Africa for the uplift and improvement of the native. This improvement can better be carried out if the mind of the native and of the missionary are working and designing together.[17]

Unlike Domingo, Chibambo never broke away from the Livingstonia Mission. He remained one of its leading figures. His words therefore carry a representative character, indicating the lack of respect widely experienced by Malawians loyal to the Livingstonia Mission during this period.

Possibly the person who experienced this lack of respect most acutely was Yesaya Zerenji Mwasi, who in 1914 was one of the first three Africans to be ordained to the ministry within Livingstonia Mission. A Tonga, born around 1869-70, Mwasi had entered the Overtoun Institution in 1897, taking the Arts course from 1897 to 1899, graduating from the theology course in 1905 and being licensed to preach the following year. During this time he established a reputation for outstanding intellectual ability, formidable gifts of leadership and a fiery temper. When he was called in 1916 to be minister of the Sanga congregation, near Chintheche, he became the first African to enjoy the full status of parish minister. He went on to become the first African Moderator of Livingstonia Presbytery in 1918 and then served temporarily as its Clerk in 1921. Such a track record might suggest that Mwasi had led the way in establishing the full equality of African leaders within the Livingstonia Mission. In fact, he became the leading figure in establishing that such equality did not exist.

A mesmerising preacher, Mwasi was also known among the Tonga as a rainmaker and miracle-worker. When the West Nyasa Native Association was formed, Mwasi was elected its Secretary and such was his influence that the District Commissioner reported that: "... this is a *one man* Association – Revd Yesiah Mwase".[18] He had the standing which gave him the confidence to challenge his Scottish colleagues and has been described by D.D. Phiri as, "most vocal and arch-critical of the missionaries."[19] A series of clashes occurred which culminated in 1932 when the Livingstonia Presbytery took disciplinary action against Mwasi in which he believed the Presbytery had flouted its own procedures in order to victimise him, thus demonstrating its lack of respect for its

African ministers. This was the last straw for Mwasi who prepared a document entitled *My Essential and Paramount Reasons for Working Independently* and formally withdrew from the Livingstonia Mission on 26 September 1933.[20] Much of his eloquent statement is concerned with due process in disciplinary cases but underlying the technical argument is a sense of outrage at the tacit racism which Mwasi believed ran through the life and government of the Livingstonia Mission. In 1935 he joined forces with two other prominent Livingstonia secessionists, Yaphet Mkandawire and Charles Chinula, to form the

Ordination of Livingstonia's first Malawian ministers, May 1914. (Front) Yesaya Zerenji Mwasi, Hezekiah Tweya, Jonathan Chirwa; (back) A.G. McAlpine, Walter Elmslie, Robert Laws

defiantly named *Mpingo wa Afipa wa Africa* - The Blackman's Church of Africa.

103

Though Mwasi has gone down in history as someone who broke away from Livingstonia Mission, a widespread perception among the Tonga is that Mwasi's secession was, in fact, a fulfilment of the vision of the first Livingstonia missionaries, though he was in conflict with the missionaries who came later. Wesley Manda, a Livingstonia minister born in 1916, noted a sense of common cause between Mwasi and Robert Laws:

> Dr Laws left Malawi in 1927 and this Laws told Mwasi that the new and young white missionaries were not going to respect Africans and this really came to pass and Y.Z. Mwasi decided to break away as a result. Mwasi decided to break away from the Free Church because of the failure of the "new arrivals" to respect educated blacks.[21]

This appears to reflect a perception, common in the Chintheche area, that Mwasi was striking a blow against rising white racism and that, in doing so, he was being true to the original vision of Livingstonia, thus enjoying the approval of Laws and "higher authorities". Timothy Happy Chirwa commented:

> The reasons that made Rev Y.Z. Mwasi to break away from CCAP include: he did not want to be under the leadership of the white missionaries; and he was against segregation in the CCAP, where whites regarded Africans as second class people and themselves as first class.... Rev Y.Z. Mwasi, soon after breaking away from the Livingstonia Mission, informed the Scottish body in Scotland of his resignation and the authorities in Scotland accepted his move or approved his move.[22]

While the latter assertion is not literally true, it reflects an accurate perception of a broad development taking place in the 1920s and 1930s as a new generation of Scottish missionaries took over from the first generation. In contrast to the early leaders of the Missions like Laws and Scott, the missionaries arriving in the years after the First World War found Africa under colonial rule and their own assumptions and attitudes were moulded by colonialism and racism, perhaps more than they realised. Men like Mwasi were highly sensitive to paternalism or racism and the results were explosive. Malawians and Scots found themselves at odds in a struggle which turned out to be the growing pains of the movement which would enable Malawi, thirty years later, to break the colonial system and emerge as an independent nation.

Crucibles of Nationalism

Though the Scottish Missions were, at times, a source of much exasperation to progressive Malawians, there is also another side to the story. As Shepperson and Price observe, Livingstonia was the seed-bed of the Nyasaland African Congress - closely followed, it may be added, by Blantyre.[23] This judgement is substantiated by the fact that when Native Associations came to be formed in the years after the First World War, they were found mainly in the north and drew their leadership and membership mostly from "graduates" of Livingstonia. Many were church elders who, as John McCracken points out, "... practised in Kirk Sessions and Presbytery procedures of discussion and debate, of the keeping of minutes and the passing of resolutions, which they were to employ successfully in the political associations they later founded."[24]

Scottish missionaries fostered and encouraged the emergence of Native Associations. Already in 1907 Robert Laws wrote in these terms:

> Some constitutional means should be provided whereby the natives who form the majority of the population should have by native council or otherwise the means of expressing a legitimate opinion on legitimate changes which concern themselves. Were this done, and done early, we believe the gradually increasing educated native community would be so enlisted on the side of constitutional government and peace and so be prevented from becoming in the future the prey of any noisy demagogue.[25]

Laws was as good as his word. In 1912, when a group of predominantly Tumbuka teachers and clerks proposed to establish the North Nyasa Native Association, Laws granted permission for them to hold their meetings in the Livingstonia reading room at Karonga. At this early stage

the Native Associations were "essentially outcrops of the mission".[26]
Indeed some of them were regularly attended by Scottish missionaries.

As they developed in the 1920s and 1930s, they began to develop their own character and momentum though still largely made up of men who had been educated at Livingstonia. "It is a peculiar thing," wrote the Karonga District Commissioner, "that almost every highly educated native of the Livingstonia Mission is politically minded and race conscious and always on the look out for some stigma."[27] In the aftermath of the Chilembwe Rising they came to terms with the reality of colonial rule and did not offer any direct challenge to it. They limited their ambitions at this stage to improving conditions for Africans within the prevailing colonial system. Nonetheless, they fostered a political consciousness and developed the beginnings of political organisation. They were seedbeds from which a nationalist movement would eventually grow that could succeed in overthrowing colonial rule and achieving independence. The Scottish missions, which in this period had accommodated themselves to British colonial rule, at the same time played a not insignificant role in the early beginnings of a political movement which would ultimately lead to the dismantling of the colonial system.

Alongside associational life and the early development of political aspirations went the growth of cultural pride – something which would also be important in the building of a movement which could overcome colonial rule. This too was a realm where the collaboration of Malawians and Scots made a significant contribution, none more so than the Livingstonia missionary Thomas Cullen Young whose appreciation of the human quality in African community life was noted in the last chapter. Young was an admirer of traditional Tumbuka community life, commenting on one occasion:

> It is hardly an exaggeration to say that primitive African life was, essentially, a finer thing than that which succeeded it, since its finer qualities were community qualities, whereas under the succeeding regimes such qualities as, say, consideration for others could only be maintained in individuals against a terrific weight of unsympathetic

general tendency.... Africa's contribution to the problems of human progress may therefor [*sic*] be expected along the lines of loyalty to the early ideal of the "good village" with the boundaries of the village extended to match the extended interests and concerns of men in the modern world.[28]

Young's approach to the history and culture of Malawian communities has been described as "progressive traditionalism" and can be regarded as having prepared the ground in important ways for a full-scale nationalist movement.[29] Among his close associates was Levi Mumba, his former student, for whom cultural nationalism led directly to political activity. After a long career in the leadership of the Native Associations, in 1944 Mumba was appointed as the first President-General of the Nyasaland African Congress.

Young also played a role in the construction of the cultural nationalism of another of his former students, Hastings Kamuzu Banda, who would become the first President of independent Malawi. The two collaborated closely as co-editors of a volume entitled *Our African Way of Life* which was prominent among the earliest published expressions of Malawian cultural nationalism.[30] More will be said in the next chapter about the remarkable relationship of Banda and Young and their encounters and interaction in Malawi and in Scotland. Meanwhile, the conclusion drawn by Young's biographer, Peter Forster, is that: "It would be fanciful to declare dogmatically that Cullen Young was the architect of cultural nationalism in modern Malawi. Yet it would be equally hard to deny that Cullen Young was a crucial influence upon Banda's thinking at a particular period in his life.... Cullen Young served a maieutic function; that is to say, he performed a midwife's services to Banda's thoughts and ideas."[31]

In 1928 Young was appointed founding editor of a Livingstonia-based Tumbuka-language periodical entitled *Vyaro na Vyaro* ("Other Lands"). For Young this was a natural extension of the "talking-place" on which he had set such store in his appreciation of village life. He was intrigued that many of the early authors of letters to the editor began their contributions with the question: "may I be allowed to speak at the *mphara* [talking-place]?"[32] This, for Young, provided the clue as to the role which a newspaper could play in the urban life now emerging in Africa. One of its most notable deficiencies was:

> ... the absence of the village or community "talking-place", the place which every African man, as he reaches maturity, is taught to honour as his "seat of learning", the place provided in every part of native Africa for "the intelligent use of leisure time". It is the complete absence of this central thing in African life which makes an emptiness for the African in our townships and labour centres. And it is this empty place which the newspaper fills, provided that it throws its columns open to the African contributor.[33]

The new periodical therefore aimed to encourage Malawians to air their views on topics of their own choice. As editor, Young sought to foster a democratic ethos. His article on the "native newspaper" reveals how much store he set by vernacular literature and open discussion and debate.[34]

Young was also a moving force behind some of the first books and scholarly articles to be published by Malawian authors. As early as 1909 he had been handed an anonymous history of the Tumbuka people. The author turned out to be Saulos Nyirenda, a Livingstonia-trained teacher who had become a telephonist. While stationed in Zomba and feeling homesick, he wrote his history of the Tumbuka on the blue forms used by the Telegraph Company. Many years later Young managed to get Nyirenda's text published in the anthropological journal *Bantu Studies*.[35] In his preface he expressed his confidence that Nyirenda would come to be recognised as the "Father of History" so far as Northern Nyasaland is concerned.[36] Another of his protégés was Levi Mumba, first President-General of the Nyasaland African Congress, whom he had known as a "little schoolboy". Young was able to arrange for Mumba's essay on traditional Tumbuka religion to be published in the *International Review of Missions* in 1930.[37] A short introduction by Young reveals his deep admiration for Mumba, though very oddly it does not mention him by name so the article appears anonymously.

When Samuel Yosia Ntara's *Man of Africa* was the International Institute of African Languages and Culture's prize winning biography in 1933, Young translated it from Chinyanja to English, wrote a preface and saw it through to publication.[38] He made a similar contribution many years later when Ntara wrote a biography of the Chewa headman Msyamboza which Young translated and published in English under the title *Headman's Enterprise.*[39] He remained enthusiastic about what Nthara had to offer, writing in the *Nyasaland Journal*: "I may, perhaps, take this opportunity of bringing to more public notice the work in authorship and historical research which has been going on for 30 years in quiet seclusion at Mkhoma by Mr Samuel Nthara. In no other land has comparable work been done by any man of the first literate generation and we would, as a protecting Power, honour ourselves by taking some opportunity to honour him."[40] Though his own research and writing had been concentrated on Tumbuka history and culture Young was also enthusiastic about books which offered analysis of the life of the Chewa. He played his part too in study of the Ngoni, particularly by promoting the publication of Yesaya Chibambo's *My Ngoni of Nyasaland* to which Young contributed some footnotes.[41]

Young was indeed a midwife in regard to the early emergence of Malawian literature. This literary endeavour did much to foster identity and national pride, countering the denigration of African life which held sway during the colonial period. While many of the Scots who were living in Malawi during the first half of the 20th century colluded to some degree with the European colonialism which was the order of the day, some like Cullen Young also contributed to the expression of the cultural nationalism which proved to be an ideological basis for the eventual overthrow of colonial rule.

The slowly emerging national consciousness which was apparent in the 1920s and 1930s rose to a new level after the Second World War. Many Malawians had fought with the Kings African Rifles in the War. This exposed them, e.g., to the efforts being made in India to attain independence and raised in their minds the question why they should not be working towards independence in their own context? Some were involved in the victory of the KAR over the Italian colonists in Ethiopia – as Jonathan Sangaya, who later became the first African General Secretary of Blantyre Synod, would put it – "an African army freeing an African country".[42] The experience of Malawian troops in the course of the War made independence much more thinkable than it had been before 1939. There was now fertile ground in which the seeds of political association and cultural nationalism might grow.

Conclusion

The years between the two World Wars were, for Malawi, a period when colonial rule appeared to be the settled order. Everyone involved had to come to terms with it. For the Scottish Missions, the friction which had characterised the early years of their relationship with the British administration gave way to a comfortable acquiescence. Indeed, the Missions themselves absorbed and expressed colonialist values. Perhaps this was seen most clearly in the steady erosion of the vision of Scott and Hetherwick that worship at the Blantyre Church would be marked by racial unity. From the 1890s it increasingly became established practice, both in Blantyre and Zomba, that the Europeans and Africans formed separate worshipping communities. Finally, in 1926, this was formalised with the creation of a colonial congregation of the Church of Scotland with its own minister in Blantyre, entirely separate from the Blantyre Presbytery of the Church of Central Africa Presbyterian.[43] This ensured that Scots living in Malawi, in their church life, could remain quite separate from Malawians.

Even the missionaries, whose professed *raison d'etre* was the advancement of Malawian communities, became much more distant than had been the case in earlier years. In the first days of the Scottish Missions only relatively small numbers of Malawians were directly involved with the life of the Mission. Relationships were close and deep. As the movement expanded there inevitably developed much greater distance between the small number of Scots and the thousands of Malawians who were becoming involved. Already by 1902 Charles

Stuart of Livingstonia was lamenting: "We do not seem to get into close enough touch with the people in their village life, meeting with them mostly, as we do, in school and in church and in the ordinary work of the station."[44]

It has to be acknowledged, however, that there was more to it than simply the pressures brought to bear by an expanding organisation. In the late 19th and early 20th century Social Darwinism emerged as a prevailing ideology of empire. It posited a hierarchy of races, giving Europeans the confidence that they were at the top and the conviction that Africans were culturally inferior. This ideology influenced the thinking of people growing up in Europe in that period, including the Scots who would come to make their life in Malawi. In marked contrast to David Livingstone, Robert Laws and David Clement Scott, they expected little from African leadership during their lifetime. John McCracken finds a clue to the underlying attitudes in "the fact even in 1920, the senior African assistant at the Overtoun Institution, Yuraya Chirwa, was being paid little more than a third of what George Williams had received in 1888, £48 as compared with £130."[45] These figures provide hard evidence of the direction which was being taken during the inter-war years. The Scottish missions were implicated in the injustices of colonialism in ways which ensured that they would provoke the outrage of their most able Malawian protégés. However, Scots were also contributing in significant ways to the construction of the equipment with which Malawi would one day throw off the yoke of colonial rule and achieve its independence.

---

[1] Hetherwick, *The Romance of Blantyre*, p. 199.

[2] John McCracken, "Church and State in Malawi: The Role of the Scottish Presbyterian Missions 1875-1965", in Holger Bernt Hansen & Michael Twaddle ed., *Christian Missionaries and the State in the Third World*, Oxford: James Currey & Athens: Ohio University Press, 2002, pp. 176-193, at p. 182.

[3] Lewis Bandawe, interview by Andrew C. Ross, 9 January 1964, Ross, *Blantyre Mission*, p. 185.

[4] Paul Bwembya Mushindo, *The Life of an African Evangelist*, Lusaka: University of Zambia Institute of African Studies, Communication, No. 9, 1973.

[5] *Ibid*, pp. 23, 42, 46; cit Thompson, *Christianity in Northern Malawi*, pp. 203-04.

[6] Vera Chirwa, *Fearless Fighter: An Autobiography*, London & New York: Zed Books, 2007, pp. 4-5.

[7] Anne Hepburn, *Memories of Malawi and Scotland*, Edinburgh: privately published, 2011, p. 11.

[8] Thompson, *Touching the Heart*; Jack Thompson, *Ngoni, Xhosa and Scot: Religious and Cultural Interaction in Malawi*, Zomba: Kachere, 2007.

[9] Thompson, *Ngoni, Xhosa and Scot*, p. 22.

[10] James Stewart to Robert Laws, 25 August 1886, cit. Thompson, *Ngoni, Xhosa and Scot*, p. 65.

[11] Quoted in Jack, *Daybreak at Livingstonia*, p. 100.

[12] Harvey J. Sindima, *The Legacy of Scottish Missionaries in Malawi*, Lewiston/Lampeter/Queenston: Edwin Mellen Press, 1992, pp. 86-87.

[13] Donald Fraser, *The Autobiography of an African*, London: Seeley, 1925, p. 207.

[14] Charles Domingo to Joseph Booth, 19 September 1911; cit. McCracken, *Politics and Christianity*, p. 259.

[15] Charles Domingo to Joseph Booth, 20 September 1911, cit. Kenneth R. Ross ed., *Christianity in Malawi: A Sourcebook*, Gweru: Mambo Press, 1996, pp. 155-59, at pp. 135-36.

[16] Chirwa, *Fearless Fighter*, pp. 6-7.

[17] Letter of Yesaya Chibambo, Minutes of Livingstonia Mission Council, July 1921, pp. 352-57, Malawi National Archives 47/LIM/3/17; repr. Kenneth R. Ross ed., *Christianity in Malawi: A Sourcebook*, Gweru: Mambo Press, 1996, pp. 155-59, at p. 157.

[18] Annual Report for the West Nyasa District 1931, Malawi National Archives NNC3/1/4; cit. McCracken, *Politics and Christianity*, p. 276.

[19] D.D. Phiri, *Charles Chidongo Chinula*, London: Longman, 1975, p. 16.

[20] Yesaya Zerenji Mwasi, *My Essential and Paramount Reasons for Working Independently*, Blantyre: CLAIM, 1999; original manuscript 12 July 1933.

[21] Turner Banda, interview with Rev. Wesley Manda, 2 March 1998.

[22] Turner Banda, interview with Timothy Happy Chirwa, 13 March 1998.

[23] Shepperson and Price, *Independent African*, p. 414.

[24] McCracken, *Politics and Christianity*, p. 304.

[25] *Aurora*, December 1907, cit. McCracken, *Politics and Christianity*, p. 304.

[26] McCracken, *Politics and Christianity*, p. 313.

[27] Letter from District Commissioner, Karonga, to Provincial Secretary, 27 January 1931; cit. Pachai, *Malawi: History of the Nation*, pp. 228-29.

[28] T. Cullen Young, *Notes on the Customs and Folklore of the Tumbuka-Kamanga Peoples*, Livingstonia: Mission Press, 1931, pp. 146-47; cit. Forster, *T. Cullen Young*, p. 62.

[29] Forster, *T. Cullen Young*, p. 115.

[30] Cullen Young and Hastings Banda ed., *Our African Way of Life*, London: United Society for Christian Literature, 1946.

[31] Forster, *T. Cullen Young*, p. 165.

[32] T. Cullen Young, "The Native Newspaper", *Africa*, Vol. 11 (1938), pp. 63-72, at p. 70.

[33] *Ibid.*, p. 64.

[34] *Ibid.*

[35] Saulos Nyirenda, "A History of the Tumbuka-Henga People", translated and edited by T. Cullen Young, *Bantu Studies* Vol. 5 (1931), pp. 1-75.

[36] *Ibid.*, p. 3.

[37] "An African" [Levi Mumba], "The Religion of my Fathers", *International Review of Missions*, Vol. 19 (1930), pp. 362-71.

[38] Samuel Yosia Ntara, *Man of Africa*, translated and arranged from the original Nyanja by T. Cullen Young, London: United Society for Christian Literature, 1934.

[39] S.Y. Ntara, *Headman's Enterprise*, London: United Society for Christian Literature, 1949.

[40] Cullen Young, "Place-Names in Nyasaland", *The Nyasaland Journal*, Vol. VI No. 2 (July 1953), pp. 35-36, at p. 36.

[41] Y.M. Chibambo, *My Ngoni of Nyasaland*, London: United Society for Christian Literature, 1942.

[42] Ross, *Colonialism to Cabinet Crisis*, p. 45, n. 65.

[43] Ross, *Blantyre Mission*, p. 191.

[44] Livingstonia Mission Report 1902, p. 73; cit. McCracken, *Politics and Christianity*, pp. 230-31.

[45] McCracken, *Politics and Christianity*, p. 242.

7. Deepening Friendship

Language of the Heart

Notwithstanding the fact that Scottish missionaries were, to no small degree, implicated in colonial rule and therefore legitimate targets for its critics within African communities, even in this antagonistic environment there were factors which made for the cultivation of mutual respect and friendship. Not to be underestimated, for one thing, is the requirement for the missionaries to learn the local vernacular languages – Chinyanja, Chitumbuka, Chiyao, Chitonga, Chinkhonde and others. One of the first projects to which Scottish missionaries applied themselves was the translation of the Bible into these languages. They were among the first to reduce Malawian language to writing and their achievements in the realm of Bible translation were prodigious. As early as 1884 Robert Laws published the first Chinyanja translation of the New Testament and subsequent years would see an intensification of Bible translation efforts which culminated in the completion of a Chinyanja translation of the Bible in 1922 under the leadership of William Murray at Nkhoma. While missionaries brought drive and leadership to the project they were highly dependent on Malawian collaborators who had the advantage of speaking Chinyanja as their mother tongue. The countless hours spent sitting together wrestling with the challenges of accurate and appropriate translation, besides resulting in a vastly influential text, had significant by-products as well.

At an interpersonal level, facility in vernacular languages allowed Scottish missionaries to communicate with Malawian associates and contacts in their mother tongue, the language of the heart. It also enabled them to develop a deep understanding of Malawian culture and community life, as had been demonstrated in the early years by Clement Scott with his Mang'anja dictionary. By no means all missionaries advanced so far in developing a sympathetic understanding of Malawian life and culture. In the high colonial period, as we have seen, there was often a degree of aloofness and paternalism on the part of the missionaries which perceptive Malawians were not slow to detect. There was, however, an unbroken succession of Scottish missionaries who made themselves familiar with the vernacular languages and the vernacular world which these brought to expression. This did not guarantee mutual respect and strong friendship but it did make it possible.

Robert D. McMinn, born at Dailly in Ayrshire in 1870 and a missionary of the Livingstonia Mission from 1893 to 1934, is a good example of a Scot who made a major contribution to the study of Malawian (and Zambian) languages.[1] As soon as he arrived he applied himself with enthusiasm to mastering the local language, Chitonga. He went on to learn Chinyanja and Chitumbuka. He contributed to Bible translation and to the production of vocabularies and grammars in these languages. In 1913 he was appointed to Lubwa, one of the stations established by the Livingstonia Mission in the north-east of Northern Rhodesia (now Zambia). David Kaunda, father of the future Zambian President Kenneth Kaunda, had pioneered the establishment of this station. To build on these foundations McMinn found that he had to learn the Chibemba language. He became an authority on the subject and was one of the leading contributors to the translation of the Bible into Bemba. In-depth knowledge of local languages enabled the Scots to share at an intimate level with the African communities among whom they were living and working.

Another notable linguist was Tom Price who served with the Blantyre Mission from 1929 to 1947 and then returned after independence to serve for a further ten years, 1964-74, as a Bible Society consultant. In collaboration with Professor George Shepperson he produced the study of John Chilembwe which remains the outstanding historical study of the colonial period in Malawi.[2] According to his *Independent African* co-author, "... he was a quintessential Scot: an interesting example of what has been called the Caledonian antisyzygy. He combined a deep faith in Christianity with a scepticism towards many aspects of modern life, ecclesiastical as well as secular."[3] He found his forte in Malawi in the work on vernacular languages for which the Blantyre Mission had been distinguished from the beginning. He produced three readers for schools – *Tinkhani*, *Nkhani Zolongosolera* and *Tiyeni Tiyemekeze*, all published by Hetherwick Press on the Blantyre Mission. Perhaps his most influential work was *The Elements of Nyanja for English-Speaking Students*, published by Hetherwick Press in 1941. He later brought his linguistic expertise to the service of the Bible Society, working on translations into Chichewa, Chilomwe, Chiyao and Makua.

In 1963 Price wrote a short article entitled "African Language, Incorporated" for *The Glasgow Herald* in which he discussed examples of English words which had been adopted by Chinyanja speakers. He commented particularly on the word for electricity – *magezi*, pointing out that this word derives from "gas" which had never been manufactured or used in Malawi. "One can only conjecture that the flippant cry of 'Light the gas' as an instruction to houseboys to switch on the electric light was heard so often from the Glasgow men imported by the missions and the African Lakes Company that it became standard. The main vowel of *magezi* may be traceable to Kelvinside and Pollock-Shields."[4] Cullen Young is another who, according to George Shepperson, believed that the Scottish way of speaking English had an influence at the linguistic level. He also argued that the Scots form of English enabled Scots to better appreciate Malawian languages.[5]

Institutions and Values

The Blantyre and Livingstonia Missions made early and substantial commitment to the development of such institutions as schools, churches and clinics. These provided the context for day-to-day contact between Scots and Malawians, for the exchange of ideas and the growth of relationships. It was often through the life and work of such institutions that a sense of affinity developed. For example, in her study of the development of the town, now city, of Zomba, Karolin Stahl recalls that: "Since the Church of Central Africa Presbyterian was not then thought of, the African Christians considered themselves to be 'Askotilandi' and collaborated heartily in providing materials and building the church which still stands by the golf course and was completed in 1896."[6]

William Watson, an influential Livingstonia missionary in the middle years of the 20th century, on one occasion duly reported on the progress of the various institutions but then went on to remark: "Behind all is the sharing of the life of the Christian congregations by missionaries and Africans, in worship, in social and personal contacts, in work and recreation. Every missionary – and missionary's wife – has close contact with a group of Africans, a training class, or a voluntary gathering."[7] In the Southern Province it was said of Alexander Hetherwick that, "He knows every evangelist and teacher intimately; he knows their difficulties and temptations in their isolated outposts, and no one is more welcome when he visits them. He is their champion and friend; one whom they can absolutely trust and confide in."[8]

The first half of the 20th century was the period of steady development of African leadership of the missionary institutions, a process which drew heavily on the quality of relationships which were established. This led by the 1950s to the kind of situation which Stephen Kauta Msiska described in the following terms: "*Church and Mission*: Although new problems and difficulties arise to hinder the progress of integration, we have managed to have our 'Education Committee with powers'. We are evangelising different districts together and in fact the name 'Church' is beginning to absorb its mother the 'Mission'. Church and Mission now become the ears and eyes of one body."[9]

Where relationships between Scots and Malawians were particularly formative was in the context of the mission schools. As Nyamayaro Mufuka observes: "Since education in Nyasaland was wholly in missionary hands, there was ample time and opportunity for the exchange of ideas between missionaries and the teachers.... Under the influence of such men as [Tom] Colvin, [Andrew] Doig and [Neil] Bernard, the Church of Scotland policy of democratic control of Church affairs became a springboard for political control of the nation."[10] Moreover, the curriculum offered an exposure to Scottish history which proved stimulating to critical young Malawian students. When Orton Chirwa, first President of the Malawi Congress Party and independent Malawi's first Minister of Justice, recalled his school days he remarked: "We loved to hear of Wallace and Bruce and the Scottish War of Independence, you did not need to be a genius to apply the lesson to our own situation."[11]

To illustrate how educational institutions could be influential in the formation of values, Mufuka considers the question of ethnic identity: "In a close examination of missionary sermons and texts in Malawi, it appears that the theme of brotherhood was by far the most important in the early days."[12] This challenged the tribal identity which had earlier predominated and played a crucial role in laying the foundation for the emergence of a national identity. Missionary teaching inculcated a sense of social justice which extended to all rather than being restricted by tribal loyalty. As Mufuka comments: "The Blantyre missionaries ... schooled the young Africans in their charge to abhor racial and tribal privilege under any guise whatever. The only judgement a man [sic] deserved was on the basis of his own merit and performance. The fact of his birth or skin colour was irrelevant. God was no respecter of races or the colour of the skin."[13]

The missionary message was reinforced by the socialization experienced in the mission schools. As Mufuka observes: "The future leaders of Nyasaland went through the initiation ceremonies at mission schools. These rituals were applicable to every boy irrespective of his tribe. Here boys and girls from the Ngoni, Tonga and Wahenga peoples lived in the same boarding houses. The Ngoni boys had to learn to accept the leadership of whoever the missionary chose as Head-Boy or Head-Girl for the particular year. Similarly, the Tonga had to cooperate with Ngoni boys if the school were to function at all."[14]

Late in his life Cullen Young reflected on the impact of the many Malawians who passed through the educational institutions of the Scottish missions:

> After 1895 there began to appear not only the telegraphist to work for Rhodes, but the carpenter, the builder in brick and in stone, the store-man, the printer, the clerk, the teacher, the evangelist, the hospital assistant. And later, even the beginnings of an African Civil Service. All this to such a growing extent that both government budgets and the profit and loss accounts of the trading community began to show

some advantage from the unexpected availability of indigenous as against imported, and expensive, employees at lower levels. Not a year began to pass, also, but somewhere in one or other of the territories some individual African was seen taking a step up into more responsible duty, or striking out for himself as petty merchant or such, to stand or fall by his own capacity.... A new African was on the stage.[15]

Education in institutions established and run by Scottish missionaries not only provided the training which equipped Malawians for these various roles but instilled values which all involved carried with them into their subsequent endeavours.

Malawians in Scotland

It has to be conceded that traffic in the Scotland-Malawi relationship has been heavily one-way. Certainly in its early years it was very much a matter of Scots coming to live and work, for longer or shorter periods, in Malawi. However, it would be wrong to suggest that there was no movement at all in the opposite direction. From early in the shared history there were Malawians who visited Scotland for periods of time. Among the first were Henry Kapito and Donald Malota who studied in Scotland in the early 1880s, returning to Malawi in 1884 to take up leadership positions within the Blantyre Mission. Mungo Murray Chisuse and Nacho Ntimawanzako travelled to Scotland with David Clement Scott, the head of the Blantyre Mission, in 1885. Chisuse had come to live at the Blantyre Mission around 1880 and from 1881 worked as "house-boy" for Clement Scott. He became part of a group of young men whom Scott trained for leadership roles and the trip to Scotland was part of this project. While in Edinburgh he attended Stewart's College, an educational experience which stood him in good stead when he began work as a printer on his return to Blantyre. In 1892 he was appointed one of the seven deacons chosen by David Clement Scott as the first Africans to hold office in the fledgling indigenous church which was emerging at the Blantyre Mission.[16]

Chisuse developed an interest in photography and this inspired the idea of another trip to Scotland which he undertook with his fellow-deacon James Gray Kamlinje in 1897. Clement Scott persuaded the owner of Rennie Lines to allow them to work their passage as stewards in the galley and his aunt, Miss Marjory Scott, provided accommodation for them in Edinburgh. John McCracken outlines the programme which they followed:

> Chisuse spent four months training at Nelson's printing works while Kamlinje received lessons in book-keeping from an Edinburgh accountant. Both learnt to ride bicycles, probably the first Malawians to do so; both were taught to play the violin: Kamlinje, who was subsequently to play solos at concerts in Blantyre, with much greater success. In an important development, Chisuse also "received much kindness" from a former Stewart's College schoolmate, one Mr Inglis, described by Scott as "now a photographer in Edinburgh, near Calton Hill."[17]

It seems likely that the kindness offered by Inglis centred around an introduction to photography, imparting skills which Chisuse would later use to good effect when he became the first Malawian photographer, with a studio in Blantyre. Clearly he also formed enduring friendships in Scotland, setting a trend which would be followed by many others right down to the present day.

One case in the long succession of Malawians who have spent time in Scotland merits particular attention. In 1937 a young Chewa medical doctor arrived in Scotland from the USA with a view to gaining the British qualifications he judged necessary if he were to return to Malawi to practise medicine. His name was Hastings Kamuzu Banda and, though no one would have guessed it at the time, three decades later he would become independent Malawi's first Head of State. Though he was a newcomer in Scotland, his connections went back to his early life growing up in Kasungu at a time when that district fell under the influence of the Livingstonia Mission. Banda's early education took place at a "bush school" administered by one of the early African ministers of Livingstonia Mission, Rev Lameck Manda. He became a catechumen and was baptised into the Church of Scotland by Dr George Prentice, the missionary responsible for the Kasungu district. He took as his Christian name the surname of another missionary he admired, John Hastings.[18]

An ambitious young man, soon afterwards he took the decision to leave his homeland with a view to enrolling at the Church of Scotland's Lovedale Institution in South Africa, at that time one of very few institutions offering higher education to Africans. Travelling on foot, he met up with his uncle Hanock Msokela Phiri in Rhodesia and the two proceeded onward to South Africa. One encounter which remained in their memory was with an elderly Scots eccentric named MacArthur. As Philip Short recounts: "Hearing Banda and Phiri speaking with Scots accents, he inquired where they were from, and on learning that the two young men were from Nyasaland and that they could read the Bible, offered them a place to sleep in his house."[19] They literally dined out on the Scotland-Malawi connection. From South Africa he eventually proceeded to the USA where he advanced his education and qualified as a medical doctor.

Still burning brightly was his youthful ambition to serve his people as a doctor and he was clear that his route had to take him through Scotland where he aimed to secure British medical qualifications through the Royal College of Physicians and Royal College of Surgeons. Besides professional development, his time in Scotland was to be important for other reasons also. It was during his three years in Scotland that he began to take an active interest in Central African politics. Not unrelated to this were the friendships which he developed with Scots who were associated with the Livingstonia Mission. He appears to have been very reserved and almost reclusive during his time in the USA but in Scotland he came out of himself and made friends. He reconnected with the Church of Scotland, attending Guthrie Memorial Church where in due course he was elected to the eldership, a clear mark of the esteem in which he came to be held. He often accepted invitations to meals at the Manse and grew close to the minister, Rev Hector Macpherson, and his family.[20] One of Macpherson's sons, Fergus, became particularly friendly with Banda.

Fergus was contemplating missionary service in Central Africa and took the opportunity to have personal tuition in Chinyanja from Banda. The two were to be life-long friends, notwithstanding disagreements in later years when Banda was ruling Malawi.

Banda also became part of a circle of Scots with strong Malawi connections. As Short recounts:

> The influence of the missionaries and other returned Scots expatriates continued throughout Banda's stay in Edinburgh, affecting his personality no less than it affected him politically. With Cullen Young, the Rev. Matthew Faulds from Karonga, the brothers John and Frederick Moir ... and with the family of his former missionary in Kasungu, Dr George Prentice, Banda could discuss the old days and debate the shape of the new. He came to feel less detached from Nyasaland, and hence more secure, and with some of these men formed the first deep friendships he had made since leaving Kasungu.[21]

For Banda, Edinburgh was a special place: "the very home and Mecca of the Church of Scotland."[22]

Of all the friendships which he struck up during this time none was more remarkable than that with Cullen Young. They had met before, as may best be explained in their own words:

> In the year 1915 an examination was due for the Teachers in one of the Districts under the Livingstonia Mission in Northern Nyasaland of the then United Free Church of Scotland. Selection of men to go to the training centre for the course leading to full certification was the purpose of the examination and there presented himself a very youthful pupil-teacher, small also in stature. He was not more than thirteen years old, but from the age of about ten he had passed all the tests open to him. At the other end of the scale, as it were, was a European who happened to be available for the conduct of the examination, though not attached to the District and therefore not intimate with the teacher personnel. The number of examinees was large, the examination hall – actually the Station Church – was small but the unlucky small pupil-teacher found himself in a distant seat, too far from the blackboard easily to see the questions thereon written. At one point he stood up in order to see more clearly over the shoulder of

the man in front of him. The European misconstrued the action and debarred the boy from further participation in the examination.[23]

More than twenty years later, when the two men bumped into each other on the street in Edinburgh, Banda immediately recognised Cullen Young, "the ex-missionary who had brought down about his ears ... the house of his dreams."[24] Only much later, after they had collaborated in a number of projects, including the editing of a set of essays which provided one of the first attempts to describe and analyze Chewa culture, did Banda reveal to Young his identity with the boy who had been expelled from the examination room. According to Banda, it was this event which precipitated his departure for South Africa and it therefore occupies a not insignificant place in Malawi's history.

By this time Cullen Young was working for the United Society for Christian Literature in London and was well connected in the circles which linked Britain and Africa. In 1939, when the British Government invited Chief Mwase Kasungu to visit the UK, it was Young who arranged for Banda to act as companion to the Chief, recommending him as "... a very sound fellow of good judgement and character."[25] It was encounters like these which reconnected Banda with his homeland and drew him into active consideration of its destiny. The Bledisloe Commission was sitting at this time to consider the possibility that Malawi might be constitutionally linked with Southern Rhodesia. The people of Malawi were strongly opposed to this suggestion and their views were echoed by Church of Scotland missionaries and their supporters at home, among whom Banda was now well connected. With their encouragement he made a written submission to the Commission.

Cullen Young's influence on Banda was to be far-reaching in many ways, perhaps not least in the choice of name for his homeland after it attained independence. It is thought that the first written reference to the name Malawi is found in their co-edited book *Our African Way of Life* and that it can be attributed to Young's influence. After alluding to the various Nyanja-speaking peoples, they conclude that, "it is practically certain that *aMaravi* ought to be the shared name of all these peoples".[26]

124

It was also during his time in Edinburgh that Banda had to come to terms with the end of his dream of serving as a doctor in Nyasaland. He had offered himself for service with the Livingstonia Mission and the initial response was encouraging. However, as Fergus Macpherson recalls: "I remember Banda's sorrow, expressed with no hint of bitterness, when he told me that he had to lay aside his hope of working at the hospital at Livingstonia because, so he had heard, some of the mission staff had declared their unwillingness to work under a black doctor."[27] Here was evidence of how far racist attitudes, at the height of the colonial period, had infiltrated even a body with the high ideals of the Livingstonia Mission. Banda received a similar response when he offered for service with the Government in Nyasaland. He determined to change direction and seek an opportunity to join a medical practice in the UK. Soon he departed for Liverpool and embarked on medical practice there.

Despite the setback to his own professional ambitions, Banda continued to respect the role of the Scottish missionaries in his homeland. He regarded Livingstonia Mission as the seedbed of the native associations which began the political movement on which the Nyasaland African Congress would later build in its drive for independence.[28] Twenty years later, when Banda was preparing to return to Nyasaland to lead the movement for independence, he revealed his continuing appreciation of the Scottish missionary contribution in a letter to Tom Colvin, a young Scot who was based in Blantyre: "It is very encouraging to me to know that we still have your type of European among us in Nyasaland. Rev. Andrew Doig is another. I can assure you that it is you, Rev. Doig, and a few others, who realise that we, too, are human beings, who are the real builders of a lasting British Commonwealth."[29] The quality of mutual respect, which Banda had so appreciated during his Edinburgh years, was clearly something he still cherished as he contemplated his eventual return to Nyasaland. It was to Colvin that he would turn when it came to the practical matters of securing property and establishing his home and medical practice.

Meanwhile, one institution in Scotland which proved to be an enduring magnet for visiting Malawians was the Scottish National

Memorial to David Livingstone, established at his birthplace in Blantyre in 1929.[30] Donald Fraser was back in Scotland by this time and contributed very significantly to the massive effort required to establish the museum. As James MacNair recalled: "his presence at our rather depressed meetings seemed to lift the sky."[31] Malawi experience played a big part in creating the Memorial.

Fraser, Robert Laws and Alexander Hetherwick were all present at the opening. It would never fail to make a profound impression on visiting Malawians over the years as they found a corner of Scotland which told their story.

Personal Friendships

In assessing the contribution of Donald Fraser, Jack Thompson remarks that, "... when all is said and done, Fraser's most important contributions might be thought to have been simply in the friendships and relationships which he made with many Malawians, such as Daniel Nhlane, Jonathan Chirwa and

Donald Fraser (oil painting) of Loudon Mission, Embangweni, served with the Ngoni from 1896 to 1925

Clements Kadalie".[32] Particularly poignant is the close friendship which formed between Donald Fraser and Jonathan Chirwa, whom he described in the language of the time as "my beloved native helper"[33] The friendship was tested in 1918 when Chirwa, one of the first African ministers within the Livingstonia Mission, confessed to adultery and resigned from the ministry. In line with the strict standards of the Mission, he was suspended from church membership. A year later the suspension was lifted but senior missionaries like Robert Laws and A.G. MacAlpine were adamant that he could never be restored to the ministry. Year after year petitions came to the Presbytery from the Ngoni community which was convinced of the sincerity of Chirwa's repentance. Year after year these petitions were resisted by missionary leaders concerned to set high standards for the fledgling Christian ministry.

Jonathan Chirwa, shortly after being restored to the ministry in 1924

In these debates Fraser was unwavering in his insistence that Chirwa should be restored. The two were working closely together and Fraser had no doubt that his friend would prove worthy of restoration. Finally, in 1924 Andrew Mkochi and Donald Fraser successfully moved that Chirwa be restored.[34] To take this position involved Fraser in a head-on confrontation with such senior colleagues as Laws and MacAlpine but such was his confidence in Chirwa that he did not hesitate. The strength of their friendship was demonstrated after Fraser's death when his widow Agnes brought his ashes to be buried at Loudon alongside the remains of Jonathan Chirwa.[35] The two friends share the same gravestone, with the simple inscription: "In Memory of Donald Fraser and Jonathan Chirwa". As Jack Thompson remarks: "Here, under a mixture of Scots pines and African indigenous trees, Fraser and Chirwa lie side by side – symbolising both their friendship, and the mixed nature of the church (both African and Scottish) which they, and many others like them, helped to create amongst the Ngoni.[36]

Of all the accounts of Scots who lived and worked in Malawi a special place must be accorded to the published letters of Mamie and Jack Martin, a couple based at Bandawe from 1921 to 1928. It is a love story for it tells of the early married life of a couple who had waited for one another through the long, dark years of the First World War when Jack was serving in the army. It is also a tragedy for it leads to the death of Mamie at the age of thirty-seven as a result of blackwater fever, shortly after the still-birth of her baby son. Though her time was to be cut short Mamie threw herself into life at Bandawe with extraordinary gusto. Not only that but she wrote vividly of her experiences in regular letters to her parents-in-law and in her personal diary. After her death her letters were put in a trunk where they lay undisturbed for more than 50 years until discovered by her young great-grandson in 1988. Her daughter Margaret, who had been just a baby when Mamie died, set about preparing the letters for publication and the result is an utterly gripping book.[37]

It reveals the quality of the relationships which the young, newly-married couple were able to form within the Tonga community where they were living and working. As Isobel Reid observes: "Working as a team they formed relationships of mutual respect with village leaders, teachers and evangelists."[38] In face of opposition from the Livingstonia Mission hierarchy, Mamie pursued her vision of developing education for girls by establishing a Girls Boarding School at Bandawe. This provided a context in which she could form close friendships with both staff and students, an opportunity of which she took full advantage. It would be hard to find more heartfelt testimony to the quality of friendship enjoyed between Scots and Malawians in the inter-war years than is offered in letters written by her Malawian friends to her parents after Mamie died. One came from members of the Makuzi and Mazembe congregation. Here is an extract:

> We are not writing this only for Mr Martin but for the father and mother and relations and for the child who has been left to us, that they may know that we weep with them and share in their sorrow. We

sympathise exceedingly in the bereavement that has come upon us, so startlingly, for we never thought she would leave us, our Mother whom we loved.

Mrs Martin kindly undertook with true interest to assist us in the School work especially in Method. All we teachers were very glad of her help. She was our friend and loved to teach. Another action of hers which gladdened us was that she loved to teach the girls to sew and was keen and painstaking in teaching sewing. She loved the older women as well as the girls so she was loved in return by many. She was known by nearly all the teachers and was a friend to some and kind to all.

When she came to a village with her husband she loved to mix with the women and chat with them. Though her work here has ceased, her words and character still preach after her. Her life was like salt and light to many people.

May the Lord comfort all you our friends, her father, her mother and her sisters and her father and mother in law, Mr Martin's parents and also her brothers in law.

Farewell all.

We are your black friends,

Robert Banda, Yekoniya Kaunda, Sam Banda, Timote Mphande, Samuel Longwe, Hanok N'Goma, Yekoniya Phiri, Jonathan Phiri, Samuel Banda, Yisake Kamanga.[39]

Another who wrote was Filemon Chirwa:

Mrs Martin who died on the 24th of this month by her death has brought great sorrow here among all her friends in Tongaland because she was the beloved of the multitude of those she has left. She was a Dona [title referring to a European woman] without ever a cross look, gracious and loving to old and young. Her life was to help everybody. Thus she began a school to teach the girls to sew and to train them in pot-making, so that all who stayed with her are expert in sowing and pot-making.

She was a Dona who helped the teachers exceedingly in their school duties, showing them the way to teach properly; everywhere she went in the schools with her husband she made this her duty. She was a

129

Dona without meanness, interested in the lives of others and she was pitiful [compassionate]. She used to send her own European food to girls who were ill even though they were far away and she was loving to the children and helped them with medicine of her own that she used with her own child. Indeed she was so fond of helping that she shared much with the children of us black people.

If women came to the house to see the children she let them sit and chat with her in a friendly way. She was well known to many and knew them well and so many loved her very much as if she were black like themselves. Of all the girls whom she taught none ever forgot her, even if they were married, they brought presents to her as if she were her own mother. Her death has impoverished Tongaland so the wailing among those who loved her was very great. Among all the Atonga there was a great sympathy.[40]

Though these letters reflect the superior social status which was accorded at this time to a white missionary, they also demonstrate the extent to which Mamie was able to break through the barriers separating white and black people and to forge deep and happy friendships. As mother of a young child she was able to share at a deeply human level especially with women and girls. In this way she exemplified the kind of friendships which would feature recurrently in the lives of Scots in Malawi though seldom so vividly described as in the case of Mamie. It is fitting that the Mamie Martin Fund, established by Mamie's daughter Margaret, continues to support the education of girls in northern Malawi.

Another Scottish missionary who broke through the conventions of the time to form personal friendships with Malawian leaders was James Rodgers of the Blantyre Mission. The first half of the 20th century was a period when socialism, spearheaded by such luminaries as Keir Hardie, James Maxton and Ramsay Macdonald, inspired many in Scotland. Among them was Rodgers who was happy to share his enthusiasm for socialism with his Malawian friends. Reflecting on the formation of the African National Congress in 1944, Nyamayaro Mufuka observes that "... the founding members of Congress, Levi Mumba, Frederick Sangala and Kenneth Matupa were elders of the Church of Scotland at Blantyre. There, they frequented the house of J.A. Rodgers, a quiet missionary who was known to be an expert on Federation and constitutional affairs. Rodgers belonged to the Left Book Club of London and passed some of his reading material to them. He helped in the formulation of evidence and memoranda submitted by these politicians to the Bledisloe Commission. He also helped in the drafting of the first Congress constitution."[41] The unassuming Scot in this way quietly contributed to Malawi's political development.

Rodgers was deeply concerned by the effects of labour migration on communities in Malawi and highly critical of the British administration for its complacency in regard to the economic development which would be needed in order to provide adequate employment opportunities for the people. He commented: "Ultimately there seem to be two courses open to us. Firstly that we frankly adopt a policy of inertia and exploit the capital value of our labour reserves for revenue purposes. This course is the total abrogation of all Britain stands for. And secondly that we adopt a policy whereby the resources of Nyasaland are developed to support its population so leaving the Native effectively free to emigrate or not as he wills.... In practice we have fallen below our high ideals of trusteeship. The present position gives credence to those detractors of British colonial policy who accuse us of using Trusteeship merely as a cloak for selfish Imperialistic aims."[42]

Not all Scottish missionaries were as politically aware as Rodgers but many had comparable qualities of friendship. In Matthew Faulds' case he won a special place in the hearts of the Nkhonde people of the Karonga area. The reciprocal quality of his friendships can be seen in the account he gives of a night he spent in a Malawian home. He found it reminiscent of Robert Burns' "Cottar's Saturday Night" which had evoked for generations of Scots the dignity of an ordinary family holding their prayers. After extolling the hospitality with which he was received at the home of the Rev Yoram and Mrs Lily Mphande, he offered this description of the household evening prayers:

> Yoram is growing old, and his voice has a curious break in it; there he sat in an old deck-chair, Lily, his wife, on the floor nearby. Carefully and slowly he adjusted his spectacles; with solemnity and dignity he

took the Bible in his hands and read that incomparable 35th chapter of Isaiah, which speaks of "streams in the desert." Then a prayer in the native tongue - a little long, perhaps, but intense and earnest, every word a breathing out of the soul to God, beseeching Him for Africa, for her people, for the cause of Christ. We were all on our knees, and only the minister's quavering voice broke the stillness; all around was the silence of night, the darkness lit only by the flickering rays of a small oil lamp.[43]

Robert Laws, Leader of Livingstonia Mission 1878-1927, died 1934

Sharing in such experiences led to the forging of deep friendships. Richard Baxter was one who enjoyed similar experiences in the 1950s and 1960s, remarking on one occasion, "I have greatly enjoyed this chance of getting out to the villages and of being with people in their homes, of conversation and singing together and joining in family prayers."[44]

Even the high tide of racism and colonialism did not remove the possibility of a deep mutual appreciation of human qualities between Malawians and Scots. W.P. Young, Principal of the Overtoun Institution in the 1930s, gave an account of the memorial services held at Livingstonia to mark the death of Robert Laws in 1934 which included this observation:

> The local minister spoke of his nearly forty years' experience of Dr. Laws at the Institution. What was most noticeable was that there was little reference to the wonderful things Dr Laws had done – the

132

bringing of electricity, the laying of pipes for water, the well-equipped hospital, and the other buildings. These were not mentioned. His talk was all of the man Dr Laws was, and how he proved the truth of his message by his life.[45]

Out of such friendship and appreciation the special relationship of Malawi and Scotland steadily grew.

---

[1] See C.M. Doke, "The Linguistic Work and Manuscripts of R.D. McMinn", *African Studies*, Vol. 18 (1959), pp. 180-89.

[2] Shepperson and Price, *Independent African*.

[3] George Shepperson, "Thomas Price (1907-1988): A Tribute", *The Society of Malawi Journal*, Vol. 49 No. 1 (1996), pp. 77-82, at p. 77.

[4] Thomas Price, "African Language, Incorporated", *The Glasgow Herald*, 19 July 1963; cit. Shepperson, "Thomas Price", pp. 81-82.

[5] George Shepperson, interview, 30 November 2009.

[6] Karolin Stahl, "Some Notes on the Development of Zomba", *The Society of Malawi Journal*, Vol. 63 No. 2 (2010), pp. 39-55, at p. 51.

[7] W.H. Watson, Report of Mission Council Secretary, Livingstonia Mission, Nyasaland, 1953, NLS MS Acc. 7548 C.11.

[8] Livingstone, *A Prince of Missionaries*, p. 171.

[9] S.K. Msiska, "Report on Life and Work of the Church", Livingstonia Mission, Nyasaland, 1953, NLS MS Acc. 7548 C.11

[10] Mufuka, *Missions and Politics*, p. 169.

[11] Cit. Andrew C. Ross, "The Mzungu Who Mattered", *Religion in Malawi*, Vol. 8 (1998), pp. 3-7 at p. 6.

[12] Mufuka, *Missions and Politics,* p. 92.

[13] *Ibid.*, p. 104.

[14] *Ibid*, p. 96.

[15] T. Cullen Young, "Understanding the Old", *International Review of Missions*, Vol. 40 (1951), pp. 450-55, at p. 453.

[16] John McCracken, "Mungo Murray Chisuse and the Early History of Photography in Malawi", *The Society of Malawi Journal*, Vol. 61 No. 2 (2008), pp. 1-18 at p. 4.

[17] *Ibid.*, p. 4.

[18] Philip Short, *Banda*, London and Boston: Routledge & Kegan Paul, 1974, p. 8.

[19] *Ibid.*, p. 15.

[20] Ross, *Colonialism to Cabinet Crisis*, p. 121.

[21] Short, *Banda*, pp. 34-35.

[22] Cit. *ibid.*

[23] Young and Banda ed., *Our African Way of Life*, p. 26.

[24] *Ibid.*, p. 27.

[25] Cit. Ross, *Colonialism to Cabinet Crisis*, p. 122.

[26] Young and Banda ed., *Our African Way of Life*, p. 10.

[27] Fergus Macpherson, *North of the Zambezi: A Modern Missionary Memoir*, Edinburgh: The Handsel Press, 1998, p. 11.

[28] Shepperson & Price, *Independent African*, p. 414.

[29] H.K. Banda to Tom Colvin, 9 March 1957; cit. Ross, *Colonialism to Cabinet Crisis*, p. 134.

[30] James L. MacNair, *The Story of the Scottish National Memorial to David Livingstone*, Blantyre: Scottish National Memorial to David Livingstone Trust, n.d.

[31] *Ibid.*, pp. 9-10.

[32] Thompson, *Ngoni, Xhosa and Scot*, p. 88.

[33] United Free Church of Scotland Monthly Record, June 1924, p. 264; cit. T. Jack Thompson, *Christianity in Northern Malawi: Donald Fraser's Missionary Methods and Ngoni Culture*, Leiden: E.J. Brill, 1995, p. 206.

[34] Livingstonia Presbytery Minutes, 11 September 1924; cit. Thompson, *Christianity in Northern Malawi*, p. 207.

[35] Thompson, *Christianity in Northern Malawi*, p.274.

[36] Jack Thompson, "Remembering the Past, Celebrating the Present: the Centenary of Loudon Mission, November 2002", *The Society of Malawi Journal*, Vol. 56 No. 1 (2003), pp. 24-32, at p. 30.

[37] Margaret Sinclair ed., *Salt and Light: The Letters of Mamie and Jack Martin from Malawi (1921-1928)*, Blantyre: CLAIM, 2002.

[38] I.E. Reid, "Myth and Reality of the Missionary Family: A Study of the Letters of Rev. J.R. (Jack) Martin and His Wife, Mary Evelyn (Mamie) Written from Livingstonia Mission, Malawi, 1921-28, with Particular Emphasis on the Position of Missionary Wives", M.Th., University of Edinburgh, 1999, p. 35.

[39] Sinclair, *Salt and Light*, pp. 346-47.

[40] *Ibid*, pp. 347-48.

[41] Mufuka, *Missions and Politics*, p. 132.

[42] J.A.R. [James Rodgers], "Emigrant Labour", *Central Africa News and Views*, Vol. 1 No. 4 (April 1936), p. 19.

[43] M.H. Faulds, "An African Family Altar", *Other Lands*, July 1930, pp. 134-35.

[44] Richard Baxter, Partner Plan letter October 1960, from Mlanje, NLS MS Acc 10104 B.15.

[45] W.P. Young, "Dr Laws: Memorial Services at Livingstonia", *Other Lands*, January 1935, pp. 53-54.

8. Together Against Federation

A significant milestone was passed in the early 1950s with the deaths of the last Malawians who had a personal memory of David Livingstone's arrival in Malawi. Cullen Young took note of this development in an article entitled "End of an Era in Livingstonia: Death of Two Men Who Remembered Livingstone".[1] These were Yuraya Chatonda Chirwa, who had been Robert Laws' right hand man and "for forty years the leading African personality upon that Plateau of Khondowe on which was built the Overtoun Institution,"[2] and Edward Bote Manda, another Tonga, who was among Livingstonia's earliest African ministers and "was irresistibly drawn into any kind of political controversy."[3] Direct, personal links with the origins of the Malawi-Scotland connection were inevitably weakening after more than ninety years. This, however, was not to mean a diminishing role for the Malawi-Scotland axis – far from it. In fact, the 1950s were to see the relationship come to centre stage in a political crisis which was to have far-reaching repercussions for both nations and for Malawi in particular.

A prescient Scot like Donald Fraser had already discerned the emergence of a nationalist movement in Malawi. In the late 1920s he remarked with reference to the Native Associations which by then were becoming well established:

> Some of these associations, under wise leadership, are becoming schools of training in national self-responsibility, and give opportunity for the expression of grievance and aspiration. All this means that the day is rapidly dawning when educated Africans will not be content with the paternal government of chiefs or Europeans, where they have no share in bearing the burdens of administration or in shaping its policies. Social and economic injustices will be demanded by the progressive African with more and more articulate force.[4]

For Fraser this was something very much to be welcomed: "We cannot keep a people for ever in a state of tutelage, nor should we look with alarm on their growing desire for self-expression in helping to control their own government. We must recognise that they too have right to manage their own affairs, and it is better to prepare a people to exercise that right, and willingly concede it when they are ready, than to have them force it from us with bitterness and resentment."[5] Unfortunately there were also forces at work which would lead to the people of Malawi becoming trapped in a set of political arrangements which seemed to most of them to be diametrically opposed to the vision expressed by Fraser.

The Origins of Federation

In the years following the First World War the idea of an amalgamation of the two Rhodesias and Nyasaland began to be mooted within the British Colonial Service. It appeared to offer economic advantages and also to be beneficial administratively. The idea was strongly supported by white settlers across the three territories who assumed that they would be given responsibility for governing the amalgamated region. In 1923, however, the British Government announced a colonial policy statement for East Africa through the Devonshire Declaration that, "the interests of the African Natives must be paramount, and that if and when those interests and the interests of the immigrant races should conflict, the former should prevail."[6] This worried settlers in the two Rhodesias who stepped up the pressure for amalgamation.

The British Government responded in 1927 by setting up the Hilton Young Commission to investigate the possibility of closer political union among the Central and Eastern African Territories. Andrew Ross observes that:

> Initially the members of the Commission were sympathetic to the settlers' position that they as "men on the spot", should control "native policy". However, two leading members of the Commission, Sir George Schuster and J.H. Oldham, were converted by evidence presented to them by Scottish missionaries in Nyasaland to a different position – to which they won over the other members of the Commission but failed to move its chairman, Sir Edward Hilton Young.[7]

The result was a minority report by the Chairman which favoured amalgamation and a majority report by the rest of the Commissioners which not only opposed amalgamation but also opposed the granting of responsible government to a white electorate, as had already been done in Southern Rhodesia. They visited Malawi and were influenced by evidence offered by Levi Mumba and other leaders of the Native Associations.

The outcome of the Commission was that in 1930 Lord Passfield, the Colonial Secretary published a Memorandum re-asserting the principle of the Devonshire Declaration that in all territories north of the Zambesi the primacy of "native" interests would be maintained over those of immigrant races. This was a vindication of the long-held view of the Blantyre and Livingstonia Missions as to the purpose of the Protectorate. It offered strong reassurance to the emerging Malawian political leaders who were already very clear that they must resist, at all costs, any extension to Malawi of the system which their compatriots had observed when they went to work in Southern Rhodesia. So much so that when, in the 1950s, British policy changed this was widely regarded by Malawians as the betrayal of a sacred trust. On the other hand, settler leaders were dismayed and redoubled their determination to achieve an amalgamation of the three territories which would be ruled from Salisbury in order to escape control from London.

Active campaigning in favour of amalgamation continued in the early 1930s. Three times – in 1933, 1935 and 1936 – the Southern Rhodesian Government petitioned the British Government for a conference on amalgamation. They enjoyed the sympathy of the Governors of Northern Rhodesia and Nyasaland, the vast majority of white settlers and significant economic pressure groups such as the British Empire Producers' Organisation. By way of response, the Native Associations in Malawi began to campaign against amalgamation. In 1935 the Blantyre Native Association petitioned the Governor to resist any suggestion of amalgamation with Southern Rhodesia. They insisted that many Malawians had worked there and they knew what conditions were like for Africans south of the Zambesi.[8]

Thus were the battle lines drawn around what would prove to be the defining political issue in Malawi for the next thirty years. An influential contributor at this early stage in the debate was the Blantyre missionary James Rodgers who was close to Malawi's emerging political leaders and often entertained them in his home. In a 1935 issue of *Central Africa News and Views*, a quarterly journal of the Blantyre and Livingstonia Missions, Rodgers resisted the argument of European advocates of Federation who believed that safeguards vested in the Governor-General would be sufficient to keep the influence of Southern Rhodesia's native policy at bay. Rodgers believed that this was a fallacy: "In this connection the experience of South Africa is illuminating. When the National Convention met to consider the subject of union and to draw up a constitution, the fact that the native question touched at some point almost every subject and cut across every line of division led the convention, after prolonged debate, to decide in favour of union rather than Federation."[9] Federation between the Rhodesias and Nyasaland, Rodgers argued, would only be the preliminary step towards complete amalgamation.

Rodgers had been influenced by the strength of feeling behind the petition lodged in 1935 by the Blantyre Native Association, pointing out that: "3000 natives petitioned the Secretary of State against any such federation believing that their interests could only be safeguarded under the control of the Colonial Office."[10] He was very clear about how negative the proposed Federation would be from a Malawian perspective: "What the future native policy of Southern Rhodesia will be we do not know, but it is generally recognised that our native policy is much more liberal and progressive. Also that our neighbour is tending to a colour bar where the interests of the European will be paramount.... In the Salisbury Parliament we would have very few members and a feeble voice in its affairs. Southern Rhodesia's interest in Nyasaland is mainly in our labour supply. The few Nyasaland members would be helpless to stem any legislation inimical to the Nyasaland native."[11]

Despite this trenchant opposition, the proponents of Federation continued to press their case and in 1938 the British Government appointed a Royal Commission, chaired by Lord Bledisloe, to consider the issues. The six-person Commission spent three months travelling throughout the three territories taking evidence. It became abundantly clear to them that in Northern Rhodesia and Nyasaland, African opposition to amalgamation, indeed to any closer relationship with Southern Rhodesia, was overwhelming. It was clear that the African community in Nyasaland was vigorously and unanimously opposed to the amalgamation proposals. They had no wish to expose themselves to the systematic dispossession and humiliation which they knew was the experience of their fellow-Africans in Southern Rhodesia. To this chorus of opposition were added the voices of Scottish missionaries in Malawi who left the Commission in no doubt that amalgamation was against the wishes and interests of the African population.

They also used their influence to persuade the 1938 Church of Scotland General Assembly to oppose the imposition of amalgamation so long as this was contrary to the clearly expressed wishes of the African population. It agreed to send a letter to the Secretary of State for the Colonies insisting that there should be no amalgamation against the will of the African people.[12] Nonetheless, although the Bledisloe Report recommended that there should be no imposition of amalgamation so long as the majority of the people of Nyasaland opposed it, it did approve of it in principle and suggested that it would ultimately be adopted. This encouraged white settler leaders like Godfrey Huggins in Southern Rhodesia and Roy Welensky in Northern Rhodesia to continue to campaign for amalgamation. Throughout the Second World War, when Central Africa was hardly at the top of the agenda for the British Government, Huggins and Welensky continuously pressed London to agree, at least in principle, to the amalgamation of the three territories.

Malawian troops returned home from the Second World War with a sense of excitement about the political direction of their homeland. Working within the framework of the Protectorate, many hoped that the time was ripe for the African community to take increasing political responsibility until the day arrived when Nyasaland would take its place amongst the free and independent nations of the world. When the

Nyasaland African Congress was constituted early in 1944 it called for rapid constitutional movement towards self-government. Leaders like James Frederick Sangala and Charles Matinga injected new urgency into what Sangala called the "fight for freedom".[13] They made their case on the basis of confidence in the long-held promise that the paramountcy of African interests was the key to British colonial policy north of the Zambesi. Their urgency was driven by their realisation that on the other side of the Zambesi a very different vision of the political future of central Africa was being cultivated.

Malawi Facing the Reality of Federation

In the years after the War, the leaders of the white community in Southern Rhodesia adopted a change of tactics. Rather than pressing for amalgamation, they made what appeared to be a more moderate proposal: the three territories could form a federation. It is clear, however, that their intention was to so manipulate the constitutional arrangements that the Federal Government, which the white settler community would control, would hold the real power. It could then work swiftly towards the attainment of Dominion status, making it effectively a self-governing country.[14] Playing their trump card that a Federation, supposedly, would make for greater economic prosperity for all, the white settlers gradually wore down the historic commitment of the British Colonial Office to the paramountcy of African interests.

On a visit to London in 1948 Huggins and Welensky persuaded Arthur Creech-Jones, Colonial Secretary in the Labour Government, to agree that, although he opposed amalgamation, some form of federation might be possible. It became apparent that the British Government was seriously entertaining the proposals being advanced by the white settlers. Just as the Congress movement in Nyasaland was stepping up its campaign to accelerate the movement towards self-government, the British Government was showing sympathy with Southern Rhodesian proposals which led in the opposite direction. As Andrew Ross summarises the issue: "It was a clash between white supremacy and the paramountcy of native interests; a clash between no skilled jobs for 'natives' in the south and African engine-drivers and telephonists in Nyasaland, between Sangala hopefully pressing for an African majority in Legco [the Legislative Council] in Nyasaland and Huggins asserting that the natives must be ruled by 'a benevolent aristocracy'."[15] The struggle between the conflicting visions of Rhodes and Livingstone was about to reach its denouement.

In January 1949 a conference was held at Victoria Falls to inaugurate the new campaign for federation. Soon afterwards, however, the political landscape in Britain changed when, at the 1950 General Election, Labour was returned to power with a paper-thin majority. Creech-Jones lost his seat and was replaced as Colonial Secretary by James Griffith. With the Labour party focussing all its energies on holding on to office, Griffiths had limited interest in the federation proposals. Huggins and Welensky, however, were relentless. Finally, Griffith consented to a conference of officials tasked to work out what the proposed federation might look like. Civil servants from the Colonial Office, the Commonwealth Relations Office and each of the three territories set about their work and quickly appreciated that differences in "Native Policy" on either side of the Zambesi. However, they brushed this aside and their favourable view of federation was welcomed, ominously, by influential voices in the Tory party.

Griffith visited Malawi in 1951 and, like all visitors who took time to listen, was impressed by the vigour and unanimity of the African opposition to federation. Chief Mwase addressed him in these terms:

> Africans still refuse federation in any form because the experience has shown that federation can only benefit Europeans to have more land and more power over Africans, that Africans should remain hewers of wood without any voice in Government. All what is said is only to bluff the Africans, therefore we refuse federation and we shall refuse it even [if] it will mean death.[16]

Griffith nonetheless agreed to attend, together with the Commonwealth Secretary, yet another Victoria Falls conference of politicians from all three territories in September of that year. The three African delegates from Malawi made it clear that their only purpose in being there was to reiterate the total opposition of the African people of Malawi to any closer association with Southern Rhodesia.[17] It was all to no avail. The Conservatives won the 1951 General Election. Oliver Lyttelton was appointed Colonial Secretary and quickly made it clear that he enthusiastically agreed with the federation proposals. He immediately overthrew his predecessor's concept of "federation only by consent", saying that if Africans could not or would not see the obvious benefits of federation, it would have to be imposed on them. It was now only a matter of time before the Federation would become a reality.

Scottish Opposition to Federation

During the post-war years Huggins and Welensky gradually gained the sympathy of first the Labour and then, more decisively, the Conservative Governments for their federation proposal. Their trump card was the sensitivity of the British politicians to the need to help the ailing British economy. Sir Stafford Cripps had stated that: "The whole future of the sterling group and its ability to survive depends on the quick and extensive development of our African resources."[18] The white settler leaders argued that if Britain wanted to benefit from the mineral and other resources of Central Africa, they should support the creation of a stable and friendly state run by white settlers. Furthermore, they claimed that a Federation would raise the standard of living of all the people of the three territories. They also made the case that, following the landslide victory of the National Party in the 1948 General Election in South Africa, the Federation could act as a counter-balancing force, sympathetic to Britain, in the southern African region.

To most British politicians these economic and political arguments proved to be compelling. When Kamuzu Banda and Harry Nkumbula of Northern Rhodesia argued, in their pamphlet *Federation in Central Africa*, that Federation would lead inexorably to amalgamation and Dominion status, resulting in all protection for African rights being swept aside, their arguments fell on deaf ears. So great were the perceived political and economic advantages of Federation that the leadership of both the Labour and the Conservative parties convinced themselves that somehow the African people would come round to appreciating its benefits. Optimistic talk of "partnership" between the races was allowed to mask the fact that the African people of the northern territories, whenever consulted, expressed their total rejection of the Federation proposals

It was only in Scotland that the sense of betrayal experienced by the people of Nyasaland in 1951-52 was understood and keenly felt. Through the closeness of Scottish missionaries to the people on the ground, the Church of Scotland was alert to the total opposition to Federation which prevailed in Nyasaland. This was unequivocally expressed in a statement issued by the Blantyre Mission Council in 1952. At the prompting of its Secretary Andrew Doig, the Council recorded its opinion that any attempt "to force Federation against solid African opposition would increase racial tension and would delay the hopes for real partnership between the races." Furthermore the Council challenged the Church of Scotland General Assembly to come to a similar conclusion. Failure to do so would be "a betrayal of trust by the Church of Scotland."[19] Thus the Church of Scotland was challenged to become the champion of opposition to Federation in the UK context. Its Committee on Church and Nation took up the question of Federation in its Report to the 1952 General Assembly, stating that: "There is no more important question today in the colonial field. In no part of Africa has the Church of Scotland closer and more intimate relations with the Africans than in these territories. In general missionaries who are or have been working there are gravely perturbed, and believe that the question has a definite and serious bearing on their work."[20]

Its assessment of the Federation proposals was damning: "The official policy of Great Britain has been to help the Africans to develop politically, socially and economically, so that they may be able to take their full share in the government and administration of their territories. The proposals ... do not appear to further this policy, and the representation proposed appears to Africans to ensure a permanent white

144

domination of the legislatures."[21] On the basis of this Report, the General Assembly: "noting with interest the movement towards a Central African Federation, but viewing with concern the actual proposals now being made, urged that full consideration be given to African opinion and that no scheme should be adopted without the consent and cooperation of the Africans."[22] Under the influence of conservative leaders in the Church and following intense lobbying in the run-up to the Assembly, it stopped short of giving outright support to African opposition to the Federation scheme, as the Blantyre Mission Council had wished.[23] However, the seeds of a popular movement of solidarity with Malawians in their rejection of the Federation had now been planted.

By now a cross-party political movement in opposition to Federation was emerging. During 1952, Dr Hastings Banda was frequently invited to speak on the issue to well-attended meetings in different parts of Scotland. A delegation of chiefs from Nyasaland, having been refused permission to present a petition to the Queen, made a successful speaking tour in Scotland. In January 1953, a mass meeting was held in Edinburgh on the "Crisis in Central Africa", chaired by the Very Revd Dr John Baillie, former Church of Scotland Moderator and featuring speeches from Nkhosi ya Makhosi M'mbelwa (the Ngoni Paramount Chief from northern Malawi), Lord Hemingford, a Conservative Peer, and John Dugdale, a Labour MP. Finally, a "Petition from the People of Scotland" with 27,000 signatures, many of these a minister and elder signing on behalf of their congregation, was prepared for presentation to the Queen. However, the delegation attempting to present it was refused access to the Queen, so determined by now was the Conservative Government to proceed with the plans for Federation.[24]

All of this was front-page news in Scotland. *The Scotsman* newspaper gave prominent coverage to the debate over Federation. Its own position was made clear in its editorial leader on 4 November 1952 which argued that the proposed federation should be postponed until the African people of Malawi could be convinced of its worth by clear practical steps in areas such as conditions of employment. The correspondence columns of *The Scotsman*, *The Glasgow Herald* and other newspapers were full of letters about the Federation issue, the great majority championing the rights of the people of Malawi to determine their future. The Scottish Council on African Questions, particularly through the tireless work of

Nkhosi ya Makhosi M'mbelwa (left) on his visit to Scotland in 1953

its Secretary Kenneth Mackenzie, who had served as a missionary in Malawi and Zambia, was a considerable force in orchestrating the popular campaign. With the public mood becoming very clear, it is not surprising that leading members of both Conservative and Labour parties in Scotland defied their London leaders and firmly opposed the adoption of the Federation proposal. "It was only in Scotland," comments Andrew Ross, "that there was a continuing and significant widespread popular cross-party concern over the threat of Nyasaland being incorporated into a new state against the wishes of the African people."[25]

The historian George Shepperson has suggested that this cross-party and well-supported movement in Scotland indicated that the issue of Federation in Central Africa had touched a nationalist nerve among the Scottish people.[26] Through the many connections which had united Scotland and Nyasaland over almost one hundred years, Scots of all stripes had an affinity with the Protectorate which made them instinctively rise to its defence when its people raised the alarm over the Federation proposals. This Scottish response stood in stark contrast to that which prevailed in England where, by and large, people were coming to accept the economic and political arguments in favour of Federation and where even those who had earlier expressed reservations were suggesting that the best course of action was to give Federation a chance.

When Chief Kuntaja wrote to express thanks to the "Scotch" people for their hospitality and support during the chiefs' speaking tour, he made much of the need to pray that the "English" leaders in Parliament might change their mind about Federation.[27] The contrast between Scotland and England had not been lost on the visitor from Malawi. It is hard to dispute the judgement of Andrew Ross that: "The campaign against Federation had a great deal more strength in Scotland than in Britain as a whole. As Nathan Shamiyarira, a young [Rhodesian] journalist said, "When we complain, who listens? When you Nyasas complain, Scotland complains as well."[28]

At this moment, however, Scotland's complaining was to no avail. The opposition to Federation in Scotland had no more effect than that of the unanimous opposition of the African population of Nyasaland. For the time being, Malawi and Scotland lost out to the new alliance between the settlers of Southern Rhodesia and the British Government in London. With the Conservative Party in power it was clear that the Federation was going to become a reality and that the constitutional arrangements would give the white settlers effective control, with scant provision for the safeguarding of "native interests". To the profound shock of the leaders and people of Nyasaland they found that they were no longer to be governed by an authority committed to protect them from external threats, including that posed by the white racist regime on the other side of the Zambesi. Instead, the British Government had formed an alliance with the white settlers of Southern Rhodesia to impose a Federation on terms which would never be acceptable to the African people of Nyasaland. Lord Llewellyn took up his post as Governor General of the new Federal state in September 1953. The Federation was now a reality.

In Malawi the Nyasaland African National Congress instituted a campaign of civil disobedience which precipitated outbreaks of violence in Ntcheu and in parts of the Southern Province. This was quickly crushed and its leaders were sent into internal exile. Scottish missionaries were sufficiently closely integrated to appreciate the extent of the dismay which was almost universally felt amongst the Malawian population. Anne Hepburn recalls, as a young teacher at Blantyre Mission, being asked to give celebratory label badges to the children at the school, on the occasion of the coronation of Elizabeth II in 1953. As part of its protest at the imposition of Federation, Congress was boycotting celebrations of the coronation. Thus the young Scottish teacher was met not with the usual politeness from her pupils but with a surly "*sitifuna*" ("we do not want it").[29] The astonishingly high level of political consciousness among the six and seven year olds revealed the extent to which the Malawian community was clear and united in its hostility to the Federation.

Nonetheless, reluctantly Congress concluded that it had no option but to accept the new political reality, put up candidates for the Federal Parliament and try to make the best of it. At Blantyre Mission James Rodgers pondered the significance of what had taken place: "1953 will be remembered as the year of the troubles. The happy relationship between Europeans and Africans, of which we were proud, has been marred and will never be quite the same again. Things have been said and done on both sides which will not be forgotten. On the surface we are back to normal, underneath there is a lining up according to colour. Largely because of its definite stand against Federation the Mission suffered less than might have been expected but the new situation will make our work more difficult from now on."[30]

Federation: Dilemma for a Scot in Malawi

This new political development soon posed a dilemma for a Scottish missionary in Malawi, the Revd Andrew Doig. Since the Legislative Council had been established in 1908 there had been a tradition that there was a seat for a missionary member who was expected to provide "an independent representation of the native community".[31] In practice, the seat had always been occupied by a missionary from either the Blantyre or the Livingstonia Mission. On his return to Nyasaland after the War, Doig took up this appointment and attempted to follow in the tradition of Hetherwick, Laws and others who had preceded him. In 1951, for example, he had joined with the African members Ellerton Mposa and E.A Muwamba in moving a motion urging the British Government not to go back on its past commitment to give up its authority only to the people of the Protectorate.[32] As Doig recalls, "I had no hesitation in weighing in on the Anti-Federation side and made my speeches in Legislative Council to that effect. My contacts built up with African political leaders, not all of whom appreciated my representing African interests but increasingly expressed delight, amazement and support for the stand I was taking."[33] Doig had also been the primary author of the 1952 Blantyre Mission statement which expressed outright opposition to the Federation proposal.

Now that what he had feared had become a reality with the imposition of Federation, he faced a dilemma. Doig was invited to occupy the post under the Federal Constitution that allowed for a Nominated European Representative of African Interests. "At first I recoiled. Would not my acceptance be seen as a denial, betrayal, surrender of all I had been saying and standing for over the years. How would the African in the Church and in the wider Nyasaland fellowship interpret my action? So I turned it down. There followed a period of anxiety and inner conflict. African opinion came to me loud and clear, saying, 'We'd rather see someone in the post whom we can trust to interpret what happens in the light of our hopes and fears and future than a Yes-man for the Federation, aiming to get a view across whatever we might think. Having thought it through, I accepted the appointment. It was probably the hardest decision of my life."[34] When he took his seat in the Federal Assembly he was not slow to make his mark. According to the Southern Rhodesian newspaper *The Citizen*, Doig "brings the murmur of the Covenanters with him – a typical member of the Scottish Church, fired with missionary zeal, eternally conscious of the traditions which his church holds in Nyasaland."[35] The African Affairs Board was tasked to provide African

MPs with "guidance and restraint". In the opinion of Southern Rhodesian Prime Minister Lord Malvern, Doig "never provided either guidance or restraint and indeed … only tried to lead every extremist movement."[36] Such a judgement may be taken as a measure of how far Doig had gone in serving the Malawi cause during his years in the Federal Parliament.

Mission and Church: A Quiet Revolution

To the dismay of Andrew Doig and many others, the century-long involvement of Scots in Malawi had led, through the establishment of the British Protectorate, to the imposition of the Federation of Rhodesia and Nyasaland in 1953, a set of political arrangements viewed by both Malawians and Scots with deep foreboding. This was a bleak moment indeed. However, it was not the only development taking place in the 1950s. The Scottish involvement had also led, through the steady work of the Blantyre and Livingstonia Missions, to the emergence of a vibrant Presbyterian Church. One factor which exposed the racism and injustice of the Federation in the minds of many Malawians was that their experience of church life provided them with contrasting experience and expectations. As has been seen, African leadership was encouraged from the earliest days of the Missions. Indeed much of the growth and development of their work came as a result of Malawian leadership. At the same time, the Missions were not immune to the colonialist assumptions which prevailed during the first half of the 20th century. The process of "handing over" authority to local leadership was slow, to the exasperation of some of the most able Malawian leaders who emerged within the Missions. Nonetheless by the middle of the 20th century a strong sense was emerging that the time had come to fulfil the long-held hope that the Mission would "hand over" to the local Malawian church.

Cullen Young recalled an occasion when he came out of a Presbytery meeting, in which a small group of whites had argued with five times their number of blacks over some point of church discipline or order. One of the Malawians turned to him and remarked:

You whites are trying to guide us; we know and we try to understand and be patient. But Jesus seems sometimes to speak differently to us. And then you have that Blue Book of yours always on the table, which annoys us because it comes out of your past, not ours.[37]

By the 1950s, however, there was a growing confidence and determination among Malawian church leaders that the time was arriving for them to take full responsibility for the affairs of their churches. In part, this flowed from the theological conviction, adopted by growing numbers of Malawians, that the African past has validity in relation to the profession of Christian faith. Rather than abandoning or disrespecting their cultural and religious heritage they found that it could be affirmed in the course of embracing the new faith.[38] Young recalls another conversation which one of his fellow-missionaries had on the lakeshore. He was in a gathering of headmen and counsellors for discussion of current issues when one of them told him: "Sir, don't think that the things you are telling us contradict what we used to believe; no! but they complete what our old folk taught us."[39] Rather than Christian faith being received as something entirely new it became apparent that, for many of the Malawians who embraced it, it was the fulfilment of their ancestral heritage. As an elderly lady once informed Cullen Young: "I always knew there was a God like that."[40]

The Malawian Christianity which emerged from mid-century was marked by growing confidence in its African character. The large and influential Presbyterian churches carried with them the influence of their Scottish foundation but they were increasingly confident in giving expression to the four "selfs" – self-governing, self-supporting, self-propagating and self-theologizing. Malawians participating in this movement had an experience and a vision which stood in stark contrast to the political arrangements associated with Federation. This proved to be a source of strength in their determination to resist it. In a context of dramatically deteriorating race relations, the experience of Scots working with the Missions stood in sharp contrast, as Hamish Hepburn reported at the height of the troubles in 1953: "During August and September 1953 Nyasaland received unwelcome publicity on account of disturbances in certain parts of the country.... In all the parishes in which I have stayed during the past two years I have been most hospitably treated, but I never received more generous treatment than I did in a parish in which I stayed immediately after the period of the disturbances. There I received so many gifts of eggs that they became something of an embarrassment!" Such relationships at the human level were not without significance in relation to the wider political context.[41]

In a letter home during the Federation years the Blantyre missionary Chad Musk observed that:

> ... fellowship is soon found with an African Christian in which colour is quickly forgotten. However, race relationships appear to be deteriorating outside the Christian Church; this is a matter of grave concern for all of us. Inside the Church there is a strengthening of bonds between African and European, as the Church of Scotland Overseas Presbytery moves towards unity with the Church of Central Africa Presbyterian. Soon The Church, made of Africans and Europeans, will take over management of those affairs which are at present the responsibility of the Mission. This is a great and thrilling development.[42]

For Musk too this was more than a matter of ecclesiastical arrangements. The warmth of human relationships was a key factor in shaping his understanding. He wrote, for example: "We are glad to have one spare bedroom so that we can put up people passing through Blantyre on their way north, or coming in for meetings from out stations. One of our most delightful guests was Rev Frederick Chintali, minister of the 1800 strong African congregation in Zomba. We were very impressed by his outstanding grace and humility. He is a man of great wisdom and a much respected leader of the Church. Like many of our guests he enjoyed some music with us."[43]

The outcome of these developments at the level of church life was such that the Church of Scotland magazine was able to report, at a time when the crisis over Federation was at its height, that: "A quiet revolution is about to take place at Blantyre, Nyasaland. In a few months time the Mission Council will cease to exist and control of all its work will pass to the Church which will govern through a General Administration Committee and a number of sub-committees, all responsible to the Blantyre Synod of the Church of Central Africa Presbyterian.... Also in the North at Livingstonia the same revolution is taking place.... A quiet revolution this indeed, as the indigenous Church gets self-government in a land where the seeking and refusing of self-government has become a burning problem."[44] Malawians who were happily engaged in taking over full responsibility for the running of their own church were hardly likely to be complacent when the Federation was moving in a direction which would deprive them of any meaningful say in the government of their country. Nyamayaro Mufuka accurately observes the close interconnection between ecclesiastical and political life in Malawi: "As late as 1960 these graduates of Scottish missions so dominated the political life of the country that a meeting of the African Congress Party was barely distinguishable from a synod of the Church of Scotland."[45]

---

[1]   Young, "End of an Era at Livingstonia", p. 83.

[2]   *Ibid.*

[3]   *Ibid.*, p. 84.

[4]   Donald Fraser, *The New Africa*, London: Edinburgh House Press, 1927, p. 160.

[5]   *Ibid.*, p. 190.

[6]   Cit. Pachai, *Malawi: The History of the Nation*, p. 256.

[7]   Ross, "Scotland and Malawi", pp. 295-96.

[8]   Minutes of the Executive Council of Nyasaland Protectorate for 1935. Minute 166, Malawi National Archives, Zomba, cit. Ross, "Scotland and Malawi", p. 297.

[9]   J.A. Rodgers, "Safeguarding Native Interests in Federation", *Central Africa News and Views*, Vol. 1 No. 2 (October 1935), pp. 12-13; cit Mufuka, *Missions and Politics*, p. 152.

[10]   Ibid., p. 12.

[11]   Ibid., p. 13.

[12] Ross, *Colonialism to Cabinet Crisis*, p. 40.

[13] *Ibid.*, p. 43.

[14] See *ibid*, pp. 52-53.

[15] *Ibid.*, p. 58.

[16] Cit. Pachai, *Malawi: The History of the Nation*, p. 259.

[17] *Ibid.*, p. 260.

[18] Cit. Griff Jones, *Britain and Nyasaland*, London: Allen and Unwin, 1964, p. 136, quoted by Ross, "Scotland and Malawi", p. 301.

[19] Blantyre Mission Council, minutes, 12 February 1952; cit. John Stuart, *British Missionaries and the End of Empire: East, Central and Southern Africa, 1939-64*, Grand Rapids and Cambridge: Eerdmans, 2011, p. 87.

[20] *Reports to the General Assembly*, Edinburgh: Church of Scotland, 1952, p. 318.

[21] *Ibid.*

[22] *Ibid.*, p. 331.

[23] See Stuart, *British Missionaries and the End of Empire*, pp. 87-88.

[24] Ross, *Colonialism to Cabinet Crisis*, pp. 70-71.

[25] *Ibid.*, pp. 56-57; see further Andrew C. Ross, "The Kirk and Colonial Policy 1864-1964" in James Kirk ed. *The Scottish Churches and the Union Parliament 1707-1999*, Edinburgh: Scottish Church History Society, 2001, pp. 125-160.

[26] Cit. *ibid.*, p. 71.

[27] Chief Kuntaja to Duncan Finlayson, 11/3/53, Box 3 David Lyon Papers, New College Library, University of Edinburgh; cit. Ross, *Colonialism to Cabinet Crisis*, p. 71.

[28] Cit. Ross, "Scotland and Malawi", p. 283.

[29] Anne Hepburn, personal recollection.

[30] J.A. Rodgers, Annual Report, Blantyre Mission, Nyasaland, 1953, NLS MS Acc. 7548 C.11.

[31] Andrew B. Doig, *It's People That Count*, Edinburgh: The Pentland Press, 1997, p. 28.

[32] Ross, *Colonialism to Cabinet Crisis*, p. 70.

[33] Doig, *It's People That Count*, p. 33.

[34] *Ibid.*, pp. 33-35.

[35] Cit. Doig, *It's People That Count*, p. 37.

[36] J.R.T. Wood, *The Welensky Papers*, Durban, 1983, p. 574; cit. Ross, *Colonialism to Cabinet Crisis*, p. 86.

[37] T. Cullen Young, "Understanding the Old", *International Review of Missions*, Vol. 40 (1951), pp. 450-55, at p. 453.

[38] See e.g. Stephen Kauta Msiska, *Golden Buttons: Christianity and Traditional Religion among the Tumbuka*, Blantyre: CLAIM, 1997.

[39] *Ibid.*, p. 454.

[40] Young, *Contemporary Ancestors*, p. 138.

[41] J.L. Hepburn, Annual Report, Blantyre Mission, Nyasaland, 1953, NLS MS Acc. 7548 C.11.

[42] Dr Chad Musk, partner plan letter from Blantyre, November 1957 NLS MS Acc 10104/B17.

[43] *Ibid.*

[44] "A Quiet Revolution in Nyasaland", *Other Lands*, May 1959, pp. 35-36.

[45] Mufuka, *Missions and Politics*, p. 106.

9. Achieving Independence

The State of Emergency in Malawi

After the failure of its initial programme of civil disobedience, the Nyasaland African Congress concentrated its efforts on the Nyasaland Legislative Council where some of its articulate young leaders, like Masauko Chipembere and Kanyama Chiume, demanded Malawi's withdrawal from the Federation. To the surprise and dismay of the Government, *Hansard* became a best seller as African readers developed their political consciousness by reading the speeches which their leaders had made in "Legco". The opposition to Federation steadily hardened in Malawi. In 1957 matters came to a head. In the Federal Parliament, the Constitutional Amendment Bill and the Federal Electoral Bill, both provisions which would weaken African representation in the Federal Parliament, were passed into law despite the opposition of the African Affairs Board. This was the last straw for Andrew Doig: "The action of the Governments in insisting upon a fundamental change to the Federal Constitution while African support has still not been won for the Federation at all ... forms a course of action I could not possibly defend or commend to the African and I feel compelled in the interests both of the Africans and of the peace of these territories to protest further by my resignation."[1]

To make matters worse, the Federal Prime Minister Roy Welensky had concluded a deal with the British Government that in 1960 a review of the Federal arrangements would take place with a view to the Federation being granted Dominion status – a move which would further entrench white supremacy. The African people of Nyasaland now felt utterly betrayed by the British Government and the political temperature rose to boiling point. Meanwhile in Scotland public opinion had been kept well-informed by the work of the Scottish Council on African Questions. Its Secretary Kenneth Mackenzie, who had served as a missionary in Malawi and Zambia, had an extraordinary gift of holding together people of different backgrounds and political persuasions.[2]

Hence there was a remarkable degree of cross-party consensus in Scotland that the direction being taken by the Federation was a betrayal of the people of Malawi.

The Nyasaland African Congress now decisively stepped up its campaign for independence. Given the youth of its most articulate leaders, it took the strategic decision to recall Dr Hastings Kamuzu Banda, who had long been an overseas "elder statesman" in the Congress movement, to lead the campaign. As a man of mature age and considerable accomplishment he could hold the respect of village elders in a way that younger leaders, regardless of ability, never could. Congress built up a messianic expectation around his arrival and soon he was touring the country to address massive crowds, promising to secure Nyasaland's withdrawal from the Federation and to make swift progress towards independence.

In the course of Banda's nationwide tour, an incident occurred which reveals the strength of the Scotland-Malawi connection and the personal relationships in which it was grounded. As Banda reached the north of Malawi, the Livingstonia Presbytery was meeting at Muhuju, at the foot of the Henga Valley. The Presbytery agreed that Dr Banda should be invited to address their meeting. When it came to the question of how to deliver the invitation, the Presbytery turned to the Scottish missionary Fergus Macpherson, Principal of the Overtoun Institution at Livingstonia: "We do not know him. You do. So you should carry our invitation."[3] This recalled the fact that Banda had been a close family friend of the Macphersons during his years in Edinburgh.

When Macpherson appeared at a political gathering with the invitation, Banda immediately accepted it – much to the consternation of his accompanying Congress officials - and the two set off together for Muhuju, followed by the Congress landrover. Banda decided that he would address the Presbytery in English so the Moderator asked Macpherson to translate into Chitumbuka. The latter recalls that: "Much of his address was about my late father and about Banda's happy relationship with my family in Edinburgh. Then in a word, he summarised his political message and sat down to hearty applause."[4]

157

Before long the two men were heading up on to the plateau at Livingstonia where Banda was delighted to accept the hospitality of his old friend and spend the night at the famous "Stone House", originally the residence of Robert and Margaret Laws, which was the Principal's residence.

As the Congress campaign gathered momentum, it became clear that the British Administration would either have to accede to it or confront it head-on. On 3 March 1959, the Governor, Sir Robert Armitage, declared a State of Emergency. Three hundred leading Congress members were arrested in a dawn swoop code-named Operation Sunrise. Hastings Banda and the senior leaders of Congress were taken to prisons at Gweru and Khami in Southern Rhodesia while other detainees were held in newly constructed camps in Malawi. The people of Malawi were astonished. Crowds gathered and were dispersed only with great difficulty. At Nkhata Bay, at least twenty people were killed when police lost their nerve and opened fire on an unarmed crowd. Similar confrontations occurred over the next few days in all three provinces, leading to a total death toll of more than fifty.

It was an unprecedented time of fear and repression in Malawi. Among the few Europeans who stood in solidarity with the Malawian people were Scottish missionaries like the doughty Helen Taylor of Livingstonia. She described some of her experiences in a letter written soon after the declaration of the State of Emergency:

> Our concern now is not for the safety of the Institution, but for the poor people terrorised by the security forces. On 19th one local Congress leader, Chakalipa Phiri, asked us to provide transport for him to Rumpi, where he wished to give himself up, to save his family and this area from further terrifying visitation by security forces; they come by night, breaking open doors, flashing lights in people's faces, beating and damaging property, and going off with agricultural implements. We had heard so many of these tales that we decided to interview the Provincial Commissioner about them, and other matters. So we went on the 20th taking with us another Congress leader, Jonas Kaunda, who was giving himself up for the same reason. Rumpi District Commissioner had arranged an interview for us and we had it,

from 2.00 pm till 5.40 pm. Haskard [the Provincial Commissioner] was very pleasant, though he said some cruel and unjust things about the C.C.A.P. and about people at Kondowe with rose-coloured spectacles.[5]

She concludes with a telling remark about the reaction of local people as they drove from Mzuzu to Livingstonia: "On our journey to and from Mzuzu people fled from the sound of a car; but ran out with greetings when we waved and called and they saw who we were. 'We knew our missionaries would come to us as soon as the road was open.' There is terror over the land."[6]

At the other end of the country, at Mulanje Mission station, Hamish and Anne Hepburn received some unwelcome visitors. Anne recalls that: "... a truckload of Rhodesian troops arrived on the station and the officer-in-charge asked if we felt safe. Of course we did, the only danger was from their presence. As soon as they had left Hamish phoned the District Commissioner and told him that he did not want to see the troops on the Mission ever again. African colleagues gave Hamish a new nickname, *Nyalugwe ya Mulanje*, the Leopard of Mulanje."[7]

The solidarity of Scottish friends was important for the detainees. Vera Chirwa recalls her experience when, together with Gertrude Rubadiri, she was in prison in Salisbury: "Reverend Doig, who was head of mission in the Presbyterian Church in Blantyre ... came to see us. Being British himself I suppose he managed to persuade the Governor to allow him to visit his church members. The reverend's visit occasioned quite a few improvements and we were moved to a new wing and allowed to do exercises in the courtyard. We told him everything – also that Gertrude was expecting. She must have been about three months pregnant by then and she was vomiting seriously."[8] Shortly afterwards the two women were repatriated and they knew the explanation: "Reverend Doig had gone straight to the Governor. 'Since when has it become an English practice to detain pregnant women? What is happening here?'"[9] The situation of the detainees was not easy even upon release. Here again Scottish friendship proved valuable, as Vera Chirwa recalls: "We had to pick up our life again after prison. They had emptied

159

Orton's offices, closed down our house and removed all our belongings, but Reverend Doig, who had visited us in prison, offered to have us in the Blantyre Mission station till we found a house."[10]

Intimacy at the personal level at this time is well illustrated by the case of Andrew Ross who, as chaplain to the Kanjedza Detention Camp, formed enduring friendships with the detainees. These relationships were, at once, pastoral, political and personal. Of the thousand men and three women who were judged to be the hard-core Congress leadership and imprisoned in the camp, Ross discovered that approximately seven hundred of the men and two of the women were members of the Church of Central Africa Presbyterian (CCAP).[11] Indeed, there were enough church elders among them to allow the formation of a new congregation of the CCAP within the camp. Besides regular pastoral ministry, Ross had the opportunity to become intimate with the principal leaders of Congress.

As he recalls: "During the cold season of 1960, I spent one afternoon a week with [Masauko Chipembere, Dunduzu Chisiza and Yatuta Chisiza] in Kanjedza [Detention Camp] in my capacity as Chaplain. During these visits we talked about the future of Malawi and of Africa and discussed the problem areas in economics and religion and culture as well as politics narrowly defined."[12] As the young Congress leaders took him into their confidence, Ross became aware of the growing tensions in their relationship with Dr Banda – a matter to be further considered in the next chapter. It is clear that these visits meant a great deal to the detainees. Rose Chibambo, the first woman to hold senior office in the Congress movement and one of the few women leaders who was detained during the State of Emergency, recalls: "Politically the missionaries were very sympathetic to our cause. It meant so much when you are in prison when you see friendly faces coming to see you. Andrew Ross lent me the pram of their daughter, I used their pram in prison in Zomba; they were very marvellous, I must say."[13]

The State of Emergency: Reaction in Scotland

The reaction in Scotland was immediate and extensive. The Scottish Council on African Questions organised the production of pamphlets and the writing of letters to the newspapers on a large scale. The correspondence columns of *The Scotsman* and *The Glasgow Herald* during March and April 1959 had to be expanded from the customary two columns to occupy a whole page in order to accommodate the volume of correspondence about the State of Emergency in Malawi. The Council appealed to the long history which united Scotland with Malawi: "We remind your readers that David Livingstone discovered Lake Nyasa in 1859 and that the first band of Scottish missionaries began work there in 1875. In 1891 Nyasaland was taken over as a Protectorate by the British Crown 'with the consent and desire of the chiefs and the people'. This was done on the recommendation of Scottish missionaries."[14] The Committee appealed also to the principle which had underpinned this long history of connection: "We [the Church of Scotland] believe that God created all men in his image ... and that the Church is a fellowship which should not know the distinctions of bond or free, Jew or Greek."[15]

It quickly became a national issue. Andrew Ross records that: "Professor [George] Shepperson suggested to a class in the University of Edinburgh that for the Scottish people Nyasaland was the success that had made up for the failure of the late seventeenth century colonial venture at Darien, and London must not be allowed to do down Scotland again."[16] There can be no question that the issue had touched a nerve in Scotland and it became regular front-page news during the Spring of 1959. Not only the future of Malawi but Scottish national pride was felt to be at stake. The importance of Scottish anti-Federation opinion was recognised by the Federation authorities in Central Africa who did their best to discredit it. A colleague of Welensky's advised him that the Federation had two main opponents in the UK: "the Church of Scotland and Labour extremists".[17]

A secret and confidential report was produced by Federal civil servants. On the assumption that the African ministers and elders who had passed motions opposing the continuation of Federation in both the Blantyre and Livingstonia Synods could not have been able to think for themselves, it alleged that: "The Church of Scotland and their Foreign Mission Committee in the United Kingdom are directly responsible for the attitude of their Church [i.e. the CCAP] with regard to Federation in that they have sent into the Mission field in Nyasaland persons with extreme left-wing political views who have had the effect of greatly exacerbating African opposition to Government, and of impairing race relations generally."[18] The report concluded in desperation that the Scottish missionaries are obsessed with one goal: "that of delivering Africans from European oppression, and of setting African feet firmly on the way to political independence."[19] Its authors showed their blind-spot in their inability to understand that the ministers and elders of the CCAP were well able to reach their own judgement in regard to the Federation. However, credit must be given to the Federal civil servants for recognising that the Church of Scotland represented a major threat to the survival of the Federation. Their judgement was vindicated by what transpired at the 1959 General Assembly.

The 1959 Church of Scotland General Assembly

The 1958 General Assembly had appointed a Special Committee anent Central Africa which was tasked to prepare a Report for the next Assembly, due to meet in May 1959. The Convener of the Committee was the Very Rev Dr George MacLeod, Moderator of the 1958 Assembly and one of Scotland's most influential church leaders during the second half of the 20th century. Its Secretary was Kenneth Mackenzie, the moving spirit of the Scottish Council on African Questions. MacLeod visited Malawi in his capacity as Moderator in June 1958 and came away utterly convinced that the Church of Scotland must take its stand with the people of Malawi in resisting Federation. He was in a position to wield influence and did not hesitate to do so.

The Special Committee's assessment of the results of Federation was dismal: "Within the last two years the power of the Federal Government relative to the UK Government and to the population of Central Africa has grown immensely. Parallel to this has gone a grave deterioration in African goodwill. Efforts to translate 'partnership' into reality have failed to be fast enough or to have a sustained appeal."[20] The Committee concluded that the time had come for a "fearless examination of the possibility of the refashioning of the present Federal structure along lines that will go further to meet the criticisms of the Africans, especially the inhabitants of Nyasaland..."[21] Between the completion of the Report and the General Assembly, however, the State of Emergency had been declared. The Committee therefore prepared a Supplementary Report to take account of recent developments. Its conclusion went further: "The time has passed for working with nicely balanced arrangements relating the Colonial Government, the European inhabitants, and the African population. *The time has come for a daring and creative transfer of power to the African people*."[22]

When the Assembly met to debate these Reports, *The Scotsman* reporter stated that he had not seen such a full or tense house since the debates in the late 1920s that had led up to the Church Union of 1929.[23] The British Government took the debate seriously enough to ensure that Rab Butler, the Home Secretary, Lord Home, Minister at the Commonwealth Office, and Lord Perth, another Cabinet Minister, were in the gallery to hear the entire debate. Commissioners arrived at the Assembly to find in their mail-boxes a pamphlet entitled *The New Face of the Kirk in Nyasaland*, produced by activists sympathetic to the Federation. It was heavily based on the secret and confidential report produced by Federal civil servants and highly critical of Church of Scotland policy and personnel. This intensive lobbying further raised the temperature.

As Convener of the Special Committee, MacLeod presented its Reports. His speech included one passage which epitomised the Scotland-Malawi relationship as he recalled an evening he had spent in the company of David and Gertrude Rubadiri in Blantyre:

> When I was on my Moderatorial year in your name I was introduced
> to the most brilliant man I met in the whole of my Moderatorial year

anywhere, he was an African. He had an equally brilliant wife, utterly composed, and this man without an atom of bombast held forth on the decay of France, the future of Europe, and various other topics, and for four hours he entirely dominated the discussion; he told me, this brilliant teacher in a Government school, that there were not four European houses where he felt at home to go. One early morning in March he and his wife were awakened, and without a change of clothing were marched out of the Protectorate into Southern Rhodesia, leaving their one year old son for anyone to look after. Not many days ago his wife was released and is in close arrest at her home. He is still in prison, and a few days ago he wrote this to the man who was our host that night: 'We are all well here, all things told. Food has improved a bit. We have more time outside to play football or just talk. The community feeling is excellent, and we pray together every morning and every evening. We hope and pray that the same spirit will in the truth that has been so grossly neglected make us all a community that looks for the good in all.' I would like to think that if the most brilliant man in this country were similarly arrested and held without trial for nearly three months he would still be writing like that.[24]

Mutual respect, indeed admiration, rooted in a depth of personal relationship that was incomprehensible to the champions of Federation, gave a distinctive character to the Scotland-Malawi connection and greatly intensified the outrage which was felt in Scotland in relation to the political situation in Central Africa. In what his biographer describes as "one of the most unforgettably eloquent orations ever heard in the Assembly Hall", MacLeod concluded:

> The ship of state that is the Federation is dangerously keeling over to starboard, and a heavy list is occasioned by the weight of the detainees battened down beneath the hatches of the starboard side. They must be brought up into the fresh air, they must be brought up into the centre of the deck and be divided off either for trial or for hope; only so will the ship of state find a more even keel for the days that lie ahead in 1960. At that point, and for the time being, someone must speak for the Africans, and that someone will be the General Assembly of the Church of Scotland.[25]

"It was passionate, magnificent, ringing oratory on behalf of the Africans of Nyasaland," writes Ronald Ferguson, "and it represented one of the General Assembly's finest hours.... There was an expectant sense of history in the making."[26] The recommendations of MacLeod's Committee were approved by large majorities, despite opposition from Commissioners who felt it had depended too much on the views of outspoken missionaries on the ground.

The missionaries, however, were only reflecting what they heard from the ordinary people with whom they were in daily contact. Nonetheless, their role is not to be underestimated. As John McCracken concludes: "... it was the special achievement of Scottish missionaries attached to the Church of Central Africa Presbyterian (CCAP) that, for a brief period, they won the support of the great majority of the members of the socially conservative Church of Scotland to a policy diametrically opposed to that of the British Government."[27]

Neal Ascherson views the Church of Scotland action in relation to the Federation as a key to interpreting the meaning of Scottish missionary endeavour during the 19th and 20th centuries. Commenting on Scottish foreign missionaries he observes that: "... their influence on empire was deep and paradoxical, at once the advance guard of colonialism and the engineers of its fall. In Africa, above all, Church of Scotland mission colleges would educate critical generations to struggle against the racism of white settlers. As a journalist on the *Scotsman* in 1959, I saw at first hand how the Church of Scotland missions in Nyasaland (now Malawi) successfully crippled the British government's sinister 'federation' scheme, designed to put all Central Africa under the control of white Rhodesia."[28]

Ascherson recalls how the *Scotsman* came to have a "world scoop" through the Scotland-Malawi connection. After introducing the state of emergency, the British Government imposed a news blackout and briefed London journalists about the fictional "murder plot". *Scotsman* editor Eric Mackay decided to telephone the Scottish missionaries:

> Telephoning Nyasaland in those days was no simple matter, even before the emergency. It took two days and nights for the call to come

through, but finally – as the London staff left their desks and crowded round the editor's door to listen – Eric Mackay found himself talking to his old Aberdeen friend the Reverend Andrew Doig. What he said completely debunked the official version of the "riots" and the murder plot and day after day Doig and his colleagues at Blantyre and Livingstonia dictated long despatches about police repression and the united but peaceful rejection of federation by the African population. With the borders closed no other paper had such a source.... The *Scotsman* had a world scoop. The government was appalled.[29]

The Scottish Missions: Standing in Contrast

In Malawi too the Church had been active, particularly the Church of Central Africa Presbyterian – the church which had emerged from the Blantyre, Livingstonia and Nkhoma Missions. Blantyre Synod produced a Statement which stated clearly its outright rejection of the Federation and support for the independence movement. This would come as a surprise to no one since the Congress which now embodied the movement for independence was dominated by people who were products of the Blantyre and Livingstonia Missions.

The biblical text Ephesians 2-14 laid out in white bricks on the ground at Livingstonia in 1959

The church in Malawi influenced events not only by words but also by actions. A striking event took place at Livingstonia during the State of Emergency. On 6 March 1959 the Provincial Commissioner sent a message indicating

166

that a Nyasa Railways launch, the *Ncheni,* would be anchored off Chitimba at 0530 the next morning and that any missionaries who wished to be evacuated and preserved from the presumed dangers of living in the midst of an African population would be taken to Nkhata Bay. When the Senatus, the governing body of the Overtoun Institution, met it was agreed that no one wished to be evacuated and the community would stick together.[30]

Furthermore, it was decided that they would communicate their solidarity to the outside world by arranging whitewashed bricks so that they spelt "Ephesians 2-14". Airmen who flew over the Mission, on return to base consulted the Bible and read the text: "For He [Christ] is our peace, who hath made both one and hath broken down the middle wall of partition between us." They also photographed the bricks from the air and within a few days the photograph was published in the press in Southern Rhodesia and Britain. An article in *The Observer* commented: "A new form of aerial warfare has appeared in Nyasaland. Rhodesian fighter pilots, flying on patrol, have noticed white stones outside the Church of Scotland Mission at Livingstonia – a Mission well known to be sympathetic to Congress. The stones spelt the message 'Ephesians ii 14'."[31] The point was made.

Another influential action was the passing of authority in church life from European to African hands. Though the Scottish Missions, from the early years of the 20th century, had been vulnerable to criticism for their slowness in handing over responsibilities to local Malawian leaders, by the 1950s they were making up for lost time. Tom Colvin remarked that: "... very considerable affairs of the Church are being controlled and furthered by committees with strong African majorities and in many cases Africans have been appointed to take over work previously done by Europeans. This is all in line with our policy of tutelage towards independence."[32] A particularly symbolic move which was made at this time was highlighted by Andrew Doig who pointed out "the importance of the appointment of Rev Sinoia Nkowane as Principal of the Overtoun Institution at Livingstonia. The first African in a long line of missionary

Principals, he will preside over a Senate that is predominantly European."[33]

The handover to African leadership, Eric Jeffrey suggests, "... made real impact not only in church circles but throughout Malawi and beyond as the implications of what occurred sank in. The Church was demonstrating the wind of change not only to the authorities in Malawi but also to the British Government in Westminster. It made the movement towards independence and self-rule much smoother than it might have been."[34] When the CCAP Blantyre Synod released a statement following Operation Sunrise in 1959 it lamented the fact that the Federation leadership had neglected to appreciate the positive possibilities of the African nationalism which was stirring throughout Central Africa. What lent power to its lament was that it spoke "as a Synod whose affairs have been in mainly African hands for many years and who are now well-nigh completely independent in control of our own affairs..."[35]

Independence Attained: the Role of the Scots

The crisis over Federation, and the drive for independence which followed, had tested and proved the strength of the special relationship between Malawi and Scotland. When the Devlin Commission, which was appointed by the British Government to investigate the underlying causes of the State of Emergency, was touring Malawi, its Secretary Anthony Fairclough remarked that it was only at Livingstonia that they found any real fellowship between Europeans and Africans.[36] Malawians and Scots worked together to ensure that the Commission was made fully aware of the strength of Malawian opposition to the Federation. On the day of the debate on Central Africa at the 1959 General Assembly, Kanyama Chiume sent a cable on behalf of the banned Nyasaland African National Congress. It read: "In this perilous time in the history of my country when the civil liberties and freedom of my people are shamefully scorned and suppressed, may I, as a member of the Church, assure you of the unfailing friendship and brotherhood between the people of Scotland and Nyasaland."[37]

The drive for independence, of course, was led by the Malawians who formed the Malawi Congress Party. Striking, however, is the degree to which the roots of the Congress movement can be traced back to the Scottish involvement in the country, particularly in relation to education. As Roderick Macdonald comments:

> It seems scarcely an accident that the relatively small and impoverished Nyasaland was in the van of Britain's East and Central African territories in bearing witness in late 1943 to the formation of a truly nationalist party, the Nyasaland African Congress. Those early Scottish missionaries had wrought better than they knew. Despite the evident decline throughout the inter-War period in Nyasaland's standing with regard to educational provision when contrasted with neighbouring territories, foundations had been laid in the quarter century prior to World War I that could neither be undone, nor ignored. As a cursory examination of the composition of the Nyasaland African Congress will demonstrate, that body was almost wholly dependent for its initial membership and branch organization upon the various Native Associations and their leadership whose origins dated from the decade of the 1920's and before.[38]

A variety of factors need to be taken into account when assessing how Congress became the force that could attain independence for Malawi but the long-term influence of Scottish educational institutions was undoubtedly a significant factor.

The Scottish dimension also found contemporary expression in the crisis of the late 1950s in a host of personal relationships. Amidst the State of Emergency, a 19-year old High School student named Aleke Banda was deported from Salisbury to Nyasaland, his parents' home country which he had never seen. Arriving at Limbe Railway Station he made his way to Blantyre Mission and knocked at the door of Albert and Jenny MacAdam, Scottish missionaries who were looking after Dr Kamuzu Banda's car and personal possessions while he was in detention. The MacAdams welcomed Aleke, who would soon embark on the career which would see him at the forefront of Malawi politics for the next fifty years, into their home and offered him hospitality until he found his feet. Many years later, in 2005, Aleke Banda recounted this story in the Scottish Parliament when he was a leading member of the Malawi delegation which came to Scotland for the conference which would launch a new phase in the relationship between the two nations. Deep personal relationships underlay the political initiative.[39]

Another Scottish couple who played their part in the struggle were Kate and Lindsay Robertson. They had arrived in Malawi as idealistic young Scottish missionaries in January 1958. Through membership of the Iona Community and involvement with overseas students they had come to view the Federation as a force which was driving central Africa in the direction of apartheid. They hoped to contribute in any way they could to the effort to free Malawi from the Federation and to set it on the path to independence. Based at Mulanje Mission they were remote from the main centres of political activity but soon won the confidence of the Congress leadership. It was therefore not a complete surprise when Yatuta Chisiza travelled to Mulanje to ask Kate to stand as a candidate for the Malawi Congress Party on the "upper roll" (reserved for Europeans, Asians and highly educated Africans) in Malawi's first Parliamentary elections in 1961. This resulted in Kate having many doors literally slammed in her face as she canvassed for support from the European community which was solidly pro-Federation and voted accordingly. The Robertsons, however, had the satisfaction of seeing Malawi attain independence and playing their part in building the nation thereafter.[40]

To return to political developments in the UK, Butler and Home travelled south after their visit to the Church of Scotland General Assembly with a very clear message from a body which at that time was broadly representative of the Scottish people. The Devlin Commission reported in terms which corroborated the analysis which had been offered by the Church of Scotland. British policy now began to turn in the direction of moving swiftly towards the granting of independence to Nyasaland. Such was the profile of this issue in Scotland that for a short time it carried potential electoral consequence which concentrated the mind of the Government at Westminster. In the run-up to the 1959 General Election, colonial policy, and African policy in particular, was central. Scottish opposition to Federation now found a strategic opportunity. John Hargreaves gives this assessment: "In Scotland many churchmen, alerted by persons whom the Prime Minister regarded as 'dangerous and subtle agitators', criticized the government's discharge of its trusteeship for African rights in the Federation; this possibly played a minor part in the loss of four Scottish seats, with a contrary swing to Labour of 1.4%."[41]

By now Roy Welensky was Federal Prime Minister but the days when the British Government was amenable to his arguments were rapidly passing. A new generation of leadership in Britain was thinking differently. This was seen when Harold Macmillan, the Prime Minister, appointed Ian Macleod, a young Scotsman, as Colonial Secretary in October 1959. Only weeks after taking office he confided in Fergus Macpherson that, while there might be some economic advantages to Federation, "if it will not work it will have to go, as we cannot rule by bayonets."[42] In April 1960, Macleod took the momentous decision to release Dr Hastings Kamuzu Banda from detention and to deal with him as the leader of a soon-to-be-independent nation. From that moment it was clear that Malawi would secede from the Federation and move swiftly towards independence. When the Monckton Commission, appointed by the British Government to review the Federal constitution, reported in October 1960 it found that the writing was on the wall for the Federation. Self-government was granted in stages from 1960 to 1963, culminating in the attainment of independence on 6 July 1964, with the Malawi Congress Party winning every election on its way to forming the first Malawian Government.

The influence of Scotland, and of the Church of Scotland in particular, had been decisive in the change of direction in British policy. When Federation came to an end its High Commissioner in London, Sir Albert Robinson, grumbled: "The Church of Scotland ... has carried on a campaign for the destruction of the Federation. Now its purpose has been achieved."[43] As Andrew Ross comments: "This campaign was possibly the last time the Kirk has determined and shaped Scottish public opinion. It was also the last effective impact made by the Kirk upon British colonial policy, perhaps the last impact on government by the Kirk in any field."[44]

Scots had also been involved on the ground in Malawi in the development of the Congress movement and in its drive for independence. As Harvey Sindima observes:

> ... [the Scots] became involved in discussion of Congress, even actively visible. When the decision was made to restructure the party, and have new strategies, Tom Colvin and Fergus Macpherson joined Andrew Doig, in supporting the idea by Congress that Dr Hastings Kamuzu Banda be called home to lead the Congress party. During the State of Emergency, following the new strategy under the leadership of Banda, the Scots provided unofficial chaplaincy to the political detainees. Andrew Ross, as an official chaplain, went in and out of Kanjedza Detention Camp ministering to detainees as well as passing

Andrew Ross conducts the funeral of Lawrence Makata in 1962, with Kamuzu Banda to his right and surrounded by Malawi Congress Party leaders

on information on political events outside the Camp. In short, the Scots, right from the beginning, remained part and parcel of Malawi's struggle for Independence.[45]

It might be added that it was in the home of Colin and Alison Cameron that Orton Chirwa, on his release from detention, was invited to become caretaker President of the Malawi Congress Party when, in September 1959, it was born out of the ashes of the banned Nyasaland African Congress in order to spearhead the drive for independence.[46]

When Dr Banda two years later formed his first Cabinet, it was composed entirely of Malawians, with the exception of Colin Cameron, its only white member, who served as Minister of Transport. The latter had been a strong Congress supporter and had been resolute in his solidarity with the detainees during the State of Emergency. Together with his wife Alison he made his home an open house for the Congress leaders and many significant meetings had been held there. Another strongly pro-Congress Scot, Andrew Ross, was appointed chairman of the Lands Tribunal and of the National Tenders Board. To the first generation of Malawian political leaders it was entirely natural that the Scots who had stood with them in the heat of the struggle against the Federation should be given responsibility in the soon-to-be independent country. Together they worked towards the appointed day of 6 July 1964 when Malawi duly became an independent state.

Scots like Cameron and Ross were also alert to the strains and tensions which were at play amongst the Congress leadership. They shared, for example, in the widely felt concern provoked by the death of Dunduzu Chisiza in 1962. It appeared that "Du", by this time established as the rising star of Malawian politics, had died in a tragic car accident, his vehicle having left the road and plunged into a river at Thondwe near Zomba. However, Andrew Ross was puzzled soon afterwards when he overheard some of his church members at Balaka referring to Chisiza's death in terms of "*anaphedwa*" (he has been killed). Immediately he asked, "*anaphedwa ndi ndani?*" (by whom has he been killed?) After an embarrassed silence came the response, "*anaphedwa ndi mfiti*" (he has been killed by a sorcerer). Ross put the further question: "*mfiti ndani?*"

173

(who is the sorcerer?), the answer came with a nod towards the distant Shire Highlands, where the seat of government at Zomba was to be found: *"mfiti wamkulu uja"* (the great sorcerer over there).[47] Through this discussion Ross became aware of the widely held belief among Malawians that Chisiza had been assassinated on the orders of Kamuzu Banda.[48] Even before independence had been achieved, the culture of political violence was taking hold which in later years would lead to car accident becoming code for political assassination and the verb "accidentalise" being adopted in Malawian English to describe the fate of murdered critics of the ruling regime. Scots shared in the forebodings which cast their shadow across Malawian politics at what was outwardly a hopeful time. Meanwhile, the fears and misgivings which arose from Chisiza's death were set aside in order to allow energies to be concentrated on the achievement of independence.

The events of 1959-64 bear out the conclusion drawn by John Stuart that: "... when confronted during the twentieth century with the need to consider the interests of settlers relative to those of Africans, the Scottish missions in Nyasaland supported the latter."[49] A similar conclusion was reached by Thandika Mkandawire, Director of the United Nations Research Institute for Social Development in Geneva, when he remarked that: "There is real affection in Malawi for Scotland. We don't associate Scotland with empire, really. It is seen warmly. A lot of Scottish missionaries were supportive of the independence struggle. The Scots have good standing." [50] The fact that Scots played such a prominent role in this period is an indication of the special relationship between the two nations. It would be evident again in the crisis which broke upon Malawian politics all too soon after the attainment of independence.

---

1   Doig, *It's People That Count.*, pp. 46-47.

2   Ross, "Scotland and Malawi 1859-1964", p. 304.

3   Macpherson, *North of the Zambezi*, p. 199.

4   *Ibid.*, p. 200.

[5] Helen Taylor to Secretaries of the Church of Scotland Women's Foreign Mission, 23 March 1959, NLS MS Acc. 10231/21D.

[6] *Ibid.*

[7] Hepburn, *Memories of Malawi and Scotland*, p. 31.

[8] Chirwa, *Fearless Fighter*, p. 30.

[9] *Ibid.*, pp. 30-31.

[10] *Ibid.*, p. 41.

[11] Ross, *Blantyre Mission*, p. 11

[12] Andrew C. Ross, "Some Reflections on the Malawi 'Cabinet Crisis' 1964-65", *Religion in Malawi*, No. 7 (November 1997), pp. 3-12, at p. 5.

[13] Cit. Kay, *The Scottish World*, p. 204.

[14] Scottish Council on African Questions, "Circular to Newspapers in Scotland", 12 March 1959; cit Mufuka, *Missions and Politics*, p. 186.

[15] Scottish Council on African Questions, *Our Brothers in Revolt: Some Notes of Nyasaland and Scotland 1959*; cit. Mufuka, *Missions and Politics*, p. 185.

[16] *Ibid.*, p. 305

[17] W,P. Coffin 11, File PM 60/12,Ellis to Welensky, 4 June 1959; cit. Ross, *Colonialism to Cabinet Crisis*, p. 180.

[18] Cit. Ross, "Scotland and Malawi", p. 306.

[19] Nyasaland Information Committee, *The Kirk's New Face in Nyasaland*, 1959, p. 2; cit Mufuka, *Missions and Politics*, p. 171.

[20] *Reports to the General Assembly*, Edinburgh: Church of Scotland, 1959, pp. 669-70

[21] *Ibid.*, p. 676.

[22] *Ibid.*, p. 682, my italics.

[23] *The Scotsman*, 26 May 1959; cit. Ross, "Scotland and Malawi", p. 309.

[24] Church of Scotland General Assembly 1959, Verbatim Record, Vol. V, pp.756-57.

[25] Cit. Ronald Ferguson, *George MacLeod: Founder of the Iona Community*, London: Collins, 1990, p. 300.

[26] *Ibid.*

[27] McCracken, "Church and State in Malawi", p. 182..

[28] Neal Ascherson, "The Money's Still Out There", *London Review of Books*, Vol. 33 No. 19 (6 October 2011), p. 8.

[29] Neal Ascherson, *Stone Voices: The Search for Scotland*, London: Granta Books, 2002, p. 89.

[30] See T. Jack Thompson, "Breaking Down the Barriers: Unity and Tension at Livingstonia in 1959", in Kings M. Phiri, John McCracken and Wapu Mulwafu eds., *Crisis in Malawi: the Nyasaland State of Emergency, 1959-60 and its Legacy*, Zomba: Kachere, forthcoming.

[31] *The Observer*, 22 March 1959, p. 15, cit. Thompson, "Breaking Down the Barriers".

[32] Tom Colvin, *Notes on Present Position in Nyasaland and Causes of Disturbances*, confidential memorandum, March 1959, cit. Mufuka, *Missions and Politics*, p. 170.

[33] Andrew B. Doig, *Nyasaland: Partnership in the Church*, Edinburgh: Church of Scotland Foreign Mission Committee, 1959, p. 8.

[34] Eric W.S. Jeffrey, "Roots and Fruits – Northern Malawi", paper presented to "Roots and Fruits" conference, Glasgow, 25 April 2009, p. 3.

[35] "Statement of the Synod of Blantyre of the CCAP Concerning the Present State of Unrest in Nyasaland, March 1959", Appendix I of the Report of the General Assembly's Committee Anent Central Africa, *Reports to the 1959 General Assembly*, Church of Scotland, Edinburgh, 1959, pp. 684-687 at p. 686.

[36] William M. Jackson, *Send Us Friends*, privately published, no date, p. 127; cit. Ross, *Colonialism to Cabinet Crisis*, p. 189.

[37] *The Scotsman*, 26 May 1959; cit. Ross, "Scotland and Malawi", p. 309.

[38] Roderick J. Macdonald, "A History of African Education in Nyasaland 1875-1945", Ph.D., University of Edinburgh, 1969, pp. 569-70.

[39] Ross, *Colonialism to Cabinet Crisis*, p. 195.

[40] Interview, Kate Robertson, 6 January 2012.

[41] John D. Hargreaves, *Decolonization in Africa*, London & New York: Longman, 1988, p. 187.

[42] Fergus Macpherson, note on his meeting with Iain Macleod, 2 December 1959, Helen Taylor Papers, Edinburgh University Library; cit. McCracken, *History of Malawi*, p. 363.

[43] Scotsman, 10 July 1963; cit. J.H. Proctor, "The Church of Scotland and British Colonialism in Africa", *Journal of Church and State*, Vol. 29 (Autumn 1987), pp. 475-93 at p. 492.

[44] Ross, "The Kirk and Colonial Policy 1864-1964", p. 160.

[45] Sindima, *Legacy of Scottish Missionaries*, p. 139.

[46] Ceciwa Bwanausi Khonje, personal recollection, cit. Power, *Political Culture and Nationalism*, p. 142.

[47] Ross, *Colonialism to Cabinet Crisis*, p. 214.

[48] See Power, *Political Culture and Nationalism in Malawi*, pp. 156-76.

[49] John Stuart, "Scottish Missionaries and the End of Empire: the Case of Nyasaland", *Historical Research*, Vol. 76 (August 2003), pp. 411-30, at p. 430.

[50] *The Sunday Times*, 9 February 2003.

10. One-Party Rule and the Struggle for Democracy

Shattered Hopes: the Cabinet Crisis

Malawi's first Cabinet comprised nine Malawians and one Scot - Colin Cameron, the Minister of Works. Of the Malawians, five had been educated at Livingstonia Mission schools: Hastings Kamuzu Banda, Prime Minister; Dunduzu Chisiza, Parliamentary Secretary, Finance; Yatuta Chisiza, Parliamentary Secretary, Labour; Kanyama Chiume, Minister of External Affairs; and Orton Chirwa, Minister of Justice. Two had been educated at Blantyre Mission schools: Augustine Bwanausi, Minister of Development and Housing; and Willie Chokani, Minister of Labour. Two were products of the Anglican Universities Mission to Central Africa schools: Henry Masauko Chipembere, Minister of Local Government; and John Msonthi, Minister of Transport and Communications.[1] The influence of the Scottish missions in shaping independent Malawi's first generation of political leadership was plain to see.

Beyond the institutional connections lay many deep friendships. With the exception of Kamuzu Banda himself, the Cabinet ministers were young men in their 20s and 30s. Several of them had recently married and were at the stage in life of starting their families. Together with their wives they formed a peer group with Scots such as Andrew and Joyce Ross, Colin and Alison Cameron, and Hamish and Anne Hepburn, young couples who had also recently started their families at this time. Sharing together their personal and family experiences, their involvement in church life, and their political aspirations, they formed friendships some of which remain strong today, half a century later. Malawi was now an independent nation but remained a country deeply influenced by its Scottish connections which included living relationships as well as historical foundations.

Having achieved success in seceding from the Federation of Rhodesia and Nyasaland, attaining independence within a short period of time and forming a Government which enjoyed the overwhelming support of the people, it might seem that Malawi was set for a fruitful period of united and purposeful development. It was not to be. Very soon after independence there occurred the "Cabinet crisis" which proved to be the defining event for the first three decades of Malawi's history as an independent nation. Rather than harnessing the prodigious talent assembled in the first Cabinet, Kamuzu Banda chose the path of dictatorship which involved imprisoning, exiling or murdering anyone posing real or imagined challenge to his supremacy. Matters came to a head at a Parliamentary session on 8 September 1964 when Banda dismissed several ministers and others resigned in solidarity, with the result that almost all Cabinet ministers left their posts just two months after independence. It was quickly apparent that their lives would be in jeopardy if they did not leave the country.

Heartbreaking as these events were, it cannot be said that they were entirely unexpected. In fact, independence had served to bring to the surface, with explosive effect, tensions within the Congress movement which had been deepening for several years. These had not been lost on astute Scottish observers. As early as 1959 Fergus Macpherson had written to Dr Banda complaining about the bully-boy behaviour of Congress youth in stoning teachers and threatening ministers."[2] By 1961 his Livingstonia colleague Helen Taylor was observing that: "A totalitarian state is being built here, not a pretty thing to watch, and we suffer with the good men who are its victims. Malawi are now hounding E.K. Gondwe out of his job – the fourth in a few months; and we know others who are on the list. Put a foot wrong and you are OUT. We cannot bear much more."[3] Gondwe was an elderly and highly respected education officer who was vilified by the Congress leadership on account of his decision to serve as a member of the Monckton Commission, appointed by the British Government in 1960 to consider future constitutional arrangements in Malawi. The same year, when Masauko Chipembere and Yatuta and Dunduzu Chisiza were being held at

Kanjedza Detention Camp, Andrew Ross visited them weekly in his capacity as chaplain. He recalls:

> During these visits we talked about the future of Malawi and of Africa and discussed the problem areas in economics and religion and culture as well as politics, narrowly defined. It was in these very general discussions that their uneasiness emerged. They readily admitted that the propaganda line being carried out so persuasively and effectively by [Kanyama] Chiume, hailing Dr Banda as the Saviour of the Nation, was a development of that initiated by them in preparation for his return, but they were somewhat uneasy at what they heard of its development. They also used to joke that there would be big problems if H.K.B. came to believe it. They were seriously unhappy, however, at his acting as though the Party was an agency of his personal authority. All three talked with me at different times about the traditional understanding of authority. They were each most insistent that traditionally, chiefs, however strong or popular, had to articulate popular feeling and although chiefs sought to guide such feeling they could do this successfully only through consultation. A chief always acted with his elders who all had the right to speak and be consulted. Indeed, in judicial matters cases had to be heard in public and everyone concerned had the right to speak. The term *mlandu* describes this understanding of authority and its concept [was] in marked contrast to what they heard of Banda's increasingly autocratic style.[4]

Already four years before independence people like the Chisizas, Chipembere, Ross and Taylor were discerning the tensions which would throw Malawi into the political convulsion described as the "Cabinet crisis".

In its wake it was not only the Malawian ministers and their close supporters who were forced to leave their homeland. In fact, the first minister to resign was the only European in the Cabinet, Colin Cameron. The issue which prompted his resignation was the re-instatement by the new Malawi Government of the British colonial powers of Preventative Detention without trial.[5] Sadly, this proved to be a portent of what was to come as thousands of Malawians would experience such detention in the decades ahead. The cost of resignation was high for Cameron and his family as they were obliged to leave Malawi at short notice and to remain

180

persona non grata for the next thirty years. Similar experiences befell their close friends Andrew and Joyce Ross and Hamish and Anne Hepburn. In one respect, they were separated from Malawi but in another they were closer than ever as they became part of the wide circle of exiles who had fled Dr Banda's repression.

Among them was Molly Dzabala who commented: "One thing we are grateful about the Scottish missionaries is that in 1964 we left this country, a number of us, and fled into exile. We were in Zambia, but some of them kept coming to see us in exile and stayed with us in our homes – that made us feel we're not forgotten, we were part of them … so Scotland is like home to us, the Scottish people are our brothers and sisters, and we'll never forget them." Nor did Dr Banda forget. When he bade farewell to the Malawi team travelling to the 1970 Commonwealth Games in Edinburgh he warned them that, while there, they must at all costs avoid a dangerous hyena, even the saliva of which would poison – his chosen way of describing Andrew Ross.[6] When the other "rebel" ministers fled the country in 1964, the one who remained as a rallying point for opposition to the Kamuzu regime was Masauko Chipembere. He went into hiding in the Mangochi district where he gathered a small guerrilla army and prepared for an attempted overthrow of Banda. During this period Chipembere was in close contact with Ross who was based at Balaka and supported him in various ways, including providing supplies of the medicine which he required. When Chipembere was ghosted out of the country, after the failure of his attempted coup, it was necessary for Ross also to leave at short notice.[7] Banda's bitterness arose most likely from his awareness of the close association which Ross had maintained with Chipembere during that decisive period.

Amongst the Scots who formed deep friendships with the ministers who "rebelled" in the Cabinet Crisis was Peter Mackay who has written movingly about his friendship with Yatuta Chisiza.[8] Mackay had followed family tradition by serving as a captain in the Brigade of Guards before emigrating to farm in Southern Rhodesia in the 1950s. Alienated by the attitudes of the white settlers, he became involved in the nationalist struggle and moved to Malawi. He became an activist in the

181

campaign for independence for Malawi and grew particularly close to Yatuta Chisiza, the dynamic administrative secretary of the Malawi Congress Party during the climactic stage of the struggle for independence.

Mackay recalls how Chisiza would visit him at Likubula, on the slopes of Mount Mulanje, where the two enjoyed "idealistic talks about our affairs and the new world to come."[9] Tragically, Chisiza was lost to Malawi when, together with his fellow "rebel" ministers, he was forced to flee the country following the Cabinet Crisis. Mackay describes in intimate detail the decision taken by Chisiza in 1967 to lead a military incursion into Malawi in the hope that his small guerrilla detachment would be the catalyst which would provoke a widely supported rising against the despotic regime of Kamuzu Banda. Instead, they were overwhelmed by soldiers of the Malawi Army on the banks of the River Shire. Chisiza himself was shot and killed. Mackay was in no doubt as to where his loyalty lay: "I prepared a letter to Dr Banda asking permission to arrange Yatuta's burial on behalf of his family and escort his body from wherever it lay to his home in Karonga."[10] African friends, fearing for his life, dissuaded Mackay from sending the letter but he makes it clear that he never fully recovered from the loss of his friend. In the bitter anguish of failed opposition to dictatorship in Malawi, the Malawian and the Scot were united by their shared ideals and aspirations.

Banda's Dictatorship: the Scottish Dimension

While there were strong links between a circle of Scots and the "rebel" ministers who lost out in the Cabinet crisis, equally Kamuzu Banda, now victorious and supreme, continued to lay emphasis on his longstanding Scottish connections. In particular, it was a familiar part of his rhetoric that he was an elder of the Church of Scotland (having been ordained at Guthrie Memorial Church in Edinburgh in 1941). Curiously, he never became a member of the Church of Central Africa Presbyterian, Malawi's equivalent of the Church of Scotland, and appeared at worship only on national occasions. In the business of religious-political power play, it seems that he preferred to appeal "over the head" of the local church to his status as a church elder in Scotland. This was consonant with the quasi-European persona which he developed, e.g. by always wearing an immaculate three-piece suit, raincoat and Homburg hat, and by refusing to speak any language other than English. His Scottish credentials were deployed as a potent means of legitimation in the Malawi context. As Lupenga Mphande explains: "Upon his arrival in Malawi, he publicly declared that while in Scotland he had become an elder of the Church of Scotland. With that announcement his mission and that of the Livingstonia missionaries in the country were enjoined."[11]

As the one-party Government struggled to sustain its legitimacy following the end of the Cold War in 1989, there was a renewed emphasis on Banda's status as a kirk elder. Indeed he travelled to Edinburgh in 1991 in order to receive a scroll honouring him for being an Elder of the Church of Scotland for fifty years. This was presented to him by the Moderator, Rt Rev W.B.R. Macmillan, on 29 October 1991 at a special luncheon at Edinburgh Castle hosted by Rev Charles Robertson of Canongate Kirk. This was not an event organised by the body officially responsible for relations with Malawi, the Board of World Mission and Unity, and was regarded as a private occasion arranged by a few friends of Dr Banda. It did not feature in the British press. Very different was the interpretation advanced by the Malawi Government. When Parliament opened in December 1991, members were instructed that they must congratulate the President on his achievements as an elder and make reference to the Edinburgh Castle ceremony. Many speakers in the House dwelt on the fact that the President had been recognised not only as a great statesman but also as a great churchman![12] When the government-controlled *Daily Times* reviewed the year 1991, its front page carried a colour photograph of Banda receiving the scroll from the Moderator, with Robertson and "Official Hostess" Mama Kadzamira looking on. This is described as a "TRIUMPHANT MOMENT". In the ideological apparatus which sustained Banda's dictatorship, his status as elder of the Church of Scotland is not to be underestimated.

Besides the church connection, Banda also set store by the medical training which he received in Edinburgh, making donations of £63,985 to

183

the Royal Infirmary of Edinburgh in 1977 and of £350,000 to the Royal College of Surgeons in 1982. After the extent of the corruption and repression of the Banda regime came to be widely acknowledged, there was considerable publicity about these donations and calls for the funds to be returned to Malawi.[13] He described himself as a "Black Scot" and there can be no doubt that the Scottish connections which went back to his earliest years played a significant part in his highly intriguing construction of identity.

This was recognised, strikingly, by detainees in Mikuyu Prison in the late 1980s. In his prison memoirs, the poet Jack Mapanje recalls the excitement generated in the cells when word reached the prison that human rights activists in Scotland were campaigning for his release:

> The fact that branches of PEN International and Amnesty International in Glasgow and Edinburgh have joined the protest particularly thrills those who are proud of being members of the Scottish Presbyterian Church. [Fellow detainee, Stephen] Pingeni openly declares to the entire cell: "If the campaign has reached Scotland, as your news claims, Dr Banda has no chance; Tembo and the Kadzamiras have no chance: they will have to give in and get you released. And Doc, you'll carry some of us along with you, won't you?" Boisterous laughter ensues. And suddenly feeling animated at the prospect of his imminent freedom, Pingeni declares: "You can mock me all you like for being imprisoned here as a mere young pioneer driver, but let me tell some of you a thing or two: I definitely understand the relationship between Banda and the Scottish people better than some of you - we'll be released, definitely, very soon, definitely![14]

Pingeni's convictions were, to some extent, vindicated in June 1988 when a photocopy of a letter from President Banda to staff members of the University of Edinburgh was smuggled into the prison:

Members of Staff   State House
University of Edinburgh   Zomba
EH8 7HF   MALAWI
Central Africa
2nd May 1988

Ladies and Gentlemen,

Your letters of appeal on behalf of Dr Jack Mapanje were received. It is not necessary for me to burden you with a lengthy reply.

But if you must know the facts, teachers, here, who stick to their professional work of teaching students, are not interfered with by anyone. Jack Mapanje has taught at Chancellor College for a number of years without doing anything wrong, just like all his colleagues, whether Africans or Europeans. But after all these years, he changed his mind, for his own personal reasons and started using the classroom as a forum for subversive politics. This cannot and will never be permitted in this country, particularly, in the University of Malawi. Therefore, he had to be picked up and detained.

This is Malawi in Africa and not any other country. Things have to be done according to conditions and circumstances in Malawi, Africa.

Signed

H. Kamuzu Banda[15]

Mapanje offers his assessment of the letter:

> Pingeni was right the other night. Of all the appeals and petitions for our liberation that individuals and institutions make to Banda, it's the Scottish ones that rattle him and his cabal most. I do not know what's going on out there, but I can speculate what might have happened in this case. Academic and administrative staff of the University of Edinburgh have petitioned Banda that I be charged with the crime I am alleged to have committed or be released. And Banda has responded with this angry letter. But how did the university convince Banda to reply to their petition? He never responds to anybody's protests, even from his closest friends; it's not in his blood, people say. This is a miracle. Banda routinely ignores whatever representa-

185

tions are made on behalf of any political opponent he might imprison. His court, the so-called royal family, simply refuse to tell him about them; often they do not allow even his relatives to see him; they want to protect the president from the truth, people say. But protests, petitions and appeals from Scotland in general and the University of Edinburgh in particular have a privileged status. Banda's coterie daren't stop Banda's Scottish friends from seeing him – hence this letter....

I have no significant contacts or people of influence in Edinburgh. I remember Keith Brown, my doctorate degree external examiner and professor of linguistics at the University of Edinburgh. I suppose Neil Smith would have told him about my plight: otherwise I cannot think who else could have influenced Banda for him to respond in this manner. The other Edinburgh connection I have is Angus Calder, a friend, literary critic, fine poet and author of the famous *People's War*. He teaches literature at the Open University and lives in Edinburgh. Angus Calder, the exiled South African writer Cosmo Piertese and I once co-edited an anthology of modern African poetry in English for the BBC. Perhaps Angus mobilised distinguished writers and academics in the city to campaign for my freedom. The substantive population of friends of Malawi in Scotland who are mostly connected to the Scottish Presbyterian Church might also have put in a word to Banda for me. The other obvious connection is the general historical one that every Malawian can claim to have. Dr David Livingstone of the Scottish town of Blantyre, near Glasgow, is supposed to have 'discovered' us in the nineteenth century on his famous journeys across Africa; the country he discovered became Nyasaland Protectorate; and when Banda became leader of the newly independent country called Malawi, Livingstone's Scottish missionary link was permanently established. But the most likely reason for Banda's reaction is his having been a medical student at the University of Edinburgh. This is why on political platforms Banda often calls Scotland his second home and Edinburgh a city close to his heart; he even claims to be an Elder of the Church of Scotland. All these may be reasons for his wanting to explain himself to the University of Edinburgh staff. The truth, though, is that I do not know who caused

186

Banda to write the letter whose photocopy I have before me, though I am delighted that they did – perhaps Banda will be embarrassed enough to consider the possibility of my release, and that this frank letter might be the kicks of a desperate man....[16]

Mapanje eventually does get to the bottom of the initiative which drew a response from President Banda. It is one which demonstrates in adverse circumstances the strength of the Malawi-Scotland connection:

> It was to take me more than twenty years to discover what the University of Edinburgh had done for Banda to respond to their appeal. It was Alison Girwood who instigated the protest on my behalf. I had met her at the 1986 Commonwealth Writers' Conference held in conjunction with the Commonwealth Games of that year – the games that had been boycotted by some Commonwealth countries. On 20 January 1988, after hearing that I had been imprisoned without reason, Alison wrote a very strong letter to Mr M.D. Cornish at Old College, University of Edinburgh, bringing my plight to the attention of the staff of the university. She also liaised with Drs Angela and Grahame Smith of Stirling University, who were organising a general petition from the Scottish Universities as a whole. On Friday 22 January Alison met Dr Andrew Ross of Ecclesiastical History and together they drafted the petition on Edinburgh University headed paper, which read:
>
> *To His Excellency, the Life President, Ngwazi Dr H Kamuzu Banda*
>
> *We, the undersigned members of staff of the University of Edinburgh appeal to you as a former student, on behalf of Dr Jack Mapanje. We respectfully request that he be either charged with a crime and dealt with under due legal process or released from detention. We, the undersigned individuals, wish to express our surprise and concern at the detention without trial of so distinguished a writer and leading academic, and in view of the special relationship and regard existing between Malawi and Scotland, hope that you will understand this concern and re-examine his circumstances...*
>
> Rob D. Leslie of the Department of Scots Law then sent numerous copies of the petition to all the Law teachers of the faculty. In the end, signatures of academic, library and administrative staff were collected from the university under *Name* on the left and *Title* in the middle and

Department on the right. More than four hundred signatures were collected, scaring Banda into responding as he did.[17]

Mapanje was eventually released. By no means all detainees were so fortunate. Another high-profile case was that of Orton and Vera Chirwa who were abducted from Zambia in 1981, put on trial and condemned to death in a "traditional court", a sentence which was commuted to life imprisonment.[18] Orton Chirwa died in highly suspicious circumstances in Zomba Central Prison in late 1992.[19] Burial, of course, took place in Malawi but a memorial service was held at St Giles Cathedral in Edinburgh. The huge church was packed to the doors, demonstrating once again the mutual regard and solidarity of Malawians and Scots.

Breaking the Silence: Banda Disowned

Given Scotland's special place in the ideological apparatus that supported the Banda regime, the question has been raised as to why Scotland was not more vocal in relation to the appalling abuse of human rights suffered by people like the Chirwas. In particular, in light of Banda's frequent reference to his status as kirk elder, an onus fell on the Church of Scotland. Its response to the Cabinet crisis had been based on respect for Malawi's independence and a sense that it would not be appropriate to "interfere" in the affairs of the new nation. As Stanley Hood, writing as Convener of the Church of Scotland Sub-Saharan Africa Committee in 1992, explained: "For many years the Church of Scotland remained silent on the denial of human rights in Malawi. We were much criticised for our silence. But we recognised that Malawi was a young country, and hoped that, in due time, the situation would improve."[20]

Furthermore, church leaders in Scotland were deeply conscious that any move they made that was unfavourably received by the Banda regime could have very serious repercussions for the church and its leaders on the ground in Malawi. As they explained when breaking their silence in 1992: "We in Scotland have been reluctant so far to comment publicly on these matters out of a concern not to place members of our sister church in Malawi in danger."[21] The presence of Church of Scotland personnel in Malawi, which continued throughout the one-party era, might also have been jeopardised had its leadership challenged the excesses and abuses of the Banda regime. It was not, however, a comfortable silence. David Lyon, General Secretary of the Overseas Council (later Board of World Mission and Unity) from 1974 to 1987 has recalled the "anger, disappointment and frustration" with which he regarded the Banda dictatorship and has stated that "my conscience is not clear."[22]

It was the death sentence handed down to Orton and Vera Chirwa by the "traditional court" in 1982 which provoked the only public intervention by the Church of Scotland in Malawi's internal affairs during the Banda era. The 1983 General Assembly agreed to "respectfully request the Life President of Malawi, himself ordained as an elder of the Church of Scotland, to exercise the Presidential Prerogative of Mercy."[23] Andrew Doig was sent as a special envoy to plead for clemency for the Chirwas. Though Dr Banda responded angrily and refused to see his old friend Dr Doig, the death sentence was commuted to life imprisonment. Nonetheless, Banda's very clearly expressed resentment at the Church of Scotland initiative made it clear that he would maintain his kirk elder status on his own terms and would not take kindly to any pastoral admonition from the Church. The President's anger at Dr Doig served as a warning to local church leaders who became even more careful to avoid any possible confrontation.[24]

The long history of Malawi-Scotland interaction yielded another source of potential influence on the Life President. When Banda returned to Malawi to lead the independence movement in 1958 he had been out of the country for more than forty years. Hence he had no close friends among Malawians and chose to maintain an air of austere detachment. Combined with other quirks of his personality and the politics of dictatorship, this ensured that he became an isolated figure to whom almost no one spoke on equal terms. One of the very few exceptions was Fergus Macpherson, whose father had ordained Banda to the eldership in Edinburgh in 1941. At that time, Banda was a frequent visitor to the manse and became a family friend. Later, when Fergus was preparing for missionary service in Central Africa, Kamuzu taught him the Chinyanja language. The two therefore enjoyed a longstanding intimacy and Macpherson could always be sure of access to the Life President.[25]

Sometimes he made use of this privilege to plead for clemency for particular victims of repression who were known to him and to probe for opportunities to discuss with Banda the nature of his presidency. Banda's responses were suggestive of a deeply disturbed personality as he switched between affectionate familiarity one moment and hysterical paroxysms of rage the next. This was particularly evident when Banda invited Macpherson to Gleneagles Hotel during the Commonwealth Heads of Government meeting in 1977. Macpherson's request for the release of a detainee named Mrs Serenje provoked fits of apparently uncontrollable rage before Banda finally acceded to the request.[26] The Scotland-Malawi axis, personified in the friendship of Macpherson and Banda, did make a difference at times for individual victims of the dictatorship but for the long period of thirty years it was unable to effectively challenge the system as a whole.

Biding their time with a sense of frustration and impatience, Church of Scotland leaders were ready to speak as soon as developments in Malawi provided the opportunity. The moment came with the publication on 8 March 1992 of the Roman Catholic bishops' Pastoral Letter *Living our Faith*, which proved to be the catalyst of the movement for multi-party democracy which finally brought down the Banda regime.[27] At the time, Banda reacted angrily to the Letter and, perhaps in an attempt to divide the churches at this critical point, appealed to his Scottish Presbyterian credentials. As the *Daily Times* reported: "Referring to the Irish Catholic bishop in Mzuzu [Mgr John Roche], who is reported to have drafted the pastoral letter, the Ngwazi said as an Elder of the Church of Scotland he was not surprised since the Catholics in Dublin, Ireland, did not like the Presbyterians in Scotland."[28]

Church of Scotland leaders in Edinburgh decided that now was the time to speak. On the evening of 13 March 1992 the BBC World Service broadcast an interview with Chris Wigglesworth, General Secretary of the Church of Scotland Board of World Mission and Unity, in which he

190

made it clear that he could not regard Banda as a serving elder of the Church of Scotland. This was quickly followed up by an official statement in the following terms: "We ... wish to make it a matter of public record that Dr Banda is not an elder of the Church of Scotland in any meaningful sense. While technically, ordination to the eldership is for life, a person with that status is not properly regarded as an elder unless they are a member of a kirk session (local Church committee). Dr Banda has not been such a member for nearly fifty years."[29]

In Malawi, the effect was dramatic. As it dawned on the Malawian public that there was something bogus about Banda's claims, the Ngwazi began to suffer a loss of legitimacy from which he never recovered. As one of John Lwanda's youthful informants indicated: "It was then that we knew that the 'force' was not really with this guy."[30] Banda's loss of face continued when the Church of Scotland General Assembly of 1992 agreed to "place on record that it is erroneous to describe Dr Hastings K. Banda as an 'elder of the Church of Scotland'."[31] This statement, issued in a context where the "mainline" churches in Malawi were distancing themselves from the government, helped to provoke a crisis of legitimacy which the Banda regime proved unable to surmount.

Together for Democracy

The deep-lying connections between Malawi and Scotland embraced not only President Banda but also his political opponents who prepared for the day when a challenge to the dictatorship could be mounted. Orton Chirwa was leader of the Tanzania-based MAFREMO (Malawi Freedom Movement). The leader of the United Front for Multi-Party Democracy, a movement of exiles based in Lusaka, was Dr Harry Bwanausi who was born in 1925 at Blantyre Mission where his family had lived since his grandfather was employed to carry goods from the River Shire at Chikwawa during the earliest days of the Mission.[32] The church elder who was most prominent in organising the Public Affairs Committee, the church-based body which proved to be the engine of political change in the 1992-93 period, was Jake Muwamba, grandson of the first theological student to be trained by the Livingstonia Mission.[33] Edda Chitalo, the

191

first woman to occupy a prominent position in the multi-party movement, was born and raised on Blantyre Mission.[34] These are but a few examples of the Malawian families with long Scottish associations who nurtured an alternative vision through the dark days of repression and who emerged to offer leadership to the multi-party movement when the time was ripe.

To these activists, the solidarity and support of their Scottish friends was a significant source of support as they found the courage to challenge the dictatorship. The 1992 Church of Scotland General Assembly which disowned Kamuzu Banda as an elder also called upon the Government of Malawi to provide "tangible and irreversible evidence of a basic transformation in its observance of the fundamental human rights of all Malawi's citizens" and "regretfully endorsed the action of Malawi's major donors in withholding development aid for a limited period."[35] The value of this action was expressed immediately by Dr Harry Bwanausi, leader of the United Front for Multi-Party Democracy, in a faxed message to Church of Scotland Africa Secretary James Wilkie: "Please convey the exiles' grateful thanks to Fergus Macpherson, Dr Ross and to your dearself and to the General Assembly of the Church of Scotland for the support on the Malawi issue. The Moral Authority of the KIRK [sic] will emancipate us for the second time, the first being when its resolution dismantled the Federation of Rhodesia and Nyasaland in 1960."[36] Not without some hyperbole, Bwanausi thus indicated the importance of the Assembly decision for those working for progressive political change in Malawi.

From this point onwards Scotland became the hub of efforts to provide international support for the democratisation movement in Malawi. One key player was Church of Scotland Africa Secretary James Wilkie who became "Ecumenical Coordinator" for a Malawi network within the Council of Churches for Britain and Ireland.[37] Through his offices a Church of Scotland delegation was successful in persuading the 1992 Assembly of the Conference of European Churches "to press the Government of Malawi for the release of Christian detainees and an immediate top-level conference on constitutional reform."[38]

Wilkie also played a key role in the formation of the Scottish Malawi Network in 1993. This brought together people in Scotland with Malawi connections who had a shared interest in the political crisis which now gripped the country. The Network held public meetings, often to provide a platform for Malawian visitors. It also began the publication of the *Malawi Update*, a quarterly newsletter which over the next twenty years became a respected source of information on developments in Malawi, with a special focus on its Scottish connections. Anne Hepburn, who had been, together with her husband Hamish, much involved in Malawi's struggle for independence thirty years earlier, was a natural choice as Coordinator of the Network as it gave expression to a new wave of commitment to the Scotland-Malawi connection.[39]

Influence was also brought to bear on the UK Government. Baroness Chalker of Wallesey, the Minister in the Foreign Office with direct responsibility for Britain's relations with Malawi recognised that, "the Church of Scotland's influence in Malawi and with Banda personally has been a powerful force for progress."[40] As preparations were made for a referendum on the multi-party question, the British Government were concerned that Dr Banda should not take too reactionary a line and requested the Church of Scotland to send a special envoy to see the President in person. Fergus Macpherson was given this task. At a time when almost no one outside the ruling clique could speak privately with Banda, Macpherson was eventually granted a private audience and spoke with the President of the urgent need for democratisation in Malawi.[41] The direct effect of the conversation is impossible to calculate but Banda did take a more conciliatory line towards the opposition in the run-up to the Referendum and in his acceptance of its result. Once again the Scottish connection came into play at a critical point in Malawian political history.

Meanwhile the Malawi-Scotland connection provided succour and support to leaders of the struggle for democracy. In the case of Rev Aaron Longwe, his experiences of harassment and detention attracted heightened interest in Scotland on account of his wife Alice being a Scot. The experiences of the couple featured in the Scottish press, with *The*

Scotsman on one occasion reporting Longwe's remark that, "If it were not for the Church of Scotland some of us would have been dead by now."[42] Silas Ncozana, the CCAP Blantyre Synod General Secretary, was also acutely aware of the risks he ran as he became a key figure in the organisation of the Public Affairs Committee. So much so that he provided the Church of Scotland with the code "PAUL AND SILAS REPEAT" which it was agreed he would use to signal his arrest.[43]

Scottish support was vital to such activists as they took up the very exposed position which was entailed in challenging the one-party system. This support remained in place throughout the period of the 1993 Referendum and the first multi-party elections in 1994. It included the organisation of an ecumenical church meeting with the Public Affairs Committee in Swanick, Derbyshire, which did important groundwork for the transition to democracy. Emmanuel Chimkwita, PAC's Acting Chairman at the time, considered that, "The Pastoral Letter was really a catalyst but the pivotal event in the process of change was the Swanick meeting where the strategy was formed which guided the PAC in the National Referendum and the General Election."[44] When the time was ripe for Malawi's transition to democracy, Scotland was not found wanting but, especially through the church links, proved to be a resourceful and committed supporter.

---

[1] *Malawi Independence Souvenir Programme 1964 – The Cabinet*, Zomba: Malawi Government, 1964; cit. Mufuka, *Missions and Politics*, pp. 201-03.

[2] Fergus Macpherson to Kamuzu Banda, 20 February 1959; cit. John McCracken, "Church and State in Malawi: The Church and the Role of the Scottish Presbyterian Missions, 1875-1964", in Isabel Phiri, Kenneth Ross and James Cox ed., *The Role of Christianity in Development, Peace and Reconstruction: Southern Perspectives*, Nairobi: All Africa Conference of Churches, 1996, pp. 48-73 at p. 68.

[3] Letter from Helen Taylor to Secretaries of the Church of Scotland Women's Foreign Mission, 11 January 1961 NLS MS Acc. 10231/21D.

[4] Ross, *From Colonialism to Cabinet Crisis*, p. 208.

[5] *Ibid*, p. 219.

[6]   *Ibid*, p. 225.

[7]   *Ibid*, pp. 224-25.

[8]   Peter Mackay, *We Have Tomorrow: Stirrings in Africa 1959-1967*, Norwich: Michael Russell, 2008.

[9]   *Ibid*, p. 132.

[10] *Ibid*, p. 333.

[11] Lupenga Mphande, "Dr Hastings Kamuzu Banda and the Malawi Writers Group: The (un)Making of a Cultural Tradition", *Research in African Literatures*, Vol. 27/1 (Spring 1996), pp. 80-101, at p. 86.

[12] *Hansard*, December 1991, *passim*.

[13] See e.g. Kenny Farquharson, "The Stains of Blood Money Stick", *The Sunday Times*, 9 February 2003.

[14] Jack Mapanje, *And Crocodiles are Hungry at Night,* Banbury: Ayebia, 2011, pp. 140-41.

[15] *Ibid*, p. 209

[16] *Ibid*, pp. 209-11.

[17] *Ibid*, pp. 215-16.

[18] See Chirwa, *Fearless Fighter*, pp. 88-107.

[19] *Ibid*, pp. 130-31.

[20] Letter from Rev. Stanley Hood to Hon. Dr Hetherwick Ntaba, 18 June 1992.

[21] Statement by the Church of Scotland Department of World Mission and Unity, Church of Scotland press release, 16 March 1992.

[22] Interview with Rev. David Lyon, Edinburgh, 31 October 1996.

[23] Minutes of the General Assembly of the Church of Scotland, 1983, p. 71.

[24] Interview with Silas Ncozana, Blantyre, 28 June 1995.

[25] Interview with Fergus Macpherson, 18 August 1994.

[26] Interview with Fergus Macpherson, 20 November 1996.

[27] See Kenneth R. Ross, *Gospel Ferment in Malawi: Theological Essays*, Gweru: Mambo Press, 1995, pp. 9-29.

[28] *Daily Times*, 13 March 1992.

[29] Statement by Church of Scotland Board of World Mission and Unity, Church of Scotland press release, 16 March 1992.

[30] John L.C. Lwanda, *Promises, Power, Politics and Poverty: Democratic Transition in Malawi (1961-1999)*, Glasgow: Dudu Nsomba, 1996, p. 108.

[31] Minutes of the General Assembly of the Church of Scotland, 1992, p. 61.

[32] Interview with Harry Bwanausi, Zomba, 8 December 1994.

[33] Interview with Jake Muwamba, Blantyre, 4 January 1995.

[34] Interview with Edda Chitalo, by Dr Isabel Apawo Phiri, Blantyre, 15 May 1995.

[35] Minutes of the General Assembly of the Church of Scotland, 1992, p. 61.

[36] Faxed letter from Dr H.W. Bwanausi to Rev. James Wilkie, 20 May 1992.

[37] See Kenneth R. Ross, "Malawi's Peaceful Revolution 1992-94: the Role of the Church of Scotland", *Scottish Church History Society Records*, Vol. XXVII (1997), pp. 280-304.

[38] Church of Scotland press release, 9 September 1993.

[39] Hepburn, *Memories of Malawi and Scotland*, p. 92.

[40] Letter from Baroness Chalker of Wallesey to Sir David Steel, quoted by Jill Clements (secretary to Sir David) to Dr Chris Wigglesworth, 25 March 1993.

[41] Fergus Macpherson, "Personal Record of a Special Visit to Malawi, 31 January to 7 February 1993".

[42] *Scotsman*, 23 February 1993.

[43] Letter from Silas Ncozana to Jim Wilkie, 8 May 1992.

[44] Interview with Emmanuel Chimkwita, by Dr Klaus Fiedler, 4 December 1994.

11. Malawian Democracy, Scottish Devolution and Partnership Renewed

Relations Rekindled in the 21st Century

The decades which followed Malawi's independence in 1964 saw a continuation of the special connection with Scotland but it would not be unfair to conclude that it had moved into a lower key. It became apparent around the time of the Millennium, however, that something was stirring in Scotland Malawi relations. Both nations had undergone significant political changes during the 1990s. Malawi had broken the stranglehold of the one-party dictatorship and embarked on the path of multi-party democracy. Scotland, after almost 300 years without its own Parliament, achieved a devolution settlement which provided for the re-introduction of a Scottish Parliament with extensive, though limited, powers. New political energy, both in Scotland and in Malawi, created the potential for fresh interaction between the two nations.

A spark, however, was needed to ignite the new possibilities. In the event it came from Strathclyde University, which incorporates David Livingstone's alma mater, and Bell College, the higher education institution closest to his birthplace. Together, as the year 2000 approached and institutions sought meaningful ways of marking the auspicious year, they created the Malawi Millennium Project which quickly caught the imagination of a new generation of Scots and completed significant development projects in Malawi.[1]

This fresh enthusiasm gave rise to a new round of networking, bringing together groups large and small whose work expresses the close relationship between the two nations. Public lectures in Glasgow, by Peter West of Strathclyde University, and in Edinburgh, by Andrew Ross of Edinburgh University, rallied support. The Lord Provosts of both Glasgow and Edinburgh gave their backing as a formally organised Scotland Malawi Partnership came into being in 2004. In their invitation to the launch they invoked the historical memory: "As the Lord Provosts of Glasgow and Edinburgh, we have agreed jointly to launch a campaign to have Scotland commit itself to extending its support for Malawi. The original name of the country, Nyasaland, was given to it by David Livingstone, who is revered there. Over the succeeding 150 years, the force of Scottish opinion has twice saved Malawi. Now it needs further help….."[2]

Becoming a registered charity in 2005, the Scotland Malawi Partnership took shape as a civil society alliance bringing together a wide variety of organisations concerned with Malawi. It aimed to increase collaboration and multiply best practice. Its stated objective is "to inspire people and organisations of Scotland to be involved with Malawi in an informed, coordinated and effective way so that both nations benefit."[3] Simultaneously in Malawi, through the good offices of British High Commissioner Norman Ling, a Committee was formed to build up the Malawi end of the renewed partnership. In July 2004 this Committee, together with their Scottish counterparts, met with the new President of Malawi, Bingu wa Mutharika, who announced his backing.

This rekindling of Scotland's relationship with Malawi coincided with the early years of the devolution settlement. Though foreign affairs is a "reserved power" at Westminster, May 2005 saw the Scottish First Minister, Jack McConnell making an official visit to Malawi. A reciprocal visit to Scotland by President Bingu wa Mutharika, on the occasion of the seminal Scotland Malawi Conference in November 2005, featured the signing of a Cooperation Agreement between Scotland and Malawi. The Agreement states that: "Scotland and Malawi have a long history of collaboration, particularly in health and education. Both countries share a wish to build upon this history by actively engaging through partnership. This is a reciprocal partnership based upon sharing experiences and skills. It is an opportunity to learn from each other and to recognise the needs of our two countries."[4] It identifies civic governance and society, sustainable economic development, health and education as broad themes on which collaboration will be developed.

Through the newly established International Development Fund, the Scottish Government began to make grants to support initiatives in these areas, with £2.4 million being granted in 2005.[5] Adjoa Anyimadu has noted the distinctive and innovative features of this initiative: "The first decision taken about the Scottish development policy was that it should focus on encouraging links between communities and schools in Scotland and those in a partner region or country on the basis of the mutual exchange of knowledge and skills. Both sides were to benefit from the experience of linking. The Scottish Executive championed this idea of reciprocity, and it was spoken of as the heart of the policy – signalling a move away from the traditional donor–recipient aid relationship."[6]

When the Scottish National Party came to power in May 2007 there was some uncertainty about whether it would continue the Malawi commitment which had become something of a flagship policy of the preceding Labour administration and, in particular, was identified with the personal commitment demonstrated by Jack McConnell as First Minister. However, the result of an extensive consultation exercise was a substantial increase in the funding committed to the International Development Fund, rising from £3m to £6m per annum in 2008-09 and 2009-10, and to £9m in 2010-11.

Moreover, among six distinct programmes, the Malawi Development Programme was the only country-specific programme and had a ring-fenced allocation of £3m. In practice, it was this programme to which the lion's share of the available resources was committed. For the financial year 2008-09 the Malawi programme received an allocation of £4.2m, exceeding the ring-fenced £3m. Following the completion of an independent review in 2008, the Scottish Government (as the Scottish Executive was renamed in 2007) affirmed the themes agreed in the initial Cooperation Agreement: civic governance and society, sustainable economic development, health, and education. Within and across those strands, cross-cutting themes were identified:

Vocational training and education
Gender issues and equality
Enterprise development
Strengthening the context for enhanced human rights and civil society development

These emphases are geared to meet priorities identified by the Government of Malawi and there is a commitment by both Governments to continuing consultation.

Additionally, the programme on core funding for Scottish-based international development networking organisations is concentrated on "the two main international development networking and membership organisations in Scotland – the Network of International Development Organisations in Scotland (NIDOS) and the Scotland Malawi Partnership (SMP)." The purpose of the support offered by Government is that the organisations will "effectively represent and co-ordinate the interest of the sector, hold best practice seminars and ensure effective information exchange and dissemination". A distinctive feature of the Scottish approach is that the Government itself does not run an international development programme. Rather, through judicious grant-making, it enables a wide variety of organisations to bring their particular skills and motivation to the sphere of international development, with Malawi as a particular focus. This has a multiplier effect since the relatively low level of funding releases energy, creativity and initiative with huge potential impact. It also has the effect, in the interface between Scotland and Malawi, of placing the emphasis on the relational. While the funding may be minimal against the scale of the challenges, capital of a different order is brought into play through drawing on the strength of the relationships which have united the two nations over 150 years and which are being rejuvenated today.

The fact that the links between Scotland and Malawi extend far beyond any partisan basis has been demonstrated by the strong cross-party support for re-invigorating the relationship which has been evident in the Scottish Parliament. This led to the formation in 2005 of a Parliamentary Cross-Party Group on Malawi, with Karen Gillon MSP and Michael Matheson MSP as the first Co-Conveners. Its aim is to "develop and enhance links between Scotland and Malawi and to provide a forum for discussion on these matters. In particular the Group focuses on links between the two parliaments and between civil society in each country. In order to achieve this, the Group works with parliamentarians from each legislature, with Malawians living in Scotland and with other organisations working in Malawi."[7] This agenda was taken forward by a series of visits by Parliamentary delegations, including representation from all parties.

When the European and External Relations Committee reported to the Scottish Parliament on its inquiry into international development in September 2008, it was apparent that cross-party consensus remained strong. Jackson Carlaw, a Conservative member, illustrated this when he stated: "By focusing primarily on Malawi, the Government – within a relatively short time, it must be noted – ensured that our association and contribution were widely recognised by the Scottish public. That is of enormous value and, indeed, is not always the case when aid is given. Moreover the people of Malawi have appreciated this engagement, which has genuinely strengthened the links between the two countries. Like many members, I have met those who have volunteered their services. The rewards extend in both directions.... I believe that Jack McConnell produced the goods..."[8]

The Parliamentary debate revealed that in many constituencies throughout the country the connection with Malawi was finding expression at local level. The cross-party consensus is driven by the grassroots movement which holds MSPs accountable to provide appropriate support for this vital element of Scottish life.[9] It is, moreover, at the civil society level that the aspiration for a reciprocal relationship can take effect. The Government to Government relationship draws its vitality and finds its effectiveness from the multitude of links made by civil society – schools, Universities, health boards, local government, community groups, faith-based organisations etc.

Mobilisation of Civil Society

It is here that the Scotland Malawi Partnership, as a civil society alliance, has a key role to play. The Partnership exists as an independent charitable company and is at pains to clarify that it is not an arm of Government. While it values very highly its close working relationship with the

Scottish Government, it is purposely a non-governmental body and is free to offer constructive criticism of Government policy or action when required. With the full support of the Scottish Government, the Partnership seeks to forge a new model of inter-national relations. It has stated its identity and vision in these terms: "It pioneers a new approach to North-South relations, one built on friendship and respect between two nations built up over generations of close collaboration. It works today on the basis of mobilising a network of Scottish-based commitment to Malawi in order to develop best practice and maximise impact, ensuring that the whole is greater than the sum of the parts."[10] This vision has brought together an alliance which is ground-breaking in the range and diversity which it brings to the quest for a vibrant civil society-based approach to the development of the relationship.

As at 31 December 2011, the Partnership had a total membership of 483, divided into the following categories: 131 organisational members, 197 school partnership members, 15 Local Authority members and 140 individual Associate members. The organisational members include Universities and Colleges, faith-based organisations, independent charities, community groups, commercial companies and the health sector. A new category of youth members is being developed during 2012. An important contribution is made by Associate Members - individuals who bring a wide range of experience and expertise, with many having spent significant parts of their lives in Malawi.

The willingness of many members to freely offer their time, energy and expertise to the development of the Partnership means that the value of the funding which supports the running of the office is multiplied many times over. By drawing together the personal and organisational bilateral links which were already in existence and by stimulating the formation of new ones, the Scotland Malawi Partnership has succeeded, in a relatively short time, in creating a capacity at civil society level for the implementation of an innovative approach to inter-national development. Its website is a primary source of information and guidance for those working between Scotland and Malawi. It also frequently offers workshops, seminars and conferences on relevant topics so as to increase the skills and knowledge of those engaged in work with partners in Malawi.

The scale of civil society involvement is remarkable. Using a form of the Social Return on Investment framework, Lawrence Dritsas of Edinburgh University prepared a report in late 2010 in which he estimated the numbers of people involved and the total financial value of their work. Dritsas concluded that:

The value of inputs of money, time and in-kind donations made by the membership of the SMP to Scotland's links with Malawi is at least £30 million over the twelve months previous to October 2010.

At least 1.3 million Malawians and 280,000 Scots have benefitted from these activities over the same period.

Approximately 148,000 Malawians and 85,000 Scots were actively involved in delivering these activities.[11]

On the basis of these findings Dritsas concludes that "... there is a very great deal of money, material, time and goodwill invested in the links between Scotland and Malawi. [£30 million] is an impressive figure and, in conjunction with our findings that over one million Malawians and thousands of Scots are involved in or benefitting from these activities, easily demonstrates that the links between Scotland and Malawi are extremely valuable to both countries."[12]

The Rise of Twinning: Churches and Schools

The churches, particularly the Church of Scotland and the CCAP (Church of Central Africa Presbyterian), have historically been the mainspring of Scotland Malawi interaction. With participation in church life becoming more of a minority pursuit in Scotland, it is observable that the relationship of the two nations has come to rest on a broader institutional base. Nonetheless, church life has remained an important resource for sustaining and developing the connections between Scotland and Malawi. In contrast to the numerical decline evident in the Church of Scotland, the CCAP has grown prodigiously, now having more than 3 million members and a dynamic presence in every part of the country.

Panel at Scotland Malawi Partnership 5-Year celebrations: Lawrence Dritsas, Adjoa Anyimadu, Kenneth Ross, Flossie Gomile-Chidyaonga, Yonah Matemba, Jack McConnell

The Church of Scotland still appoints staff to serve in Malawi, albeit in much smaller numbers than in earlier times, and supports programmes of the CCAP. Perhaps even more significant is a growth area in church life: a movement among local congregations to form a "twinning" with a counterpart in another country. As this movement spread during the early years of the 21st century, it was often Malawi to which local congregations looked for a "twin". By 2009, some fifty Scottish congregations were actively pursuing a twinning with a Malawian counterpart. In several cases the church-to-church links are comple-mented by parallel school-to-school relationships. This development has been widely welcomed in Malawian communities, both urban and rural.

The enthusiasm with which such twinnings have been embraced, on both sides, shows the hold on the popular imagination still exercised by the Scotland Malawi relationship. It also offers a model of relationship which is transferable to the wider development of active links between the two nations. There has been a move away from an HQ-led approach to partnership towards more of a local-to-local approach. There has been an upsurge of (region-wide) presbytery-to-presbytery and (local community) congregation-to-congregation links. In the Church of Scotland, for example, the *Church Without Walls* Report, something of a charter document as the Church entered the 21st century, called on congregations to: "research an area of the world church and establish a personal partnership with a congregation or project".[13]

In shorthand, these kind of relationships have become known as "twinnings". Rather than depending on a specialist missionary, congregations were taking ownership of particular relationships and developing them through direct involvement. To some extent this is making virtue out of necessity. The life-long missionaries around whom congregations built their global horizons in the 19th and 20th centuries were fast disappearing. If congregations were to continue having an active overseas connection they had to find a new model through which to work. Twinning was an idea whose time had come.

For congregations which have become involved in twinning with counterparts on other continents, it has been a mind-blowing and faith-stretching experience. The Church of Scotland General Assembly of 2007 heard, for example, from members of a congregation from Ruchazie, generally regarded as being among the most deprived areas of the city of Glasgow. They spoke movingly of how their church and community had been affected by a twinning with the congregation in Baula in northern Malawi. They described it as a "life-changing experience" and spoke of how they had come to think of people in Baula as part of their own family. The visit of Malawians to Ruchazie had had a startling effect. People stopped in the streets to greet them. Young people, in particular, struck up a rapport with the visitors. Many more people have come to the church as a result of the Malawi connection, speaking with the minister and church members about what it has meant to them. A community-wide impact was being made and the church members were clearly excited by the discovery of new dimensions to their faith and new possibilities for their Christian witness.[14]

Coming to appreciate how much they stand to gain from the twinning experience has been a steep learning curve for Scottish congregations which have become involved. Often they have begun with a charity model – imagining that it would be noble and altruistic to help a community that is much less well off. As the twinning has developed, however, they have realised that it is much more of a two-way exchange than they had imagined was possible. For growing numbers of Scots it is proving to be a transformative experience as their own life and perspectives are impacted by the experience of the twinning. Likewise on the Malawi side, the relationship has often begun with hopes of financial assistance, e.g to maintain the church building, but has developed into something much more mutual and comprehensive as Malawians have come to understand more of the struggles which face their Scottish counterparts.

Parallel to church twinnings, and often connected with them, have been school partnerships. Scottish life for centuries has been marked by the quest to fulfil John Knox's vision of a church and a school in every parish. The same axis of church and school has been key to Malawi's development since the late 19th century. It has therefore been a natural development for schools in the two nations to forge links. Between 2004 and 2009 the number of Malawian and Scottish schools which are in partnership rose from some 20 to around 200. The Scotland Malawi Partnership fosters certain ideals in regard to such partnerships: "At the heart of partnership are the core values of equality, mutuality and reciprocity. Partnership is not simply about providing material aid to another school, but about creating a relationship which enables pupils in both schools to develop a more critical understanding of the lives and prospects of their partner pupils. Partnership is defined more by the ongoing development of relationships than by the integration of the partnership into the wider context of pupils' learning."[15]

There is a high level of confidence about what can be achieved through a school partnership: "A successful link can lead to enthused students and an enriched curriculum and school ethos, both in Scotland and Malawi. Pupils can develop the skills and attitudes they need to become responsible citizens through the exchange of ideas with partner's pupils and the fostering of an international perspective."[16] Jack McConnell illustrated this in the Parliamentary debate of September 2008 when he spoke of a visit he had recently made to Nairn Academy, a school which had been developing a twinning with a counterpart in Malawi: "The most telling comment yesterday came from a girl who is in her sixth year at Nairn Academy. When asked to describe how she had changed as a result of her visit, she said that she and her colleagues would, for the rest of their lives, be less greedy and more appreciative and have a greater understanding of the rest of the world. That is why I want to highlight the importance of the people-to-people relationships, whose role is central to ensuring that we make the most of the resources and the effort that we put in."[17] Such an outcome is replicated in many situations around the country

In Pursuit of Genuine Reciprocity

All who have participated in twinnings of churches and schools talk enthusiastically about the two-way nature of the benefits. Where both Government and civil society alliance meet a considerable challenge, however, is in the aspiration for the partnership to be genuinely two-sided at the organisational level. Since the language of partnership was much used by proponents of Federation in the 1950s, there is an onus on those who use this language today to demonstrate that it is not a mask for domination and disrespect. Memories in Malawi are long enough to remember Lord Malvern, in a moment of candour, describing the partnership between the races as being akin to that between the rider and the horse.[18]

In today's neo-colonial world, it would still be easy to develop a partnership where authority and initiative lie entirely at the Scottish end. A very different aspiration was evident, however, at the Scotland Malawi Partnership Conference organised by the SMP and hosted by the Scottish Parliament in November 2005.[19] The inadequacies of a donor-recipient model of international development were trenchantly exposed and the value of a relationship grounded in mutual respect and a commitment to learn from each other was affirmed and celebrated. This laid down the challenge to determine how such a relationship can be developed and sustained.

A primary obstacle to a two-way partnership is the extent of the disparity in resources between the two partners. At the time of the 2005 Conference, the per capita GDP in Malawi was US$605 while in Scotland it was US$27,147.[20] In other words, the average Scot was 45 times better off than the average Malawian. No wonder that Scots visiting Malawi were struck by the shocking level of poverty which blights people's lives and determined to take action to alleviate it. This positive commitment has motivated much of the current renewal in Scotland Malawi relations.

No one could question the good intentions behind the efforts to combat poverty but these can easily be undermined by two sets of dynamics. The first is that the relationship of the two countries comes to be understood within narrow economic parameters. The second is that a "Lady Bountiful" approach is adopted whereby the relationship is reduced to prosperous Scotland sharing a small part of her bounty with her impoverished old friend Malawi. The more the dynamics move in this patronising, disempowering direction, the more they undermine the relationship of mutual respect which is the key to authentic partnership. This point was deftly made at the Scotland Malawi conference in 2005 by Matthews Chikaonda when he quoted the Malawian proverb: "no one can shave your head in your absence."[21]

Despite the good intentions with which it began, the Scotland Malawi Partnership has not been able to escape from the forces which make for imbalance and inequality. The Scottish end of the partnership can perhaps be seen as a victim of its own success. The more it has established itself and extended its influence, the more the balance tilts towards concentrating energy and initiative on the Scottish side of the partnership and consequently exposing the relative weakness of the Malawi side. The strength of its delivery in mobilising a strong civil society network in Scotland has won the confidence of the Scottish Government. It benefits from the establishment of a distinct Government programme to provide "core funding for Scottish-based networking organisations". Provision of a Government grant enables a small but highly effective office to be run. Success breeds success and the Partnership enjoys growing confidence from its membership and the wider Scottish community.

By contrast, in Malawi until 2012 there was a distinct lack of resources to develop an effective hub for the Partnership. There could be no question of the commitment of members of the Malawi Board, in principle, to the idea of the Partnership, However, given the inherited weakness of civil society in Malawi and the consequent lack of a resource base from which to develop a coordinating function at the Malawi end of the Partnership, during its early years there has not been sufficient impetus to enable the Partnership to become a functional reality at the Malawi end. It has to be acknowledged that, besides the fundamental reality that Malawi is a relatively ill-resourced country in material terms, both the colonial government and the one-party regime which succeeded it systematically inhibited the development of the kind of associational life which would make for an active civil society. Even the democratic era has seen a sustained effort to concentrate power at the centre of the political system, leaving civil society very weak.[22]

This poses a serious threat to the realisation of the core vision of the Partnership. The spectre of Lord Malvern hovers over its efforts. The greater its success at the Scottish end without corresponding development at the Malawi end, the more it is likely to lapse into the patterns of paternalism and neo-colonialism from which it set out to escape. This risk is highlighted through the difficulties which the Partnership has experienced in creating a meaningful and constructive role for Malawians living in Scotland. The presence of a relatively small but nonetheless significant Malawian community in Scotland is clearly an opportunity for the development of two-way partnership. Efforts have been made to build this kind of relationship but it has to be acknowledged that, on the whole, participation of Scottish-based Malawians in the development of the Partnership has been rather limited. It seems likely that the ethos and mode of operation of the Partnership, no doubt in subtle and unintended ways, inhibits large-scale participation of Scottish-based Malawians. This is something that the Partnership is committed to address, sensing that the Malawian diaspora in Scotland may hold some of the keys to the development of an authentically reciprocal partnership.

Meanwhile, for those with the civil society partnership at heart, both in Malawi and in Scotland, it is crucial that capacity is developed on the Malawi side which is equivalent, though not necessarily identical to, that which is developing on the Scottish side. With this in view, in late 2009 the Scotland Malawi Partnership undertook an extensive consultative exercise to elicit the views of key stakeholders in Malawian civil society as to how their interaction with Scottish counterparts could better be facilitated. Over 250 organisations and individuals fed into the research, making it one of the most extensive and inclusive needs assessments of Malawian civil society ever to be conducted. The priorities identified were: better coordination and more collaboration, increased funding, capacity building, improved relationship with Malawi Government, better education, better information dissemination, better professional training, infrastructural development, more community inclusion, and better communication. In the course of the research exercise 337 requests for new civil society partnerships were received from 187 organisations or individuals, demonstrating the appetite for increased bilateral working with Scottish counterparts.[23]

After several unsuccessful attempts to secure funding to meet these aspirations, in May 2012 the Scotland Malawi Partnership was awarded a Scottish Government grant, specifically for the purpose of establishing a membership organization with a coordinating Secretariat on the Malawi side of the partnership. The vision is that this will become a hub for Malawi's involvement with Scotland, offering training, capacity-building, advocacy and coordination. It is intentional in aiming to reach far beyond the urban elite and to enable the participation of vulnerable, isolated and impoverished communities in the further development of the Malawi-Scotland relationship. The Government of Malawi is also actively exploring ways in which it can support and collaborate with the work of the Secretariat. Besides affirming the value of the Malawi-

Scotland links, the Malawi Government sees the mobilization of civic society through Malawi-Scotland connections as a strategic opportunity to help to overcome the polarization between Government and civil society which reached crisis proportions during 2011.

It is therefore expected that 2012-15 will see the emergence of a Malawi-led and Malawi-owned national umbrella organization with a diverse and broad-based membership throughout Malawi, which is able to bring together, support and add value to the great number of grassroots links between the two countries. Through events, communication and networking, the Malawi Scotland Partnership will aim to enhance and raise the profile of the bilateral way of working being pioneered by the two nations. Through regular interaction with its Scottish counterpart it will also further strengthen mutual understanding and common purpose. The first AGM of the Malawi Scotland Partnership, held in Lilongwe in June 2012, signalled the commitment of an impressive range of stake-holders to turning this vision into reality.

"A Very Definite Radicalism"

In 1961, prior to Malawi's independence, George Shepperson drew attention to the affinity between the two nations: "The predominant European culture in Nyasaland until very recent times has been Scottish: in fact, the histories of Scotland and Nyasaland pursue remarkably parallel courses. Both are poor; but both have distinctive educational traditions which have reinforced the conviction of their many migrants that they are worth better jobs than their homeland can offer them. From such conditions, there has sprung up in both countries a very definite radicalism, at home and abroad."[24]

This radicalism is now being brought to one of the great unresolved questions of our time: that of how to reverse the widening of the rich-poor divide. The unprecedented levels of prosperity being enjoyed in the Western world contrast unacceptably with the deepening levels of poverty being experienced elsewhere, in Africa in particular. For sixty years this issue has been addressed by bilateral and multilateral aid programmes, with Western Governments being challenged to devote 0.7% of their GDP to overseas aid. However, analysts are increasingly recognising the limitations of large-scale Government-to-Government aid as a lever for economic development.

Dambisa Moyo has gone so far as to argue: "More than US$2 trillion of foreign aid has been transferred from rich countries to poor over the past fifty years – Africa the biggest recipient by far. Yet regardless of the motivation for aid-giving – economic, political or moral – aid has failed to deliver the promise of sustainable economic growth and poverty reduction."[25] Moyo argues that aid creates a vicious cycle: "The cycle that chokes off desperately needed investment, instils a culture of dependency, and facilitates rampant and systematic corruption, all with deleterious consequences for growth. The cycle that, in fact, perpetuates underdevelopment, and guarantees economic failure in the poorest aid-dependent countries."[26] Whatever the merits of such an argument, it is demonstrable that large-scale aid programmes do not have all the answers when it comes to combating poverty.

Drawing on the "very definite radicalism" identified by Shepperson as characteristic of the interaction of Scotland and Malawi,[27] the two small nations have embarked on an alternative path. The robust quality of the debate and the manifest commitment to deepen mutual understanding, apparent e.g. at the 2005 Scotland Malawi Conference, suggests that the relationship will run on different lines from the donor-client pattern familiar in the world of international aid. The conference was radical it its willingness to question received wisdom and to open up new lines of analysis. A significant lead in this regard was offered by Thandika Mkandawire who noted that the standard approach to development is the *quid pro quo* that the West offers aid provided that the recipient Governments adopt the "good policies" and "good governance" promoted by the Washington consensus. He then went on to ask "what if those policies and institutions being promoted as "good" are in fact the wrong ones, or simply not feasible at the current levels of development?"[28] The renewal of the Scotland Malawi relationship therefore began with some fundamental questioning of received wisdom and an openness to innovative approaches.

By way of response during the years from 2005 to 2010 Scotland and Malawi together forged an alternative model of international development. The Scotland Malawi Partnership has indicated that it: "promotes a people-to-people model of development, rooted in the shared history between our two countries. It focuses on active relationships between people to foster a shared understanding of the development challenges facing Malawi and to support the development of practical, sustainable solutions. It is through this deeper understanding and shared human experience that the people of Scotland and Malawi will be able to effect real and lasting change, both through their own activity and by influencing the policies and actions of governments and institutions."[29] Distinctive features of this new model include:

Ordinary people and local communities are mobilised to offer their time, energy, resources, experience and expertise to Scotland and Malawi's shared effort. This is not to usurp the role of development professionals but it is to place their work in the context of strong popular ownership and involvement.

It draws on democratic and communitarian traditions both in Scotland and Malawi to move away from hierarchical and top-down approaches in favour of working from below. It represents a vote of confidence in the people and in their capacity for active participation in the close relationship between two nations committed to working together for the common good.

It engages extreme poverty, the great moral challenge of our time, not as an array of statistics or TV footage of crisis situations, but by coming alongside in a spirit of mutual respect, forming friendships and working together practically and purposefully.

It is comprehensive and multi-sectoral, promoting mutually beneficial interaction which ranges from national Parliaments in capital cities to primary schools in remote areas. This gives it a capacity to address such pressing issues as healthcare or gender or climate change by drawing on a very wide range of perspectives and contributions.

It is committed for the long term. With already one hundred and fifty years of history behind it, the partnership is informed and inspired by challenges which have been met in earlier years. While particular projects may be time-limited, the underlying relationship will continue, drawing on the cumulative benefit of ever-growing mutual understanding.

It creates a virtuous circle between Government and people where popular support inspires Government efforts while Government support stimulates popular engagement. The result is that resources committed by Government are multiplied many times over by institutions and individuals within civil society.

While the Partnership is currently driven by the urgency of tackling the crippling poverty faced by many in Malawi, it also recognises that no society is as developed as it might be. By drawing on each other's culture, history and spirit, the two nations are able to strengthen one another in the quest for human flourishing. Reciprocity is foundational to this way of working.

The Partnership works on a basis of collaboration and networking. At both ends of the relationship a membership-based charitable company, working from a very modest resource base, acts as the catalyst for an ever expanding and maturing engagement between the people of the two nations.

Malawians are cooking partnership in their own distinctive way

As an alternative model of international development the endeavour shared between Scotland and Malawi is a work in progress. The model outlined above has been formed through hands-on experience and the learning experience continues. Already, however, it is proving strong enough to inspire tens of thousands of people to commit themselves to its outworking. Not only does it create confidence that it can change Scotland and Malawi for the better but it emerges as a model which can be commended for wider application.

Conclusion

The distinctive genius of the Scotland Malawi relationship is its grounding in the friendship – both individual and institutional – which has built up between the two nations over the past 150 years. Though the language of friendship and "auld alliance" is often used by politicians and diplomats to characterise the relationship of two countries, it is rare that this is so deeply grounded in the genuine affection and practical activism of ordinary citizens. Adjoa Anyimadu notes that: "Senior UK diplomatic officials have pointed to the focus on relationship-building as a factor which makes Scotland's involvement with Malawi stand out from that of other donors."[30]

It creates a unique kind of drive by uniting the great variety of organisations and individuals which operate bilaterally between the two nations. Benefits flow in both directions and a cumulative effect is built up, where good experiences inspire further initiatives. Only after a longer time will it be possible to assess the effects of this model of interaction on both Malawi and Scotland. Nonetheless, at this early stage it can be demonstrated both that a distinctive new model has been developed and that it is having an energising and inspiring effect both in Scotland and in Malawi. It champions the principle once stated by David Clement Scott, who did so much at an early stage to pioneer Scotland Malawi relations: "Mutual respect is the lesson we so much need to learn at this time."[31]

---

[1]   See http://www.strath.ac.uk/projects/malawi

[2]   "The Scotland/Malawi Partnership: The Warm Heart of Scotland / The Warm Heart of Africa", circular letter from Liz Cameron, Lord Provost of Glasgow, and Lesley Hinds, Lord Provost of Edinburgh, 29 March 2004.

[3]   *Scotland Malawi Partnership Strategic Plan 2008-11*, Edinburgh: Scotland Malawi Partnership, 2008, p. 3.

[4]   Cooperation Agreement between Scotland and Malawi, November 2005, "Malawi After Gleneagles: A Commission for Africa Case Study", Report of the Scotland Malawi Partnership Conference, November 2005, pp. 5-6, see http://www.Scotland Malawipartnership.org – my italics.

[5]   Scottish Executive News Release, 4 November 2005.

[6]   Adjoa Anyimadu, *Scotland and Wales in Africa: Opportunities for a Coordinated UK Approach to Development*, Africa Programme Paper: AFP PP 2011/02, London: Chatham House, 2011, p. 8.

[7]   Register of Cross-Party Groups, Scottish Parliament.

[8]   The Scottish Parliament, Official Report 17 September 2008, pp. 35-36.

[9]   As Malcolm Chisolm, Chair of the Europe and External Affairs Committee, summarised: "It was clear throughout the inquiry that there is substantial support across Scotland for building on our links with Malawi." *Ibid*, p. 15.

[10]   Peter A. West & Kenneth R. Ross, "Foreword", *Scotland Malawi Partnership Strategic Plan 2008-11*, Edinburgh: Scotland Malawi Partnership, 2008, p. 2.

[11]   Lawrence Dritsas, "Valuing Scotland's Links with Malawi: Inputs from Scotland Malawi Partnership Members", University of Edinburgh School of Social and Political Science and Global Development Academy, October 2010, p. 5.

[12]   Dritsas, "Valuing Scotland's Links with Malawi", p. 7.

[13]   *Church of Scotland General Assembly 2001, Report of the Special Commission anent Review and Reform,* Edinburgh: Church of Scotland, 2001, p. 36/5.

[14]   Church of Scotland General Assembly 2007, authorised recording of proceedings on 21 May 2007.

[15]   *Schools Partnership Guide*, Edinburgh: Scotland Malawi Partnership, 2007, p. 2.

[16]   *Ibid*, p. 9.

[17]   The Scottish Parliament, Official Report 17 September 2008, p. 25.

[18] Confidential Print, Commonwealth Relations office for Central Africa Office, 19 February 1964, cit. Power, *Political Culture and Nationalism in Malawi*, p. 57.

[19] See "Malawi After Gleneagles".

[20] *International Cooperation at a Crossroads: Aid, Trade and Security in an Unequal World*, United Nations Development Programme Report 2005, New York: UNDP, 2005.

[21] "Malawi After Gleneagles", p. 104.

[22] See further Kenneth R. Ross, *Here Comes Your King! Christ, Church and Nation in Malawi*, Blantyre: CLAIM, 1998, pp. 168-71.

[23] *Civil Society Research Exercise*, Edinburgh: Scotland Malawi Partnership, 2010, pp. 7-8.

[24] George A. Shepperson, "External Factors in the Development of African Nationalism, with Particular Reference to British Central Africa", *Phylon: The Atlanta University Review of Race and Culture*, Vol. XXII/3 (1961), pp. 207-28 at p. 212.

[25] Dambisa Moyo, *Dead Aid: Why Aid Is Not Working and How There is Another Way for Africa*, London: Allen Lane, 2009, p. 28.

[26] *Ibid.*, p. 49.

[27] Shepperson, "External Factors", p. 212.

[28] "Malawi After Gleneagles", p. 35.

[29] *Scotland Malawi Partnership Strategic Plan 2011-2014*, Edinburgh: Scotland Malawi Partnership, 2011, p. 3.

[30] Anyimadu, *Scotland and Wales in Africa*, p. 16.

[31] *LWBCA*, December 1897.

12. Conclusion: The Conversation Continues

Malawi's first President, Kamuzu Banda, used to say to visiting Scottish Moderators: "Had there been no Church of Scotland there would have been no Malawi."[1] From the arrival of David Livingstone, through the establishment of the Scottish Missions, through the resistance to Portuguese and Arab ambitions, through the struggle against the Federation of Rhodesia and Nyasaland, through the attainment of independence, through to Malawi's struggles of more recent times – at every turning point in history the Scottish dimension has been important for Malawi.

Less frequently recognised is the fact that Scotland too has been influenced across one hundred and fifty years by its connection with Malawi. In particular, the Malawi dimension has fostered a sense of distinct Scottish identity, not least at times when this was in some jeopardy. The failure of the Darien scheme cast a long shadow across Scottish history. With Malawi came the opportunity to wield influence in another part of the world, this time not simply with a view to commercial advantage but with high ideals of human freedom and dignity. It was fitting that when the Scottish Parliament reconvened in 1999, after an interval of almost three hundred years, the first foreign Head of State to address it was Bakili Muluzi, President of Malawi. The African nation has played an important role in fostering national consciousness in Scotland and in nurturing an outward-looking national identity.

In both nations an appeal to their shared history in the life and work of David Livingstone can be guaranteed to evoke a strong response. The scenes at Kamuzu Stadium in Blantyre in 2009 when Malawians celebrated the 150th anniversary of Livingstone's arrival in their country, described in Chapter 2, demonstrate how powerful this memory remains in the early 21st century. In Scotland too it should not be underestimated. Reflecting on the definitive event of the 1959 Church of Scotland General Assembly, John McCracken remarks: "No one single factor can explain why in 1959 the Church of Scotland intervened so actively on the side of Malawian nationalists. One reason appears to be historical: the belief that Scotland had a special responsibility for the Nyasaland Protectorate as a result of the connection with Livingstone."[2] This belief was evoked again in 2004-05 when a new round of Scottish solidarity with Malawi was launched.

All through this history a major challenge for all involved has been the level of poverty prevailing in Malawi. It was apparent during the colonial period that Nyasaland was, in economic terms, one of the weakest of Britain's many colonies. The landlocked situation and lack of mineral wealth which impeded economic development in colonial times has continued to bedevil post-independence efforts to achieve prosperity. Overcoming the poverty which blights the lives of too many of Malawi's citizens remains the priority issue whenever Malawians and Scots meet, talk and plan. Nonetheless, the relationship of the two nations is marked by a mutual respect which transcends a shocking disparity in living standards and inspires efforts to resolve it.

This mutual respect has found expression in three main features of the relationship between the two nations: the struggle for justice, the sharing of faith and the experience of friendship.

The relationship was born in a struggle for justice – namely David Livingstone's passionate opposition to the slave trade. This inspired the Scots who followed in his wake, including those who established the Livingstonia and Blantyre Missions in the 1870s, those who fought Mlozi in the "Arab Wars" of the 1880s, and those who proved to be a thorn in the side of the British Administration during the 1890s. It marked Malawi apart from the territories south of the Zambesi where racist white-dominated regimes came to hold sway. It continued to inspire the Scottish connection with Malawi and came to fruition in the struggle to overcome the Federation of Rhodesia and Nyasaland during the 1950s. Scots played a significant role in the attainment of independence and in the struggles occasioned by the dictatorship which followed. They gave significant support to the movement which brought multi-party democracy to Malawi. They continue to be actively engaged in the struggles for justice which have marked the democratic dispensation in Malawi.

At the same time the Malawi connection has played a significant part in the development of Scotland as a responsible nation. The strength of commitment to Malawi which has been evident socially and politically during the first decade of the 21st century reveals an important aspect of Scottish identity. Scotland's pursuit of social justice is not entirely a domestic matter but also marks its engagement with the wider world. The Malawi connection has been important in ensuring that devolution does not lapse into parochialism but that, on the contrary, the nation is re-energised to play its part in working for justice on a global scale.

Secondly, it is apparent that the relationship of the two nations has been marked by an experience of sharing at the level of faith. Given the strength of religion in Malawi and the fact that the Scottish connection in its early years was developed, to a great extent, by Christian missionaries, there has inevitably been a strong faith dimension to the relationship. This is seen most obviously in the fact that the Presbyterianism which represents a distinctively Scottish appropriation of Christianity has taken root in Malawi to such an extent that the membership of the Church of Central African Presbyterian today greatly outnumbers the membership of the Church of Scotland. It is apparent that there has been something of a reversal so that it is now in Malawi rather than in Scotland that there is more evidence of the vitality of the Christian faith. Church life, however, continues to be an important point of connection and sharing at the level of faith continues to bring depth and texture to the relationship. In recent times, partnership working between Islamic institutions in Malawi and Scotland has added a further dimension.

Thirdly, perhaps the most simple and yet the most profound characteristic of the relationship of the two nations is that it has been marked by friendship at the personal level. After analysing the involvement of Scottish missionaries in the 1959 state of emergency and subsequent drive for independence, John McCracken concludes that: "At a personal level the most remarkable feature of the period was the extent to which friendships forged between black and white Christians during the years of the emergency remained unbroken by the political disturbances that followed. Activist missionaries whose lives had been disrupted by the cabinet crisis ... retained an active involvement with Malawi that reached fruition in the early 1990s, when several of them were able to return."[3]

One of them was Andrew Ross who, during the last years of his life in the late 20th and early 21st century, liked to recall a conversation he had in Ndirande, as a young man in 1960, which had linked him with the early beginning of Scottish involvement in Malawi. He was speaking to a very old lady, Mrs Likagwa, who had been baptised at Blantyre by David Clement Scott in the late 19th century. Slightly confused in her old age she turned to Andrew and asked, "*Wokondewa wathu, dotoro Scott, ali bwanji masiku ano?*" ("Our beloved Dr Scott, how is he keeping these days?")[4] Scott, of course, was long dead but the warmth of affection lived on.

Such a subjective matter as personal friendship is difficult to quantify or evaluate but there is no doubt that many Malawians and Scots have drawn inspiration from the warmth of human affection they have experienced. Among them is David Rubadiri, described by George Macleod as the most brilliant man he met during his year as Moderator of the General Assembly of the Church of Scotland in 1958-59, who remarked that:

> Malawi is very much a Scottish country because of the early presence of the Scots Mission here.... Malawi is a Scotsman's country. The friends that we knew and lived with are people who, though they've retired back in Scotland, are people who are in spirit with us here. I know it doesn't make sense to put it that way, [but] what I'm saying is that when you have lived and experienced at a spiritual and human level, human issues and problems being asked and answered, those you've experienced all those questions and answers with never leave! So though I know that they are in Scotland, each time I move around Malawi, I feel them around ... because they are part and parcel of a great experience.[5]

It is the quality identified by Rubadiri which perhaps does most to make the relationship between Malawi and Scotland something quite distinctive. Many years earlier Cullen Young had learned the lesson that: "The cry in Africa ... is for the feel of human relationships and comradely activities at all costs, even if great schemes for political or educational or economic amelioration seem to be pushed into an inferior place."[6] Scots who have responded to that call have found their lives immeasurably enriched as a result.

When President Bingu wa Mutharika visited Scotland in 2005 to sign the Scotland-Malawi Cooperation Agreement, there was a moment of consternation when he was expected at the Scottish Parliament but appeared to have gone missing. Soon, however, it was discovered that a priority matter for the President had been to call on his old Sunday School teacher Dr Gwen Dabb, a long-serving medical missionary with the Blantyre Mission now retired in Edinburgh and coming towards the end of her life. Out of such cherished personal connections the distinctive relationship between the two nations has been built.

This brief set of edited highlights has now reached its conclusion. There is much more that should be said. There are many memories still to be retrieved. More importantly, there are new chapters still to be written as a new generation of Malawians and Scots work out how the distinctive relationship between their two nations can be a force for good in meeting the challenges of the 21st century. As they do so, the rich history of the interaction of their two nations during the first one hundred and fifty years forms a resource on which they will always be able to draw.

---

[1] The remark was made to Rt Revd John R. Gray in 1977 and to Rt Revd William McDonald in 1989. Hamish McIntosh, *Robert Laws: Servant of Africa*, Edinburgh: Handsel Press & Blantyre: Central Africana, 1993, p. 244.

[2] John McCracken, "Missionaries and Nationalists: Scotland and the 1959 State of Emergency in Malawi", in Afe Adogame and Andrew Lawrence ed., *Scotland and Africa*, Leiden: E.J. Brill, forthcoming.

[3] John McCracken, "Missionaries and Nationalists".

[4] Ross, "The Mzungu Who Mattered", p. 7.

[5] Cit. Billy Kay, *The Scottish World: A Journey into the Scottish Diaspora*, Edinburgh & London, Mainstream, 2006, p. 205.

[6] Young, *African Ways and Wisdom*, p. 40.

Bibliography

Primary Sources

Archives

Church of Scotland Files
Malawi Collection, Chancellor College, University of Malawi
Malawi National Archives, Zomba
National Library of Scotland, Edinburgh
Scotland Malawi Partnership Files
Scottish Parliament Records
University of Edinburgh Library Special Collections

Newspapers and Periodicals

Aurora
Central Africa News and Views
Central African Times
Life and Work in British Central Africa
Other Lands
The Glasgow Herald
The Nyasaland Journal, later The Society of Malawi Journal
The Scotsman
United Free Church of Scotland Monthly Record

Secondary Sources

"An African" [Levi Mumba], "The Religion of my Fathers", *International Review of Missions*, Vol. 19 (1930), pp. 362-71.
Anyimadu, Adjoa, *Scotland and Wales in Africa: Opportunities for a Coordinated UK Approach to Development*, Africa Programme Paper: AFP PP 2011/02, London: Chatham House, 2011.
Ascherson, Neal, *Stone Voices: The Search for Scotland*, London: Granta Books, 2002.
Ascherson, Neal, "The Money's Still Out There", *London Review of Books*, Vol. 33 No. 19 (6 October 2011).

Banda, Hastings K., "The Moirs of Nyasaland: An African's Tribute", *Other Lands*, July 1940, pp. 144-45.

Breitenbach, Esther, *Empire and Scottish Society: The Impact of Foreign Missions at Home c. 1790 to c. 1914*, Edinburgh: Edinburgh University Press, 2009.

Buchanan, John, *The Shire Highlands (East Central Africa) as Colony and Mission*, Edinburgh and London: William Blackwood, 1885.

Calder, Angus, *Scotlands of the Mind*, Edinburgh: Luath Press, 2002.

Chadwick, Owen, *Mackenzie's Grave*, London: Hodder & Stoughton, 1959.

Chibambo, Y.M., *My Ngoni of Nyasaland*, London: United Society for Christian Literature, 1942.

Chirnside, A., *The Blantyre Missionaries: Discreditable Disclosures*, London: Ridgeway, 1880.

Chirwa, Vera, *Fearless Fighter: An Autobiography*, London & New York: Zed Books, 2007.

Cole-King, P.A., "Transport and Communications in Malawi", University of Malawi, Conference on the Early History of Malawi, 20-24 July 1970.

Collier, Paul, *The Bottom Billion: Why the Poorest Countries Are Failing and What Can Be Done About It*, Oxford: Oxford University Press, 2007.

Devine, T.M., *To the Ends of the Earth: Scotland's Global Diaspora*, London: Allen Lane, 2011.

Doig, Andrew B., *It's People That Count*, Edinburgh: The Pentland Press, 1997.

Doig, Andrew B., *Nyasaland: Partnership in the Church*, Edinburgh: Church of Scotland Foreign Mission Committee, 1959.

Doke, C.M., "The Linguistic Work and Manuscripts of R.D. McMinn", *African Studies*, Vol. 18 (1959), pp. 180-89.

Dritsas, Lawrence, "Valuing Scotland's Links with Malawi: Inputs from Scotland Malawi Partnership Members", University of Edinburgh School of Social and Political Science and Global Development Academy, October 2010.

Elmslie, W.A., *Among the Wild Ngoni*, Edinburgh: Oliphant, Anderson & Ferrier, 1899.

Faulds, M.H., "An African Family Altar", *Other Lands*, July 1930, pp. 134-35.

Ferguson, Ronald, *George MacLeod: Founder of the Iona Community*, London: Collins, 1990.

Finlay, Richard J., "National Identity, Union and Empire, c.1850 – c.1970", in John M. Mackenzie and T.M. Devine ed., *Scotland and the British Empire*, Oxford: Oxford University Press, 2011, pp. 280-316.

Forster, Peter G., *T. Cullen Young: Missionary and Anthropologist*, Hull: Hull University Press, 1989.

Fraser, Donald, *The Autobiography of an African*, London: Seeley, 1925.

Fraser, Donald, *The Future of Africa*, Edinburgh: The Foreign Mission Committee of the Church of Scotland and the Mission Study Council of the United Free Church of Scotland, 1911.

Fraser, Donald, *The New Africa*, London: Edinburgh House Press, 1927.

Green, Stephen, "Blantyre Mission", *The Nyasaland Journal*, Vol. X No. 2 (July 1957), pp. 6-17.

Hargreaves, John D., *Aberdeenshire to Africa: Northeast Scots and British Overseas Expansion*, Aberdeen: Aberdeen University Press, 1981.

Hargreaves, John D., *Decolonization in Africa*, London & New York: Longman, 1988.

Hepburn, Anne, *Memories of Malawi and Scotland*, Edinburgh: privately published, 2011.

Hetherwick, A., "Livingstone's Makololo: Pioneers of Empire before Cecil Rhodes", *Other Lands*, April 1935, pp. 115-16.

Hetherwick, Alexander, *The Romance of Blantyre: How Livingstone's Dream Came True*, London: James Clarke, n.d.

Hokkanen, Markku and J.A. Mangan, "Further Variations on a Theme: The Games Ethic Further Adapted – Scottish Moral Missionaries and Muscular Christians in Malawi" in *The International Journal of the History of Sport*, Vol. 23 No. 8 (December 2006), pp. 1257-74.

Iliffe, John, *Africans: the History of a Continent*, Cambridge: Cambridge University Press, 1995.

International Cooperation at a Crossroads: Aid, Trade and Security in an Unequal World, United Nations Development Programme Report 2005, New York: UNDP, 2005.

Jack, James W., *Daybreak in Livingstonia: The Story of the Livingstonia Mission, British Central Africa*, Edinburgh & London: Oliphant, Anderson & Ferrier, 1900.

Jackson, William M., *Send Us Friends*, privately published, no date.

Jones, Griff, *Britain and Nyasaland*, London: Allen and Unwin, 1964.

Kadalie, Clements, *My Life with the ICU*, London, 1970.

Kay, Billy, *The Scottish World: A Journey into the Scottish Diaspora*, Edinburgh & London, Mainstream, 2006.

Keatley, Patrick, *The Politics of Partnership*, Harmondsworth: Penguin, 1963.

Krishnamurthy, B.S., "Aspects of Land and Labour Policies in Malawi 1890-1914", University of Malawi, Conference on the Early History of Malawi, 20-24 July 1970.

Leslie, M.E., "Pitgaveny, 1899-1905", *The Nyasaland Journal*, Vol. 4 No. 1 (January 1951), pp. 40-53.

Livingstone, David, *Missionary Travels and Researches in South Africa*, New York: Harper & Bros., 1858.

Livingstone, David and Charles, *Narrative of an Expedition to the Zambesi and its Tributaries; and of the Discovery of the Lakes Shirwa and Nyassa*, London: John Murray, 1865.

Livingstone, W.P., *A Prince of Missionaries: Alexander Hetherwick*, London: James Clarke, n.d.

Livingstone, W.P., *Laws of Livingstonia: A Narrative of Missionary Adventure and Achievement*, London: Hodder & Stoughton, 1921.

Lwanda, John L.C., *Promises, Power, Politics and Poverty: Democratic Transition in Malawi (1961-1999)*, Glasgow: Dudu Nsomba, 1996.

Matecheta, H.K., *Blantyre Mission: Nkani ya Ciyambi Cace*, Blantyre: Hetherwick Press, 1951.

McCarthy James ed., *The Road to Tanganyika: The Diaries of Donald Munro and William McEwan*, Zomba: Kachere, 2006.

McCracken, John, *A History of Malawi 1859-1966*, Rochester NY: James Currey, 2012.

McCracken, John, "Church and State in Malawi: The Church and the Role of the Scottish Presbyterian Missions, 1875-1964", in Isabel Phiri, Kenneth Ross and James Cox ed., *The Role of Christianity in Development, Peace and Reconstruction: Southern Perspectives*, Nairobi: All Africa Conference of Churches, 1996, pp. 48-73.

McCracken, John, "Church and State in Malawi: The Role of the Scottish Presbyterian Missions 1875-1965", in Holger Bernt Hansen & Michael Twaddle ed., *Christian Missionaries and the State in the Third World*, Oxford: James Currey & Athens: Ohio University Press, 2002, pp. 176-193.

McCracken, John, "Livingstone and the Aftermath: the Origins and Development of Livingstonia Mission", in Bridglal Pachai ed., *Livingstone: Man of Africa*, London: Longman, 1973, pp. 218-34.

McCracken, John, "Missionaries and Nationalists: Scotland and the 1959 State of Emergency in Malawi", in Afe Adogame and Andrew Lawrence ed., *Scotland and Africa*, Leiden: E.J. Brill, forthcoming.

McCracken, John, "Mungo Murray Chisuse and the Early History of Photography in Malawi", *The Society of Malawi Journal*, Vol. 61 No. 2 (2008), pp. 1-18.

McCracken, John, *Politics and Christianity in Malawi 1875-1940: The Impact of the Livingstonia Mission in the Northern Province*, 2nd ed., Blantyre: CLAIM, 2000.

Macdonald, Duff, *Africana*, Vols. I & II, London: Simpkin Marshall & Co, 1882; repr. New York: Negro Universities Press, 1969.

Macdonald, Roderick J., "A History of African Education in Nyasaland 1875-1945", Ph.D., University of Edinburgh, 1969.

McIntosh, Hamish, *Robert Laws: Servant of Africa*, Edinburgh: Handsel Press & Blantyre: Central Africana, 1993.

Mackay, Peter, *We Have Tomorrow: Stirrings in Africa 1959-1967*, Norwich: Michael Russell, 2008.

Mackenzie, John M. and T.M. Devine ed., *Scotland and the British Empire*, Oxford: Oxford University Press, 2011.

Mackenzie, John M. with Nigel R. Dalziel, *The Scots in South Africa: Ethnicity, Identity, Gender and Race, 1772-1914*, Manchester and New York: Manchester University Press, 2007.

Macmillan, H.W., "The Origins and Development of the African Lakes Company 1878-1908", PhD, University of Edinburgh 1970.

MacNair, James L., *The Story of the Scottish National Memorial to David Livingstone*, Blantyre: Scottish National Memorial to David Livingstone Trust, n.d.

Macpherson, Fergus, *North of the Zambezi: A Modern Missionary Memoir*, Edinburgh: The Handsel Press, 1998.

Mapanje, Jack, *And Crocodiles are Hungry at Night*, Banbury: Ayebia, 2011.

Moir, Fred L.M., *After Livingstone: An African Trade Romance*, London: Hodder & Stoughton, n.d.

Morrow, Sean, "'War Came from the Boma' Military and Police Disturbances in Blantyre, 1902", *The Society of Malawi Journal*, Vol. 41 No. 2 (1988), pp. 16-29.

Moyo, Dambisa, *Dead Aid: Why Aid Is Not Working and How There is Another Way for Africa*, London: Allen Lane, 2009.

Mphande, Lupenga, "Dr Hastings Kamuzu Banda and the Malawi Writers Group: The (un)Making of a Cultural Tradition", *Research in African Literatures*, Vol. 27/1 (Spring 1996), pp. 80-101.

Msiska, Stephen Kauta, *Golden Buttons: Christianity and Traditional Religion among the Tumbuka*, Blantyre: CLAIM, 1997.

Mufuka, K. Nyamayaro, *Missions and Politics in Malawi*, Kingston, Ontario: The Limestone Press, 1977.

Mushindo, Paul Bwembya, *The Life of an African Evangelist*, Lusaka: University of Zambia Institute of African Studies, Communication No. 9, 1973.

Mwasi, Yesaya Zerenji, *My Essential and Paramount Reasons for Working Independently,* Blantyre: CLAIM, 1999; original manuscript 12 July 1933.

Newell, Jonathan, "'Not War but Defence of the Oppressed'? Bishop Mackenzie's Skirmishes with the Yao in 1861", in Kenneth R. Ross ed., *Faith at the Frontiers of Knowledge*, Blantyre: CLAIM, 1998, pp. 129-43.

Norman, L.S., *Nyasaland without Prejudice*, London: East Africa, 1934.

Ntara, S.Y., *Headman's Enterprise*, London: United Society for Christian Literature, 1949.

Ntara, Samuel Yosia, *Man of Africa*, translated and arranged from the original Nyanja by T. Cullen Young, London: United Society for Christian Literature, 1934.

Nyirenda, Saulos, "A History of the Tumbuka-Henga People", translated and edited by T. Cullen Young, *Bantu Studies* Vol. 5 (1931), pp. 1-75.

Oliver, Roland, *The African Experience*, London: Weidenfeld and Nicolson, 1991.

Pachai, Bridglal, *Land and Politics in Malawi 1875-1975*, Kingston, Ontario: The Limestone Press, 1978.

Pachai, Bridglal ed., *Livingstone: Man of Africa*, London: Longman, 1973.

Pachai, Bridglal, *Malawi: The History of the Nation*, London: Longman, 1973.

Page, Melvin Eugene, "Malawians in the Great War and After, 1914-1925", Ph.D., Michigan State University, 1977.

Parsons, Janet Wagner, "Scots and Afrikaners in Central Africa: Andrew Charles Murray and the Dutch Reformed Church Mission in Malawi", *The Society of Malawi Journal*, Vol. 51 No. 1 (1998), pp. 21-40.

Phiri, D.D., *Charles Chidongo Chinula*, London: Longman, 1975.

Power, Joey, *Political Culture and Nationalism in Malawi: Building Kwacha*, New York: University of Rochester Press, 2010.

Proctor, J.H., "The Church of Scotland and British Colonialism in Africa", *Journal of Church and State*, Vol. 29 (Autumn 1987), pp. 475-93.

Ransford, Arthur, *David Livingstone: The Dark Interior*, London: John Murray, 1978.

Reid, I.E., "Myth and Reality of the Missionary Family: A Study of the Letters of Rev. J.R. (Jack) Martin and His Wife, Mary Evelyn (Mamie) Written from Livingstonia Mission, Malawi, 1921-28, with Particular Emphasis on the Position of Missionary Wives", M.Th., University of Edinburgh, 1999.

Robert, Dana L., *Christian Mission: How Christianity Became a World Religion*, Oxford: Wiley-Blackwell, 2009.

Rodgers, James, "Emigrant Labour", *Central Africa News and Views*, Vol. 1 No. 4 (April 1936).

Rodgers, J.A., "Safeguarding Native Interests in Federation", *Central Africa News and Views*, Vol. 1 No. 2 (October 1935).

Ross, Andrew C., *Blantyre Mission and the Making of Modern Malawi*, Blantyre: CLAIM, 1996.

Ross, Andrew C., *Colonialism to Cabinet Crisis: A Political History of Malawi*, Zomba: Kachere, 2009.

Ross, Andrew C., *David Livingstone: Mission and Empire*, London & New York: Hambledon & London, 2002.

Ross, Andrew C., *John Philip: Missions, Race, and Politics in South Africa*, Aberdeen: Aberdeen University Press, 1986.

Ross, Andrew C., "Livingstone and the Aftermath: The Origins and Development of the Blantyre Mission", in Bridglal Pachai ed., *Livingstone: Man of Africa*, London: Longman, 1973, pp. 191-217.

Ross, Andrew C., "Livingstone, David", in Daniel Patte ed., *The Cambridge Dictionary of Christianity*, Cambridge: Cambridge University Press, 2010, p. 736.

Ross, Andrew C., "Scotland and Malawi 1859-1964", in Stewart J. Brown & George Newlands ed., *Scottish Christianity in the Modern World*, Edinburgh: T. & T. Clark, 2000, pp. 283-309.

Ross, Andrew C., "Some Reflections on the Malawi 'Cabinet Crisis' 1964-65", *Religion in Malawi*, No. 7 (November 1997), pp. 3-12.

Ross, Andrew C., "The African – 'A Child or a Man'; - the quarrel between the Blantyre Mission of the Church of Scotland and the British Central Africa Administration, 1890-1905", in Eric Stokes and Richard Brown ed., *The Zambesian Past: Studies in Central African History*, Manchester: Manchester University Press, 1966, pp. 332-51.

Ross, Andrew C., "The Kirk and Colonial Policy 1864-1964" in James Kirk ed. *The Scottish Churches and the Union Parliament 1707-1999*, Edinburgh: Scottish Church History Society, 2001, pp. 125-160.

Ross, Andrew C., "The Mzungu Who Mattered", *Religion in Malawi*, Vol. 8 (1998), pp. 3-7.

Ross, Kenneth R. ed., *Christianity in Malawi: A Sourcebook*, Gweru: Mambo Press, 1996.

Ross, Kenneth R., *Gospel Ferment in Malawi: Theological Essays*, Gweru: Mambo Press, 1995.

Ross, Kenneth R., *Here Comes Your King! Christ, Church and Nation in Malawi*, Blantyre: CLAIM, 1998.

Ross, Kenneth R., "Malawi's Peaceful Revolution 1992-94: the Role of the Church of Scotland", *Scottish Church History Society Records*, Vol. XXVII (1997), pp. 280-304.

Sanneh, Lamin, *Translating the Message: the Missionary Impact on Culture*, Maryknoll NY: Orbis, 1989.

Schoffeleers, J.M. "Livingstone and the Mang'anja Chiefs", in Bridglal Pachai, *Livingstone: Man of Africa*, London: Longman, 1973, pp. 111-30.

Schools Partnership Guide, Edinburgh: Scotland Malawi Partnership, 2007.

Scotland Malawi Partnership Strategic Plan 2008-11, Edinburgh: Scotland Malawi Partnership, 2008.

Scotland Malawi Partnership Strategic Plan 2011-2014, Edinburgh: Scotland Malawi Partnership, 2011.

Scott, D.C., *A Cyclopaedic Dictionary of the Mang'anja Language*, Edinburgh: Foreign Missions Committee of the Church of Scotland, 1892.

Shepperson, George A., "External Factors in the Development of African Nationalism, with Particular Reference to British Central Africa", *Phylon: The Atlanta University Review of Race and Culture*, Vol. XXII/3 (1961), pp. 207-28.

Shepperson, George, "Malawi and the Poetry of Two World Wars", *The Society of Malawi Journal*, Vol. 53 No. 1 (2000), pp. 144-45.

Shepperson, George, *Myth and Reality in Malawi*, Evanston: Northwestern University Press, 1966.

Shepperson, George, "Thomas Price (1907-1988): A Tribute", *The Society of Malawi Journal*, Vol. 49 No. 1 (1996), pp. 77-82.

Shepperson, George and Thomas Price, *Independent African: John Chilembwe and the Origins, Setting and Significance of the Nyasaland Native Rising of 1915*, Edinburgh: Edinburgh University Press, 1958; repr. Blantyre: CLAIM, 2000.

Short, Philip, *Banda*, London and Boston: Routledge & Kegan Paul, 1974.

Sinclair, Margaret ed., *Salt and Light: The Letters of Mamie and Jack Martin from Malawi (1921-1928)*, Blantyre: CLAIM, 2002.

Sindima, Harvey J., T*he Legacy of Scottish Missionaries in Malawi*, Lewiston /Lampeter/Queenston: Edwin Mellen Press, 1992.

Smith, George, *Life of Alexander Duff*, London: Hodder & Stoughton, 1899.

Stahl, Karolin, "Some Notes on the Development of Zomba", *The Society of Malawi Journal*, Vol. 63 No. 2 (2010), pp. 39-55.

Stuart, John, *British Missionaries and the End of Empire: East, Central and Southern Africa, 1939-64*, Grand Rapids and Cambridge: Eerdmans, 2011.

Stuart, John, "Scottish Missionaries and the End of Empire: the Case of Nyasaland", *Historical Research*, Vol. 76 (August 2003), pp. 411-30.

Thompson, T. Jack, "Breaking Down the Barriers: Unity and Tension at Livingstonia in 1959", in Kings Phiri, John McCracken and Wapu Mulwafu eds., *Crisis in Malawi: the Nyasaland State of Emergency, 1959-60 and its Legacy*, Zomba: Kachere, forthcoming.

Thompson, T. Jack, *Christianity in Northern Malawi: Donald Fraser's Missionary Methods and Ngoni Culture*, Leiden: E.J. Brill, 1995.

Thompson, T. Jack ed., *From Nyassa to Tanganyika: The Journal of James Stewart CE in Central Africa 1876-1879*, Blantyre: Central Africana, 1989.

Thompson, Jack, *Ngoni, Xhosa and Scot: Religious and Cultural Interaction in Malawi*, Zomba: Kachere, 2007.

Thompson, Jack, "Remembering the Past, Celebrating the Present: the Centenary of Loudon Mission, November 2002", *The Society of Malawi Journal*, Vol. 56 No. 1 (2003), pp. 24-32.

Thompson, T. Jack, *Touching the Heart: Xhosa Missionaries to Malawi, 1876-1888*, Pretoria: University of South Africa, 2000.

von Prince, Tom, *Gegen Araber und Wahebe: Erinnerungen aus meiner ostafrikanischen Leutnantszeit 1890-1895*, Berlin, 1914.

Walker, Graham, "Empire, Religion and Nationality in Scotland and Ulster before the First World War", in Ian S. Wood ed., *Scotland and Ulster*, Edinburgh: Mercat Press, 1994, pp. 97-115.

Walls, Andrew F., "David Livingstone 1813-1873: Awakening the Western World to Africa", in Gerald H. Anderson et al. ed., *Mission Legacies: Biographical Studies of Leaders of the Modern Missionary Movement*, Maryknoll NY: Orbis Books, 1994, pp. 140-47.

Wilson, G.H., *The History of the Universities Mission to Central Africa*, London: UMCA, 1936.

Wood, J.R.T., *The Welensky Papers*, Durban, 1983.

Young, T. Cullen and Hastings Banda ed., *Our African Way of Life*, London: United Society for Christian Literature, 1946.

Young, T. Cullen, "End of an Era at Livingstonia: Death of Two Men Who Remembered Livingstone", *Other Lands*, July 1951, pp. 83-84.

Young, T. Cullen, "Place-Names in Nyasaland", *The Nyasaland Journal*, Vol. VI No. 2 (July 1953), pp. 35-36.

Young, T. Cullen, "The 'Native' Newspaper", *Africa*, Vol. XI (1938), pp. 63-72.

Young, T. Cullen, "The Battle of Karonga", *The Nyasaland Journal*, Vol. VIII No. 2 (July 1955), pp. 27-30.

Young, T. Cullen, "The New African", *Other Lands*, Vol. 7 (1927), pp. 27-30.

Young, T. Cullen, "Understanding the Old", *International Review of Missions*, Vol. 40 (1951), pp. 450-55.

Young, T. Cullen, *African Ways and Wisdom: A Contribution Towards Understanding*, London: United Society for Christian Literature, 1937.

Young, T. Cullen, *Contemporary Ancestors*, London: Lutterworth Press, n.d.

Young, T. Cullen, *Notes on the Customs and Folklore of the Tumbuka-Kamanga Peoples*, Livingstonia: Mission Press, 1931.

Young, T. Cullen, *Notes on the History of the Tumbuka-Kamanga Peoples in the Northern Province of Nyasaland*, London: Religious Tract Society, 1932; 2nd ed., London: Frank Cass, 1970.

Young, W.P., "Dr Laws: Memorial Services at Livingstonia", *Other Lands*, January 1935, pp. 53-54.

Index

Chimkwita, Emmanuel, 193
China, 19
Chinkhonde, 115
Chintali, Frederick, 152
Chintheche, 101, 103
Chinula, Charles, 102
Chinyanja, 107, 115-17, 122, 190
Chipatula, 45, 90
Chipembere, Masauko, 156, 160, 178-81
Chipeta, Mary, 64
Chipuliko, John Macrae, 65
Chiradzulu, 43, 45, 58, 79
Chirenje, 39
Chirwa, Filemon, 129
Chirwa, Jonathan, 100, 102, 126-27
Chirwa, Orton, 118, 172, 178, 187-88, 191
Chirwa, Timothy Happy, 103
Chirwa, Vera, 95-96, 159, 188-89
Chirwa, Yuraya Chatonda, 27, 110, 136
Chisiza, Dunduzu, 160, 173-74, 178-79
Chisiza, Yatuta, 160, 170, 178-82
Chisuse, Mungo Murray, 65, 120
Chitalo, Edda, 191
Chitonga, 115-16
Chitumbuka, 115-16, 157
Chiume, Kanyama, 156, 168, 178, 180
Chiyao, 115, 117
Chokani, Willie, 178
Chuma, 17
Church of Central Africa Presbyterian, 160, 162, 165-66, 181, 203-204, 220

Church of Scotland, 33, 35, 54, 83, 122, 140, 144, 152-53, 161-62, 165, 170-71, 181-83, 185, 187-91, 193, 203-204, 218, 220
Citizen, The, 149
Colenso, William, 24
Collier, Paul, 41
Colonialism, 20, 53-55, 93-103, 105, 108, 110, 115-16, 131, 137
Colvin, Thomas, 118, 125, 167, 171
Cooperation Agreement, 9, 198-99, 222
Creech-Jones, Arthur, 141-42
Cripps, Sir Stafford, 143
Culloden, 17, 27
Dabb, Gwen, 222
Daily Times, 183, 190
Darien scheme, 47-48, 68, 161, 218
Devine, Tom, 27
Devlin Commission, 168, 170
Devonshire Declaration, 137
Doig, Andrew B., 118, 125, 144, 148-49, 156, 159-60, 166-67, 172, 189
Domasi, 43, 45
Domingo, Charles, 98-99, 101
Dritsas, Lawrence, 203-204
Duff, Alexander, 47
Dugdale, John, 145
Dundee, 54
Dzabala, Molly, 181
Edinburgh, 31, 54, 123-25, 157, 161, 181-84, 197
Ekwendeni, 62, 66, 95
Elmslie, Angus, 42, 46, 60, 98, 102
Embangweni, 61, 126
Engalaweni, 66
Evangelical Revival, 15

233

Lightning Source UK Ltd.
Milton Keynes UK
UKOW05f2025260813

215996UK00005B/724/P